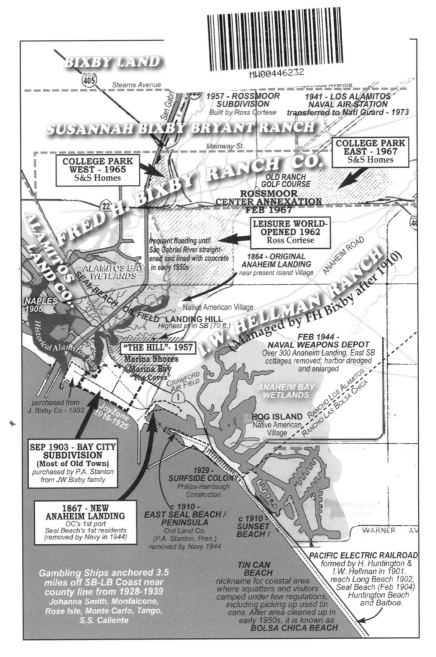

BIXBY LAND

(405) Stearns Avenue

SUSANNAH BIXBY BRYANT RANCH

1957 - ROSSMOOR SUBDIVISION
Built by Ross Cortese

1941 - LOS ALAMITOS NAVAL AIR STATION
transferred to Natl Guard - 1973

Mainway St.

COLLEGE PARK EAST - 1967
S&S Homes

COLLEGE PARK WEST - 1965
S&S Homes

FRED H. BIXBY RANCH CO.

OLD RANCH GOLF COURSE

ROSSMOOR CENTER ANNEXATION FEB 1967

(22)

LEISURE WORLD-OPENED 1962
Ross Cortese

frequent flooding until San Gabriel River straightened and lined with concrete in early 1950s

1864 - ORIGINAL ANAHEIM LANDING
near present Island Village

ANAHEIM ROAD

(40)

ALAMITOS LAND CO.

ALAMITOS BAY WETLANDS
SEAL BEACH

NAPLES 1905

Historical Alamitos Bay

Native American Village

LANDING HILL
Highest pt in SB (70 ft.)

I.W. HELLMAN RANCH
Managed by FH Bixby after 1910

FEB 1944 - NAVAL WEAPONS DEPOT
Over 300 Anaheim Landing, East SB cottages removed; harbor dredged and enlarged

"THE HILL"- 1957
Marina Shores
Marina Bay
"The Coves"

CRAWFORD AIR FIELD

ANAHEIM BAY WETLANDS

RANCHO LOS ALAMITOS
RANCHO LAS BOLSA CHICA

purchased from J. Bixby Co - 1903

JoyZone 1916-1925

(1)

HOG ISLAND
Native American Village

SEP 1903 - BAY CITY SUBDIVISION
(Most of Old Town)
purchased by P.A. Stanton from JW Bixby family

1929 - SURFSIDE COLONY
Phillips-Hambaugh Construction

1867 - NEW ANAHEIM LANDING
OC's 1st port
Seal Beach's 1st residents
(removed by Navy in 1944)

c 1910 - EAST SEAL BEACH / PENINSULA
Ord Land Co.
(P.A. Stanton, Pres.)
removed by Navy 1944

c 1910 - SUNSET BEACH /

WARNER AV

Gambling Ships anchored 3.5 miles off SB-LB Coast near county line from 1928-1939
Johanna Smith, Monfalcone, Rose Isle, Monte Carlo, Tango, S.S. Caliente

TIN CAN BEACH
nickname for coastal area where squatters and visitors camped under few regulations, including picking up used tin cans. After area cleaned up in early 1950s, it is known as
BOLSA CHICA BEACH

PACIFIC ELECTRIC RAILROAD
formed by H. Huntington & I.W. Hellman in 1901.
reach Long Beach 1902,
Seal Beach (Feb 1904) to Huntington Beach and Balboa.

Seal Beach's destiny was shaped in large part by its geography—a remote "highland" isolated by two sprawling bays/wetlands and the flat, fertile soil (and subsequent agricultural success) of the Hellman and Bixby ranches. The former made access inconvenient and hindered the early success of Bay City and the Seal Beach amusement resort, and the latter allowed those owners to keep their lands undeveloped and intact, which later made the open space attractive for the Navy and then orderly large-scale development in the 1960s.

LARRY STRAWTHER

SEAL BEACH

· A BRIEF HISTORY ·

Charleston | London

THE
History
PRESS

Published by The History Press
Charleston, SC 29403
www.historypress.net

Front cover: Two postcards, circa 1916, show the Seal Beach Pavilion and Joy Zone Amusement Area, dominated by the Derby roller coaster. Postcards hand-colored from original photos by Edward Cochems. *Back cover, top and middle*: Photos from 1914 and 1916; *bottom*: Seal Beach's first city letterhead. *From drawing by architect Edward Symmes.*

First published 2014

Manufactured in the United States

ISBN 978.1.62619.489.2

Library of Congress CIP data applied for.

Notice: The information in this book is true and complete to the best of our knowledge. It is offered without guarantee on the part of the author or The History Press. The author and The History Press disclaim all liability in connection with the use of this book.

CONTENTS

ACKNOWLEDGEMENTS

Many people have been very helpful and gracious during the research and writing of this book. My thanks to Chris Jepsen at the Orange County Archives, Charles and Marie Antos at the Seal Beach Cultural and Historical Society, Carrie Reed at the Orange County Library, Mary Wilson branch library in Seal Beach and Laura Alioto, Libby Appelgate and Michael Dobkins for sharing their vast memories of Seal Beach events.

And of course, thanks to my wife, Nancy, who is still trying to figure out why my office has to be so messy and cluttered while doing research.

INTRODUCTION

Many people know far more about Seal Beach than me. Unfortunately, with a few exceptions, those people haven't written books. And because I wanted to know more about the town—early Anaheim Landing, Phil Stanton, the red cars, Joy Zone, rumrunners, gambling ships, summers on the bay, the early days of surfing and the people who used to live here—I started doing some research here, more research there until I realized that even considering what I don't know, I still have a lot of good information worthy of a book. So here it is.

Unlike earlier city historians, I had the advantage of the Internet, which has provided access to a treasure-trove of information heretofore buried in college libraries around the country. I've incorporated much of that information in here.

Seal Beach was originally a city of hype—a real estate development where honesty and factual history took a back seat to hoopla and press releases that have been passed down as fact over the years—and over beers.

Like the issue of whether John Ord was Seal Beach's first resident. He wasn't.

Nor was the town's original name of Bay City changed because of confusion with San Francisco, and the Seal Beach amusement area (the Joy Zone) was not one of Southern California's most popular tourist areas until the Depression did it in. The Joy Zone, overwhelmed by competition from other beach cities, was a financial disappointment right from its start in 1916 and was basically out of business by 1925.

But not to worry—most of the legends are based in truth, and newly discovered facts are more impressive than the previous hype.

There is probably too much information in this book. But since the town has never had a thorough history written about it, I figured I had better cram all the info in now. Who knows how long before the next one is written?

I stop my story of Seal Beach in 1967 for what I think are extremely good reasons:

First, I didn't want to write a five-hundred-page book.

Second, by avoiding the craziness of the 1970s and '80s, I can keep friends.

Finally, 1967 was arguably the year that Seal Beach stopped being an isolated small town. Some say that happened when Leisure World opened in 1962. Or when the school districts merged in the early 1980s. But to me it was 1967—after the annexation of the Rossmoor Business Center, when the separation between Seal Beach and its neighbors to the north became seamless.

I'm sure I've left out deserving events and memorable characters. The more I learned, the more I realized how little I still knew about the town. But hopefully, I've also brought much forward that has been overlooked and given a good account of why Seal Beach is what it is.

So I hope you Old Town old-timers are willing to cut this inlander some slack. But if you aren't, then go down to Main Street, and while having a beer, start your own book or article. I look forward to reading it.

CHAPTER 1
THE BASICS

Except for Landing Hill, all seventy feet of it, Seal Beach is flat. From an elevation of thirty-eight feet in easternmost College Park East, it drops over two miles to twelve feet by the high tide line of the wetlands and local beaches. Before the straightening of the San Gabriel River and construction of the levees, this area frequently flooded when heavy rains carried water from the San Gabriel and San Bernardino mountains.

Pacific storms often stalled over these mountains, sometimes releasing incredibly heavy precipitation—a 1943 storm dumped twenty-six inches on Hoegee's Camp in a twenty-four-hour period. Annual rainfall near the coast averaged twelve inches, but in the mountains, it exceeded forty inches per year (more than Portland and Seattle). As the mountain soils saturated, debris of boulders, gravel, sand and silt fell into canyon streams and was carried along on its journey toward the ocean.

Most of the water sank into the sand and gravel soil of the San Gabriel Valley, the Inland Empire and Los Angeles basin. In some places, the gravel was six miles deep. Gravity induced most of the run-off water to sink into the large aquifers—underground reservoirs that slowly made their way through the slanted layers of sediment that descend to the ocean.

On reaching the main Los Angeles basin, the waters would sometimes spread out or form and reform channels on a whim. The San Gabriel River sometimes sent its water west to merge with the Los Angeles River, sometimes east to join up with Coyote Creek, sometimes south directly into Alamitos Bay. Farther east, the Santa Ana emptied at times into Bolsa Chica or Anaheim Bay until the floods of 1862 diverted it permanently to empty near Newport Bay. During great rainfalls, the floodwaters spread out and joined up in one vast sheet of water fifteen miles wide, allowing individuals to travel by canoe from Long Beach to Newport. The floods led the U.S. Army Corps of Engineers to consider these rivers, especially the Santa Ana, as the greatest flood threats in the nation.

Underground, the waters encountered a natural dam of clay and rock, a fault line running from Newport Beach to Inglewood. Above ground, this "dam" is visible as a string of highlands—the Bolsa Chica Bluffs, "The Hill" in Seal Beach, Bixby Hill, Signal Hill, etc. up to Cheviot Hills. This natural dam caused the gravelly soil and silt to build up behind it, only to be leveled by the inevitable floods.

Eventually, the rivers wore down and created four gaps through this natural barrier—by Newport Bay, Anaheim and Bolsa Bays (the Sunset Gap), Alamitos Bay and the Wilmington Gap. On the coast, the incoming waves and the downstream flow of alluvial silt and sand built up sand barriers that created a sheltered tidal marsh much bigger than now.[1] Portions of Alamitos and Anaheim Bays—marshy sloughs—reached up beyond the present San Diego Freeway into Rossmoor, forming lakes, ponds, marshes and peatlands, often bordered by forests of willows, cottonwoods and thick shrubs.

The wetlands left the area that would become Old Town Seal Beach accessible by only one land route—the Anaheim Landing Road—more recently called Bay Boulevard and now Seal Beach Boulevard. Even on the slightly higher land, the high water table made much of present Leisure World and College Park East areas into large alkali meadows.

The wetlands were natural cleaning agents where fish and smaller mammals thrived, which in turn attracted bigger animals—coyote, foxes, deer and, at the top of the chain, the California grizzly bear.[2]

The area's climate and abundant food supply no doubt attracted the area's earliest human settlers. Some say these first arrivals arrived 2,500 years ago and were of Hokan[3] linguistic stock. Others say the first inhabitants arrived about 40,000 years ago and were part of the Santa Barbara Oak Grove hunter-gatherer culture. Whoever these original inhabitants were, it is generally accepted that between 500 BC and AD 1200, natives of Shoshone linguistic stock made their way from the Great Basin of Utah and Nevada to the Southern California coast. This intrusion is called the Shoshonean Wedge. The early Spanish called those around here Gabrielino because of the proximity to the Mission San Gabriel.

What the Native Americans called themselves is shrouded in controversy and tribal politics. Some say they were called the Puvu, the Puvitsi and the Tongva. Another side claims Tongva is a made-up word and that the "tribe" used the word "Kizh."

The Tongva/Kizh built as many as one hundred villages in the greater Los Angeles and Northern Orange County area, leaving us with many familiar names—Pacoima, Cahuenga, Tujunga, Topanga, Azusa and Cucamonga. Tibahangna lay near the Los Angeles River on the property of Rancho Los Cerritos. The largest settlement was probably Puvungva, on Bixby Hill, by California State University–Long Beach, where the underground dam forced water up into a reliable, natural spring.

The closest village site was just north of Landing Hill by the new Heron Point homes. The hill blocked the cooler ocean breezes, and the waters of both bays were very close. Arms of Alamitos Bay reached almost to the current police station.[4] But middens (refuse heaps of shells) and other remains indicating villages have also been found on Hog Island in the Anaheim Bay Wetlands, the Bolsa Chica bluffs and along the San Gabriel River near El Dorado Park and up Coyote Creek.

Tongva society included extensive trade, technologically advanced knives and bowls, and baskets woven so tight they could hold water and also make very sea-worthy canoes.

There was a sizable Tongva population in Southern California—estimates range from five thousand to fifteen thousand—when Juan Rodriguez Cabrillo, a Portuguese navigator sailing under the Spanish flag, sailed into San Pedro Bay in 1542. Cabrillo noted the smoke from many villages, calling it the "Bay of Smokes."

California was left alone by the Spanish for over two hundred years, until other European powers, especially Russian fur traders, showed interest. To thwart Russian colonization north of San Francisco Bay, the Spaniards sent four expeditions to California. In 1769, Father Junipero Serra established Mission San Diego, the first of many missions intended to bring Catholicism to the California natives and secure the land for Spain. In mid-July 1769, a second land expedition under Don Gaspar de Portola set out from San Diego north in search of Monterey Bay.

Portola's company included friars, muleteers, servants and Indian neophytes, as well as his second in command, Captain Pedro Fages; Corporal Manuel Nieto; and privates Jose María Verdugo and Juan Jose Domínguez. Their path roughly followed what is now Interstate 5. After two weeks, they camped near present Angels Stadium, then continued north, passing through the Coyote Hills, which provided an excellent view of the land toward Palos Verdes and Signal Hill and the lush lowlands between Anaheim and Alamitos Bays.

Fages eventually became governor. Nieto was assigned to the garrison at San Diego but remembered the good land to the north. In 1784, he petitioned his former commander for the right to graze his cattle on some of it, and Fages granted him, as well as Verdugo and Dominguez, the first provisional ranchos in California. (Technically, they were grazing permits. The King of Spain still owned the land.) The Nieto "grant" was by far the largest—300,000 acres—but to resolve issues with the priests at San Gabriel, it was whittled down to a measly 167,000 acres between the ocean and El Camino Real and the Santa Ana River and the old San Gabriel River (which emptied where the Los Angeles River now empties). It was still the largest grant ever made by the Spanish or Mexican governments in California.

Nieto settled near present Downey. When he died in 1804, the land passed to his widow but was overseen by their oldest son, Juan Jose.

In the early 1830s, Mexico declared itself free of Spain. Others petitioned new governor Figueroa for the land by Alamitos Bay, saying it was not being used. Juan Jose Nieto asked Figueroa for a re-confirmation of his father's grant and requested that it be divided among Manuel's heirs. After a diseño (a survey of the land) in June 1833, Figueroa granted the separation of the vast grant into five separate ranchos: Las Bolsa, Los Cerritos, Los Coyotes, Santa Gertrudes and Los Alamitos. Perhaps not so coincidentally, a year later, Juan Jose sold the governor the Alamitos rancho at a very cheap price.

Figueroa formed a company to work the land, but his untimely death in 1835 ended that enterprise. However, the quality of the land had not been forgotten by the man who made the diseño, Abel Stearns. Stearns was born in Massachusetts in 1798. After becoming an orphan, he went to sea at age twelve. He learned the South American and China trade and then made his way to Mexico, forming good relationships with important British merchants and becoming a Mexican citizen.

By 1829, Stearns was in Los Angeles and became a leading merchant, bartering groceries, liquors and dry goods for the hides and tallow from the surrounding ranchos. He also purchased furs from the growing number of American trappers coming to California.

Stearns's influence grew even more after his 1839 marriage to Arcadia, the daughter of the influential Don Juan Bandini. Their home in Los

Angeles became a center for pueblo society for the next thirty years. In 1840, just a year after his marriage, Stearns purchased the Rancho Los Alamitos, paying around $6,000 for its "900 cattle, nearly 1,000 sheep & 240 horses," as well as "6 sq. leagues of land, a small house & a few other triflings worth some $200."

The California gold rush, and the arriving miners' appetites for beef, ushered in a spectacular boom for cattle. Once worth four dollars for their hides and tallow, cattle now sold for seventy-five dollars just for their beef. Stearns's knowledge of Southern California business affairs enabled him to add one financially troubled ranch after another to his holdings. By 1862, Stearns had built up the largest cattle empire in southern California, controlling over 200,000 acres of the choicest land in the area now comprising Los Angeles, San Bernardino and Riverside Counties and most of the land in Orange County west of the Santa Ana River.[5]

But he also invested in several unprofitable mining ventures and the celebrated Arcadia Building in Los Angeles, which stood at the southwest corner of Arcadia and Los Angeles Streets. The two-story brick building contained eight stores, and represented an investment of about $85,000.

To finish the building, Stearns borrowed $20,000, with an interest rate at 1.5 percent per month, from a San Francisco financier, Michael Reis (usually now spelled Reese). Stearns used the Alamitos as security.[6]

Stearns's predicament was not helped by Mother Nature. December 1861 saw the arrival of almost forty straight days of rain, turning the Los Angeles Basin into an inland sea. Ironically, when the rain finally stopped, the irrigated lands produced lush grasses, which made the cattle plump, causing a glut on the beef market and another drop in prices. By the spring of 1862 Stearns's obligations far exceeded his income, and a number of his notes, including one for $15,000 and another for $10,000, were "long overdue."

The floods were followed by an even more disastrous two-year drought. The bones from the carcasses of dead cattle covered the Stearns lands, including the Alamitos, and those of other ranchers for years.[7]

In 1866, the Alamitos defaulted into the hands of Michael Reese. Before he lost other properties, Stearns was rescued by longtime friend and business associate Alfred Robinson, who organized a group of San Francisco investors to subdivide and sell almost 180,000 acres of Stearns's remaining lands in Southern California. Besides being paid $50,000 and having a one-eighth interest in the new corporation, Stearns was also paid a dollar and a half per acre once the land was sold.

The trust, under the name of the Los Angeles and San Bernardino Land Company, distributed thousands of maps and flyers of the "Stearns Ranchos" throughout the United States and Europe. Agents flooded the east with literature describing the incomparable climate and agricultural advantages of Southern California. Every time a steamship left San Francisco for Los Angeles, trust agents were on board to describe the Stearns land. Twenty- and fifty-acre plots sold for five to thirteen dollars an acre.

By 1870, the syndicate had sold more than twenty thousand acres, and Stearns, fully recovered from the financial debacle of the 1860s, was on the eve of again amassing one of the greatest California fortunes when he was stricken with a sudden illness while on a business trip to San Francisco. He died there on August 23, 1871.

The next actors in our story were three cousins from Maine—Benjamin and Thomas Flint and Lewellyn Bixby. In 1849 and 1850, they came to California in search of gold and settled in the mining town of Volcano, where it was said that one miner took out $8,000 worth of gold in a few days.

Eventually, seven of Lewellyn Bixby's brothers, his two sisters and his father-in-law would migrate to California. The Maine men quickly learned that selling goods to the growing population of miners provided better financial opportunities than mining itself. The cousins made enough ($5,000) to return home in late 1852. After a short time of visiting, Benjamin, Thomas and Lewellyn took a train to its terminus in Terre Haute, Indiana. There they formed Flint, Bixby & Company and proceeded to buy two thousand head of sheep. In mid-May 1853, starting out in Council Bluffs, Iowa, they drove the sheep on a seven-month trek to California. Because of the slow pace of the sheep, the men would usually walk.

Throughout the 1850s Flint, Bixby & Company became California's most successful sheep ranching company, even more so during the Civil War, when the Union blockade of Southern cotton created a demand for wool. As wool prices soared, so did the Flint-Bixby fortunes.

The drought of 1862–64, which almost ruined Stearns, provided opportunities for the Flint-Bixby sheepmen who began buying lots of the available land in Southern California. In 1864, they partnered with Benjamin Flint's friend James Irvine of San Francisco to buy two ranchos and part of a third that together would be called the San Joaquin Ranch and later the Irvine Ranch. In 1866, on their own, Flint, Bixby & Co. bought the twenty-six-thousand-acre Los Cerritos Ranch for $20,000 in gold and asked

Lewellyn's capable younger brother Jotham to manage it, also giving him a future option to buy half the ranch.

In 1869, Jotham exercised his purchase option and a new company was formed to manage the Cerritos—J. Bixby Company, half owned by Jotham and half by Flint, Bixby & Co. The new company had thirty thousand head of sheep, with 200,000 pounds of wool being sent annually to San Francisco, often via Anaheim Landing.

The partners invested in other projects—the Coast Stagecoach line, a Northern California sugar factory[8] and the Ranchos Palos Verdes. By 1872, the men of Flint, Bixby & Co. were the largest non-railroad landholders in all of California. Their interests in eight ranchos totaled 334,000 acres—over 500 square miles.

But a mid-1870s drop in wool prices, another drought in Southern California and bad investments by Benjamin Flint almost ruined the company. Thomas Flint and Lewellyn Bixby bought out Ben, and to get out of debt, the company sold off many properties, including its share of the San Joaquin Ranch. Irvine paid the men $150,000—a nice return on their original $12,500 investment twelve years earlier.

In October 1871, another Bixby arrived in Southern California. John W. Bixby was not only a first cousin to Lewellyn and Jotham via their fathers but also a first cousin to the Flints through his mother, Deborah Flint.

He found work at the Cerritos Rancho, and then in October 1873, John W. Bixby married Susan Patterson Hathaway, the youngest sister of Lewellyn's second wife, Mary, and Jotham's wife, Margaret.[9]

The newlyweds moved to Wilmington, where their first child, Fred Hathaway Bixby, was born in 1875. Within a couple years, John and Susan were subleasing one thousand acres of Rancho Los Alamitos land when they heard that Alamitos owner Michael Reese had died and his will required that all his property be sold. John W. Bixby organized a partnership between himself, the J. Bixby Company (still half owned by Jotham and half by Lewellyn Bixby and Thomas Flint) and banker I.W. Hellman.

Hellman was president of the Farmers & Merchants Bank, Los Angeles' largest bank,[10] and already becoming the most important banker on the Pacific Coast. The *Los Angeles Express* reported on December 29, 1886, that Isaias paid the most taxes of any man in Los Angeles—more than $14,000.

Some reports have John W. first approaching the Farmers & Merchant Bank to lend him $125,000 to acquire the 26,392.5 acres of the Alamitos. Hellman reportedly said the bank couldn't assume the risk but that he personally would lend half the requested money if John W. could convince his cousins Jotham and Lewellyn to do the same. J.W. did. [11]

The new partnership formed the John W. Bixby Co., a name that did little to end confusion of the Bixby holdings. Since Thomas Flint and Lewellyn Bixby held half interest in the Jotham-managed J. Bixby Co., the Flint-Bixby Co. now held half of the J. Bixby Co.'s one-third interest in the J.W. Bixby Company. Bottom line for the Alamitos ranch owners: Lewellyn Bixby and Tom Flint each held a one-twelfth interest, Jotham held a one-sixth interest and Hellman and John W. Bixby each owned one-third.

John W. made many improvements to the ranch and its agricultural operations and made it profitable. He also laid out the five-thousand-acre town of Alamitos Beach, roughly bounded by the ocean on the south, Hathaway Street (now Pacific Coast Highway) on the north, the Los Cerritos boundary line (Alamitos Avenue) on the west and Termino Avenue on the east.

The timing seemed good. The real estate boom of the '80s was now fully underway, and just west of his new town was the growing town of Long Beach. On one January day in 1887, real estate transactions in Los Angeles surpassed $1 million. But four months later, in May 1887, J.W. took ill—presumably with appendicitis—and died. And within another four months, the real estate boom died as fast as it began.

The surviving partners separated the ranch into four parts. As the Alamitos Land Company, they would jointly control basically everything in present East Long Beach south of the Pacific Coast Highway. The rest of the rancho was equally divided into parcels of approximately eight thousand acres. The J. Bixby Company assumed the northern third (roughly north of present Stearns and Orangewood Avenues) adjacent to its Los Cerritos ranch property.

J.W. Bixby's heirs kept the middle strip—roughly east of Clark Avenue and between the present Pacific Coast Highway and Stearns Avenue in Los Angeles County and between present Orangewood and Garden Grove Boulevard in Orange County. This property included the old adobe and the name Rancho Los Alamitos.

I.W. Hellman received the Orange County land south of Anaheim Road (current 405 freeway and Garden Grove Boulevard). To achieve equal distribution, some coastal lands between Anaheim Bay and Alamitos Bay were divided into three smaller parts as well. Hellman kept the parcel closest to Anaheim Landing. Jotham and Lewellyn Bixby received what is now the Long Beach Peninsula and a little strip east of the San Gabriel River. And

When the Rancho Los Alamitos was divided among its three owners, I.W. Hellman's share included present Leisure World, "The Hill," Anaheim Landing and the Naval Weapons Station. Hellman was one of the nation's most influential bankers, and in 1901, he and Henry Huntington formed the Pacific Electric Railroad.

the John W. Bixby heirs received the piece in between—Seal Beach land that is basically now bordered by Pacific Coast Highway (PCH) on the north, the ocean on the south and between Fourth and Thirteenth Streets.

In 1889, Orange County was formed with the county line roughly following the shifting sandy beds of Coyote Creek to its confluence with the equally sandy beds of the San Gabriel River. This placed the Alamitos ranch in two counties, a separation that would have significant impacts on the growth and character of Seal Beach.

CHAPTER 2

ANAHEIM LANDING

When the Stearns Ranchos lands went on the market in 1868, some of the first lands sold were just west of the new town of Anaheim. Started in 1859 by fifty German settlers "for the purpose of manufacturing wine," Anaheim soon became the greatest wine-producing center in California, producing 125,000 gallons of wine by 1862. By 1885, the wineries, which now numbered fifty, were producing 1,250,000 gallons, much of it good enough to sell in San Francisco and New York.

The Anaheim vineyards were far from the market, and transportation was difficult. Roads were little more than bumpy wagon trails, and with no bridges, rivers had to be forded. So Anaheim growers had to find dependable, affordable transportation.

Newport Bay—at the time an estuary protected by a half-mile-wide sand spit—was considered, as was San Pedro and Phineas Banning's new port at Wilmington.

The other possible location was on Alamitos Bay, where Coyote Creek reached the tidal waters. At this time, the San Gabriel River followed the present Rio Hondo Channel and merged with the Los Angeles River to empty into the ocean near Wilmington. Alamitos Bay was only twelve miles from Anaheim, about half the distance of San Pedro, and wagons didn't have to cross any major streams.

The area had been used as a harbor before for military purposes, as in 1849, just after the end of the Mexican-American War, when Commodore Robert Stockton established a trench position near Landing Hill to repulse a suspected landing of munitions by a French schooner from Mazatlan.

Founded in 1864, Anaheim Landing was first located on Alamitos Bay (near present Island Village) until the silt from an 1867 flood blocked the harbor's ocean access. A new wharf and warehouses (shown above) were then built on Anaheim Bay. Robust coastal trade was carried on here for about fifteen years. Locals also used the Landing for recreation.

While Alamitos Bay offered protection, it was too shallow for large ships. Lighters—smaller, cable-powered boats—would have to move cargo from ships to a new pier. Despite its limitations, the Anaheim grape growers saw Alamitos Bay as their best option. So the Anaheim Lighter Company was formed to construct a pier and wharf on the slough that reached up close to present Island Village, just off Second Street/Westminster Avenue.

A twelve-mile road was blazed from Anaheim to the "Landing," which opened for business in October 1864 and became a regular stopping place for coastal steamers, joining San Francisco, San Luis Obispo, Santa Barbara, San Buenaventura, San Pedro and San Diego.[12] Among the ships that regularly stopped at the Landing were the *Senator, Commodore, Mahong, Orizaba* and *Pacific,* as well as steamers headed for Panama and Mexico.

Vessels anchored two to three miles off shore, and goods and passengers were transferred to lighters of eighty-ton capacity and taken by cable to and from the steamers. One end of the cable was fastened at the warehouse and the other near where the steamer would stop. Eight or ten men pulled the cable, giving freight and humans an interesting but often perilous ride. Depth at the port was seven feet in the slough at low tide.

Lumber from Northern California and other building materials were shipped in while wine, corn and other crops and products, including wool from the Flint-Bixby ranches, were shipped out.[13]

But in February 1867, heavy rains and flooding carried massive amounts of silt down the San Gabriel River and into Alamitos Bay, making the port impassable even for the smaller lighters.

Undaunted, the company chose a spot over Landing Hill in the waters of Anaheim Bay. In March 1868, the California legislature authorized "the right to construct and maintain a wharf...on the Bay of Bolsa Chiquita [Bolsa Chica]...thirteen and one half miles from the Town of Anaheim, and one mile and a half from the former landing of the Anaheim Lighter Company."[14] Specifically, the company was granted "a strip of land five hundred feet in width...and extending into said bay four hundred feet, or until a sufficient depth of water shall be obtained for the accommodation of commerce." This franchise was granted for a twenty-year period, and the men were required to build the facility within two years.

But apparently, the Anaheimers lacked the capital to fully develop the project, and William Workman, a major figure in early Los Angeles, was brought in as a partner. There is some evidence that Don Juan Forster, owner of Rancho San Juan Capistrano, also invested in the Landing. But Workman, who owned a large rancho near La Puente and had a large bank in downtown Los Angeles, was the key figure.

Warehouses and an office were up and running by the end of the decade. Oxen teams hauled crops from the inland ranches and farms and returned with lumber for the growing towns of Anaheim, Westminster, Orange, Santa Ana and Gallatin (now Downey). To reach the latter, much lumber was hauled over an old Spanish and Gabrielino trail called the North Walk—later shortened to Norwalk.

In 1871, California senator Eugene Caserly presented a petition "of citizens of Los Angeles County, praying that Anaheim Landing be designated as a port of entry." The motion shows the seriousness of the port's activity.

There were usually two coast steamers a week and occasionally a Panama steamer. By one 1872 report, thirty or forty teams usually made the trip daily to or from the Landing, but one day registered seventy teams of horses.

Among the more frequent visitors were 250-foot-long lumber schooners from Crescent City, able to carry 600,000 to 1,000,000 board feet of lumber. Seamen threw the larger pieces of lumber into the sea to float ashore, where they were collected and hauled away by teams of horses.

Lighters carried the smaller lumber and items like bolts, fence posts and pickets. After moving it from the ships to the mud flats with the incoming tide, the lighters were reloaded with goods (mainly wine and brandy from Anaheim) and sent back to the ships on the outgoing tide.

A captain usually owned most of the lumber he brought, and he sent his clerk ashore to handle the bargaining for his lumber. Barter was the general method of trade until 1876, when lumber companies set up stores at Anaheim Landing.

In 1873, the Landing exported six thousand tons of local products, mostly wine and grain. Another five thousand tons of product was imported, including one million board feet of lumber. Its traffic rivaled Wilmington in most products.

Businessmen were excited by the area's potential. Anaheim leaders raised $25,000 to build a railroad from San Bernardino to the Landing. Others started raising funds for a new wharf at Bolsa Chica. In January 1874, San Francisco financier Michael Reese, owner of the Rancho Los Alamitos, was granted approval to build a new wharf at the Landing. He was partnered in this venture with a Panamanian merchant, but nothing came of it.[15]

Perhaps this was due to increasing competition. At Wilmington, Banning had dredged channels to allow large ships to get closer and, by 1868, had built a railroad running to and from Los Angeles. In 1870, the McFadden brothers built a wharf at the "New Port" at the mouth of the Santa Ana River.

More influential was the coming of the Southern Pacific Railroad to Anaheim in January 1875. It now cost Anaheim farmers and merchants $2.50 a ton to ship their products by train to Wilmington, compared to the $3.50 a ton it cost to ship by wagon to Anaheim Landing.

Another factor was a national recession that began in New York in 1873, causing the stock market to close for ten days and nearly 25 percent of New Yorkers to lose their jobs. By 1875, the recession had worked its way to the West Coast, causing a run on local banks. I.W. Hellman had shrewdly prepared reserves for such emergencies, but Workman's group hadn't, and its bank failed. Workman's property was placed in receivership, and Workman put a bullet through his head.

Farmers from Westminster took over the Anaheim Lighter Company in late 1877. Well aware of the Southern Pacific's history to "charge all that the market can bear," the farmers felt an active Anaheim Landing was necessary to secure competition and reasonably priced rail transportation. Six Westminster colonists leased the landing for eighteen months, declaring they just wanted to break even on their estimated annual costs of $28,000, and solicited subscriptions from the community, part of which was used to build a new wharf in 1879.

The landing would ship freight as late as 1902, but by then the area was more used as a picnic and vacation destination for inland residents seeking a respite from the summer heat. They pitched tents on the beaches or rented space at the Landing warehouse, with blankets being used as walls between families. The blankets were taken down when the warehouse, which was about forty feet by sixty feet in size, was used for dances. The local churches in Garden Grove and Westminster also used the Landing for baptisms.

Not all residents were visitors. John Kelly, who had lost his money during the 1880s real estate bust, lived at the Landing for years, making a living by digging out clams, which he sold to restaurants in Santa Ana.

Louis Boltz, an Anaheim saloonkeeper, set up shop at the Landing in 1872, and despite being prosecuted numerous times for squatting and selling liquor without a license, he was still there thirty years later.

Boltz also rented out a room at his saloon and later some cottages. An early renter was author Henryk Sienkiewicz, a Polish emigrant who would later win a Nobel Prize for literature. He came to California in 1876 to seek a place for a Thoreau-esque commune, which was later established near Anaheim. Sienkiewicz lived in a shack at the Landing and planned out many of his later stories and novels. In his short essay "The Cranes," he describes his Landing "society" as mainly Norwegian fishermen and a German (Boltz) who feeds and lodges them. The men fished the waters by day and played poker by night. During days, Sienkiewicz walked the Landing shores while great sea lions sunned themselves on the rocks. Across the river mouth, a sandy island (now Surfside and Sunset Beach) was filled with mews, pelicans and albatrosses. Sienkiewicz rowed over to the uninhabited isle and looked out over:

> *sunsets which were simply marvelous; they changed the whole horizon into one sea, gleaming with gold, fire, and opal, which, passing into a brilliant purple, faded gradually until the moon shone on the amethyst background of the heavens, and the wonderful semitropical night had embraced the earth and the sky. The empty land, the endlessness of the ocean, and the excess of light disposed me somewhat toward mysticism. I...had the feeling that everything surrounding me formed a certain single great soul which appears as the ocean, the sky, the plain, or diminishes into such small living existences as birds, fish, shells, or broom on the ocean shore.*[16]

By 1883, the *Times* reported a "regular population of over 200" Landing-ites. It wrote, "The business portion of the town consisted of a boarding house, a feed stable and the indispensable saloon...very much like all other saloons,

After the railroad ended the Landing's days as a shipping center, it became a popular summer resort, with a population sometimes close to four hundred. The company's full-time employees, fishermen and longtime saloonkeeper Louis Boltz were Seal Beach's first permanent residents.

only more so." During the summer season, the town would swell to over 400 souls. On one warm weekend, an Anaheim reporter noted that "half its population was down there." Several neat and comfortable houses had been erected along with a "number of tents of various shades, sizes and styles." Surf bathing, boat riding and fishing were the chief attractions. Captain Wilson would occasionally drag the bay bottom with his net to remove "stingarees," but three or four persons were still stung that summer.[17]

Reports describe the Landing as "quite an important place in those days, and the scene of most holiday celebrations." Sometimes during summers, a teenager would ride a horse cart or buggy back to Anaheim to get the mail, "riding over the salt-grass pasture land, just about making their own road as they went." If one youth in a buggy met another on the same road, more often than not, a race would break out.[18] Also during summers, the Landing would host shooting contests, with marksmen from the area coming to test their skills on pigeons and quail.[19]

In August 1888, the Landing hosted the huge first encampment of the Southern California chapters of the Grand Army of the Republic, a fraternal group of Civil War veterans. The event was attended by over one thousand veterans from lodges all over Southern California and an additional five thousand to six thousand family members and friends. The campground, a tent city of well-defined streets and blocks, ran from Anaheim Bay west toward Alamitos Bay and included much of Old Town Seal Beach.[20]

When not listening to the parade of speakers—which included the governor of California—the attendees could frequent the merchants and concessionaires along First and Second Street, including butchers, candy makers, cigar stores, restaurants and barbershops. Many of the merchants came from nearby cities; Grocer T.A. Deerling was from Artesia, while Mr. Greenleaf Ana provided fun

In 1888, Jotham and Lewellyn Bixby allowed the Grand Army of the Republic to use Anaheim Landing for its first summer gathering for Civil War veterans and their families. Newspapers estimated that the ten-day event was attended by over six thousand persons.

for children of all ages on the merry-go-round he hauled over from his home in Santa Ana. "Mssrs. Sanders and Dye of Orange had a busy ice cream, fruit and confectionary stand." J.T. Bangham dispensed peanuts from "the only patent peanut roaster in the United States." Hundreds took advantage of the soothing beach waters, while the Women's Relief Corps tent stayed busy caring for ill and sunburned attendees.[21]

Liquor was not allowed in the campsite, but just outside the encampment, the Landing's saloon keepers and impromptu beer pavilions offered veterans a chance to relive tales "of food and field" and old battles. And when the Orange Municipal Band broke into "Rally Round the Flag, Boys," the whole camp joined in "with enthusiasm and patriotism of the occasion."

Every evening at 5:00 p.m., veterans who hadn't stood in formation for over twenty years fell in for a dress parade and sharply executed the commands of "countermarch" and "right wheel" as if they were still on active duty. Much of this camaraderie was caught by "Mssrs. Conaway and Hummel, photographers of Santa Ana."

After ten days, the veterans returned home, leaving the landing to be enjoyed by the usual parade of summer vacationers.

By 1890, the number of Landing visitors decreased, as Newport and Balboa grew in popularity each season.[22] Still, enough residents lived there full time that in 1890, the *Los Angeles Times* reported that Anaheim Landing was the tenth-largest community in Orange County, with a population around two hundred.

CHAPTER 3

HELLMAN AND STANTON

BEETS AND BAY CITY

In February 1890, word leaked that I.W. Hellman had obtained controlling interest in San Francisco's Nevada Bank. Funded by the Comstock Lode millionaires, the Nevada Bank had been the richest bank in the United States, but recent ventures had left it weak.

Hellman announced a plan to raise $2.5 million through a stock offering. But his reputation was so good that he was swamped with orders for over $15 million of stock from some of the nation's wealthiest men and financial institutions.

When, a month later, he said he would move to San Francisco, editorials in Los Angeles newspapers questioned how the loss of this civic force would affect their city.

He was one of Southern California's larger landowners, and his share of the Alamitos property made him more so. He had numerous agents in different parts of the county, but after he moved to San Francisco, he came to rely more and more on Los Angeles real estate agent Phillip A. Stanton.

Philip Stanton was born in 1868 in Ohio and moved to Los Angeles in 1887, ostensibly for "health reasons," but ambition had something to do with it. Within his first year, he had joined two Sons of Civil War Veterans groups, and was an officer in two additional social groups. By 1892, he was also on the city's Fourth of July Celebration Committee and in 1895 was very involved with the planning of Los Angeles' second-annual Fiesta, a week-long Carnival-like celebration that brought to downtown Los Angeles much business and many visitors, some who were more sexually active than the town morals police preferred.

To capitalize on Pacific Electric Railroad plans for a coastal line to Newport Beach, Philip A. Stanton, pictured here, formed the town of Pacific City (later Huntington Beach) and then sold his interest to fund his new town of Bay City. Stanton's Bayside Land Company dominated Bay City and Seal Beach growth and activities over its first twenty years.

He was also involved with local politics. By November 1888, the *Los Angeles Times* lists him "among the more prominent men" in the Third Ward of the Republican City Convention.

On arrival in Los Angeles, Stanton also jumped into real estate—just as the boom of the '80s went bust. Still, by 1890, Stanton was selling Stearns Ranchos properties west of Anaheim. He bought 3,500 acres himself and resold most of the land southwest of Brookhurst and La Palma Avenue.

By 1893, many of Stanton's renters were growing sugar beets, which were hauled to Chino, where Southern California's first sugar beet processing factory was built in 1891. He also got involved in an attempt to build a sugar factory in Anaheim.

By 1895, Stanton had become the real estate agent for the San Francisco–bound I.W. Hellman. Their frequent correspondence provides great details on the development of the western Orange County area.[23]

By this time, over two thousand acres—one-quarter of Hellman's Alamitos acreage—was planted in sugar beets. With so much west Orange County land now growing beets, Stanton approached Hellman about funding a beet-processing factory in Anaheim or on Hellman's land. But Hellman declined. The severe depression would make raising capital difficult.

Soon after this exchange, Lewellyn Bixby—who had invested in California's (and the nation's) first successful sugar beet factory back in 1870—tried to raise bonds to construct a beet factory on either the Rancho Los Cerritos or Rancho Los Alamitos. But while land-rich, the Bixbys couldn't finance a factory themselves. Soon after, millionaires J. Ross Clark and his brother William were enticed to build the Los Alamitos Sugar Factory, and Lewellyn and Jotham Bixby agreed to provide land for the factory and lay out a township to support it. This would become Los Alamitos.

Enthused by the news, Stanton again tried to get Hellman to lay out a town site at Anaheim Landing. The new factory would provide a guaranteed income for local farmers, who would have to go to a town to buy merchandise. Why not in a town on land Hellman owned and where Stanton could sell the lots? Although he had shown interest in doing just this a year earlier, Hellman declined at this time because he had already leased out all the land around the Landing. But leaseholders weren't the only residents on his lands.

Squatters had always been a problem at the Landing. There was legal confusion over where the Landing Company's actual property ended and where the tidelands (which were state property) officially started. This was exacerbated by an incorrectly marked boundary survey. The squatters included saloonkeeper Louis Boltz, some farmers, dockworkers and independent fishermen or merchants catering to resort visitors.

With the development of the nearby Los Alamitos sugar beet factory, more squatters moved to the Landing. In April 1897, Stanton wrote Hellman that there were now thirty-one houses on his land, only a few with proper leases.

Stanton wanted to take the squatters to court, but Hellman declined, although the threats of eviction temporarily drove off many people.

The Los Alamitos sugar factory's first campaign in summer 1897 was so successful that before the season ended, the Clarks set about doubling their plant's capacity and purchased eight thousand acres of Rancho Los Cerritos (around present Lakewood and the Long Beach airport).

The Clarks could now supply almost all the beets for their factory by themselves, which meant tenant farmers on the Hellman and Susan Bixby lands would have to sell their beets to the distant Chino factory.

There were other farming opportunities. Much of the land was planted in alfalfa, barley and vegetables or used as pasture for the dairy cattle, sheep and pigs.

But beets offered the most promise. J. Ross Clark talked openly about building a second factory nearby, and both Susan Bixby and Hellman entertained proposals to build sugar factories on their land. In late 1897, Susan Bixby optioned her Alamitos property to an English syndicate.

About the same time, Hellman was asked by an Anaheim businessman to commit enough acreage for sugar beets and a new factory to be built by the Oxnards, who owned the Chino plant. Hellman liked the project but wouldn't commit because his land was all leased out. But a few months later, in February 1898, *Los Angeles Times* publisher Harrison Gray Otis, representing Dutch capitalists, optioned all of Hellman's Alamitos lands for $650,000.[24]

Los Alamitos was the hot property in Orange County. New merchants, like John C. Ord, arrived to set up shop in a two-story building, the bottom floor of which was a store that children remembered as selling "candies and novelties." Main Street (now Reagan) was soon home to a general store, a baker, a meat market, the Harmona Hotel, a confectioner, a billiard parlor and a barber, Joseph Watts, who would be the stepfather of a Seal Beach legend.

But then the Dutch investors were scared off by the outbreak of the Spanish-American War, and three straight years of drought dramatically reduced the area's sugar output. When the factory was open only seven days in 1898, the crop's unpredictability made the Clarks lose interest in building a second factory, and they shifted their attentions to more lucrative areas—real estate and railroads.[25]

I.W. Hellman had also reached this same decision, along with his new San Francisco business partner, Henry E. Huntington. Together, in 1898, they decided to build a system of inter-urban electric railways that would connect Los Angeles with all its suburban areas. This would become the famous Pacific Electric rail system.

Henry Huntington was the nephew of Southern Pacific Railroad kingpin Collis Huntington. Henry came to California in 1892, and his skills soon had him overseeing the company's numerous San Francisco trolley systems, a mess of short, horse-drawn rail lines. The younger Huntington consolidated these under one management, converted them to electricity and then expanded them into the city's growing residential areas. To fund this undertaking, he partnered with Hellman, whose Nevada Bank oversaw the sale of $5 million worth of bonds. Hellman understood trolleys. In Los Angeles and San Francisco, before meeting Huntington, he had twenty years experience investing in local lines. The two formed a friendship and watched appreciatively as riders flocked to the upgraded cars, and new homes sprang up around the trolley lines.

Hellman knew Los Angeles offered bigger opportunities, so he and Huntington formed a plan to take over Los Angeles' hodge-podge of short rail systems and, just as they had done in San Francisco, convert them all to electricity and into a wide network. To fund the operation, Hellman organized a syndicate that alone owned 45 percent of the stock and controlled other investors. Henry Huntington and his uncle Collis owned a smaller but still significant block.

On September 14, 1898, the new Los Angeles Railway Company purchased six local trolley lines covering 168 miles of track. The new owners wasted no time upgrading the lines, reconfiguring routes and securing a deal with William Kerckhoff's San Gabriel Electric Company to provide all the electricity for the new system.

Their plans were thrown a curve in August 1900 when Collis Huntington died and the younger Huntington lost a boardroom battle for control of the Southern Pacific, which fell into the hands of E.H. Harriman, owner of the Union Pacific and the largest railroad network in the country.

Undeterred, Huntington focused on developing his electric railroad network in Southern California, funded and advised by Hellman, who had the key business relationships in Southern California. Newspaper articles of the time usually refer to them as "the Huntington-Hellman syndicate." In May 1901, Hellman wrote Huntington, "The time is on hand when we should commence building suburban railroads out of the city" and added that he had already commenced a survey of potential routes.[26]

The company's first step called for the extension of its lines from downtown south to Long Beach and ultimately down the coast to Newport Beach. It was no coincidence that this would make Hellman's Alamitos lands along the ocean far more valuable. Hellman's plan also called for new electric lines to San Pedro.

As Hellman's agent, Philip A. Stanton was aware of all this long before it was formally announced. By June 1901, he had put together a syndicate— the West Coast Land & Water Company—to buy 1,500 acres of land around present Huntington Beach, subdivide it and sell lots. After conducting a contest, the winning name for the new seaside resort was Bolsa Beach (Superior Beach was a second choice). For some reason, Stanton soon changed it to Pacific City.

Henry Huntington, depicted here, and I.W. Hellman formed the Pacific Electric Railway in 1901. Huntington's insistence on reinvesting profits and not distributing dividends led the Hellman faction to sell its controlling share to the Southern Pacific by 1904.

By this time, many rumors of the Huntington-Hellman plans were floating about publicly. In early June, the *Times* and other papers reported, "The country all around Alamitos Bay is to be transformed into a delightful resort." And two weeks later, Charles Drake, who had plans to build a resort hotel (and a giant swimming plunge) in Long Beach, requested that city's council issue a permit for "a trolley system from Los Angeles to Long Beach, 'by a syndicate headed by Henry Huntington and I.W. Hellman.'"

Huntington and Hellman weren't the only ones with electric railway projects on the mind. On September 3, 1901, there were at least thirteen different proposed electric railway projects in Los Angeles County.[27] But on October 30, 1901, the Hellman and Huntington group was awarded the Long Beach trolley franchise with a high bid of $9,600.

Over the next two weeks, Huntington, Hellman and their partners incorporated the Pacific Electric Railway in California "to build and operate over 452 miles of electric railways over seven primary lines." Huntington held 22 percent of the stock, while the Hellman group owned 45 percent.

Using the Los Angeles and Pasadena Electric Railway as its core, the company began laying out extensions to Long Beach and Pasadena and examining possible routes to Newport, Santa Ana, Whittier, La Habra, Monrovia and Riverside.

Not so coincidentally, on January 18, Stanton's West Coast Land & Water Company announced it would build a five-hundred-foot pleasure wharf at its new Pacific City site, where land company agents were hyping that "over a hundred lots had already been sold and several buildings were already going up."

Construction on the Pacific Electric's Long Beach line began February 1. Crews averaged 7,800 feet of track a day. On April 8, 1902, the *Los Angeles Times* reported, "Property along the line of the road has advanced enormously in value…Several men have made fortunes out of it."

Stanton's hopes of joining that list became even more real when the Pacific Electric Railroad officially rolled into Long Beach on July 4, 1902, with PE surveyors already surveying routes down the Orange County coast.

But Stanton's dreams encountered the Bolsa Chica Gun Club, which owned a large chunk of the coastal property on the proposed PE route, and the members didn't want a railroad traveling down the beach near the club—at least not at the price being offered.

Unfazed, Huntington indicated—he rarely said what he was going to do— that he would build his railroad to Newport Beach via a more northerly route, which would bypass Bolsa Chica and Stanton's new township at Pacific City.

Beginning in 1902, the Pacific Electric railway's "red cars" connected downtown Los Angeles with Long Beach and the area's growing suburbs. As a passenger line, the PE never turned a profit, but Huntington saw the railway as a necessary investment to establish his real estate and electricity supply operations.

Fortunately for Stanton, Huntington had to first resolve some bigger problems. E.H. Harriman let it be known that the Southern Pacific would contest Huntington at every possible opportunity. A second problem was a new competitor with even deeper pockets, the Clark brothers, William A. and J. Ross, owners of the Los Alamitos Sugar factory as well as numerous copper mines, forest lands, banks (some in Los Angeles) and newspapers. The older brother, William Andrews Clark, who had by now also added the position of U.S. senator from Montana to his portfolio, was considered at the time to be the second-richest man in the world, behind only John D. Rockefeller. In 1900, the brothers announced plans to build a railroad from the Port of Los Angeles to Salt Lake City. They had already bought the Terminal Island Railroad and now set their sights on many of the Los Angeles area's short railways that the Huntington-Hellman group were interested in. However, by 1902, it was suspected that the Clarks were acting as a front for Harriman, who had bested them the year before in a power play regarding their San Pedro to Salt Lake railroad.

This created problem number three because it alarmed Hellman, who was by now not only Harriman's banker but was also displeased that his Pacific Electric Railroad investments were not seeing dividends despite impressive revenues. Huntington continually reinvested profits in more construction and acquisitions, because his business model showed the railroad to be an investment for future revenues from the sale of real estate and electricity in the areas served by the new rail lines.

The Hellman syndicate was not an investor in these real estate projects and understandably reluctant to invest more money—especially during the depressed bond market of the time. But Huntington's plan of rapid expansion required capital. If he no longer had access to Hellman's financing sources, the railroad builder knew he would have to make a deal with Harriman, who was funded by John D. Rockefeller's banking combine (the largest of which was the Chase National Bank).

Throughout early 1903, the two transportation titans played a game of corporate chess to best position themselves for the inevitable. They even corresponded frequently and on friendly terms and exchanged a few smaller properties here and there. But in January, Huntington bought options and pieces of land in Fresno and Stockton and dropped hints that he might build a railroad line through the San Joaquin Valley to compete with the SP's older, less-efficient steam railroad. In March, his surrogates applied for franchises in the Riverside area. More significantly, in February 1903, Huntington received a franchise to build a railroad and wharf at the southernmost reaches of San Pedro. A few weeks later, he announced a million-dollar plan to build a giant wharf as well as a luxury hotel, an aquarium that would be the largest in the world, a bathhouse and a pavilion. The proposed super wharf would put a major dent in SP business.

Harriman was, by nature, a soft-spoken businessman who preferred to work out compromises that benefited all parties—he had done this when acquiring control of the Salt Lake and Santa Fe railroads. But when forced to, he could play hardball, and Huntington's acquisition of the San Pedro franchise had dramatically raised the stakes and forced the SP owner to strike back.

On April 18, 1903, William A. Clark wildly outbid Huntington for an existing interurban franchise from downtown Los Angeles to San Pedro, committing to pay almost half a million dollars. Newspapers speculated that this confirmed that the Clarks were acting on behalf of Harriman, who now controlled the Salt Lake Railroad project.[28]

Two weeks later, on May 4, 1903, another Harriman surrogate countered every bid Huntington made for a new downtown rail franchise, a franchise some estimated worth only possibly $10,000. Huntington finally stopped at $100,000, allowing the Harriman group to have it for $110,000.[29]

Neither side was surprised by the other's actions, but the excess bidding confirmed that it was time to make a deal. That night, Huntington made the trip to San Francisco and met with Harriman and Hellman. The latter still had a major stake in the game, and as the owner of the Alamitos lands in Orange County, he wanted to make sure the Pacific Electric tracks reached his property.

On May 5, a deal was worked out: the Hellman group would sell enough of its Pacific Electric Railroad stock so that Huntington and Harriman each owned 40 percent, while Hellman's group kept 20 percent. From this point on, the Pacific Electric Railroad and the Southern Pacific basically acted as one railroad, although Harriman recognized Huntington's skills and usually left him alone.

Armed with his new deal and access to East Coast financing, Huntington immediately resumed his plan of expansion. Later that same day, it was also announced that Huntington would buy out most of the assets of Philip A. Stanton's West Coast Land Company, including all lots close to the beach, and form a new company called the Huntington Beach Company. This assured that the Pacific Electric, which was already building a trestle through the Alamitos Bay estuary, would continue down the coast and reach the new town.

During the main show of the Harriman-Huntington corporate chess match, Stanton had not been idle. When the Bolsa Chica Gun Club owners had shown reluctance to grant passage through their property, Stanton saw his own real estate ambitions threatened. But now, in 1903, Stanton had an additional power base—that of being an elected official.

Over the years, as a familiar figure in the backrooms of the local Republican Party, Stanton had built up lots of favors, especially with "The Push," the Southern Pacific's statewide political machine. In the fall of 1902, Stanton ran for the office of assemblyman from the Seventy-first District near downtown Los Angeles. In the primary, with the Southern Pacific behind him, he defeated by one vote a candidate backed by *Los Angeles Times* publisher Harrison Otis. In November, again with the Southern Pacific machine behind him as well as the votes of some apparently fictitious voters, Stanton became an assemblyman.

His first term in office was unimpressive—the *Los Angeles Times* (admittedly biased because of Otis's loathing of the Southern Pacific) said you had to fumigate Stanton's record before you could look at it—but he won

P.A. Stanton bought his Bay City lands from the John W. Bixby heirs, led by Fred H. Bixby, seen here. Bixby's success at managing his own ranch and the Hellman Ranch allowed the area north of Old Town to stay undeveloped until the 1950s.

Opposite: Bay City's early promotion fell on the shoulders of John C. Ord, depicted here. Although Ord was not, as he claimed, the first resident of Seal Beach, he was the first resident of the Bayside tract and the town's first mayor, and he played a large role in the development of the Anaheim Peninsula and Surfside.

reelection in 1904, impressing his fellow politicians with his political skills.

Those same skills aided Huntington and Harriman (and himself) when he helped resolve the Bolsa Chica Gun Club issue. Huntington and other heavy hitters of the PE and SP would become members of the gun club, making the club very prestigious; gun club members received more money for granting rail rights to the PE and a train stop at the gun club.

Huntington paid the West Coast Land Company stockholders $200,000 for their assets and gave them an additional $100,000 in stock in the new Huntington Beach Company.

This deal was the first of many in Huntington's new buying binge. Over the next month, he closed deals in Placentia, Riverside, San Bernardino and Fresno, and on June 1, he invested $1 million in W.S. Collins Newport Beach Company and received a right of way for a trolley line to Santa Ana.

As the president and largest stockholder of the West Coast Land Company, Stanton received most of Huntington's cash, which he immediately put to use on another project. He began negotiations for another property on the coastal strip between Anaheim and Alamitos Bays that had been divided between the three Alamitos partners into equal parcels. Parcel A nearest Alamitos Bay went to the J. Bixby Company, which in turn conveyed it to the Palos Verdes Company. Parcel C by Anaheim Landing went to Hellman, and Parcel B, located between the two, went to the John W. Bixby heirs. This last land was isolated from the main property and was inconvenient for Susan Bixby and her children, Fred and Susannah. But it was attractive to Stanton. A land purchase was recorded in Orange County on September 2, 1903: "2 SEP, 1903—Susan Bixby, Fred H. Bixby and S.P. Bixby grant to P.A. Stanton. Notarized in San Francisco. Lot B2 of the Partition—white post of the SW corner of the SE quarter of Sec. 11, containing 119.40 acres, more or less."[30]

Basically, this was Old Town Seal Beach from Fifth Street to Fourteenth Street. Part of the Fifth Street side by Central fronted onto the Alamitos Bay sloughs. The purchase price was $100,000. Stanton brought in a partner with deeper pockets—I.A. Lothian. Lothian had come to Los Angeles in the mid-1880s. He was a relative of J. Parmer Fuller (Fuller Paints) and became the company's agent in Southern California. In addition to his paint business and real estate investments (a few weeks earlier, he had sold Henry Huntington a big chunk of property south of downtown Los Angeles), Lothian also was a partner in the Central Oil Company, which struck oil in the Whittier area.

Stanton and Lothian also purchased the Orange County snippet of Jotham Bixby's adjacent Parcel A, a finger that extended across the county line toward the Long Beach Peninsula. This section of land is now the "Gold Coast" between First and Fifth Streets.

On the same day, the Bayside Land Company incorporated with a capital stock of $200,000. Besides Stanton and Lothian, among its directors was George E. Pillsbury, the chief engineer of the Pacific Electric. It's possible he was acting as a front for Huntington. He had performed a similar role in the Brea area, and in later years, Stanton referred to Huntington and Lothian as the two major stockholders in the Bayside Land Company.[31]

Five days later, newspapers reported, "Orange County Surveyor S.H. Finley and a corps of assistants have been at work nearly a week laying out a new summer resort between Alamitos Bay and Anaheim Landing...The new town will be called Bayside, and will be reached by the electric road which will be built from Long Beach to this city. This road is already in operation as far as the new townsite."[32]

The last part was a stretch. The railroad only reached the edge of Alamitos Bay (near the western edge of present Marine Stadium). At that point, interested buyers and investors would catch a ferry which would take them through the channels and sloughs of Alamitos Bay to a new wharf in Bay City that was being built where Fifth Street reached Central Way.[33]

Finley laid out a town of just over eight hundred lots, all 25 feet in width and between 116 and 118 feet deep. When Stanton's group applied for a post office, it was told there was already a post office with the Bayside name in California (located on Arcata Bay just north of Eureka). So the new village was named Bay City.

By the end of February, the new tract had its first inhabitant, John C. Ord, whom a number of histories incorrectly cite as the first resident of Seal Beach.[34] He wasn't. As shown previously, there were numerous permanent residents at Anaheim Landing going back as far as 1872 when Louis Boltz opened his saloon, which was still open as late as 1904.[35]

However, Ord was the first resident in the Bay City subdivision and the only resident for three months until June 1904, when the Pacific Electric finally reached Orange County.

Ord was born in Vermont in 1842, and after three years in the Civil War, he came to Northern California and drifted around to a number of cities and jobs. By 1899, he was a justice of the peace and storekeeper in Los Alamitos.[36] After a couple years in Los Alamitos, he leased out his store and took a six-month trip to New Zealand.

Returning to Los Alamitos, Ord resumed his justice of the peace duties, but he apparently appreciated the potential of Stanton's new beachfront town. In February 1904, he hauled his two-story building to Bay City and located it on Main Street, where it met the Pacific Electric right of way (the southwest corner of Main and Electric).

With Stanton in Sacramento, Ord acted as Bayside Land Company's representative on site. They also formed the Ord Land and Mining Company, which had two goals. The first was to gain title to some disputed land on the peninsula across from Anaheim Landing. Initially, Stanton seems to have been a hidden partner, because in 1905, Ord opposed the Alamitos Land Company over the property that is now Surfside (and was also the Seal Beach Peninsula before the Navy changed the outlet's configuration). Since the Alamitos Company was partially owned by I.W. Hellman, it is difficult to believe Stanton would openly take on his longtime business associate. The Ord Company also bought lots in Bay City for resale after some improvements.

Ord was not the only Los Alamitos resident to have a presence in Bay City. Saloonkeeper Pete Labourdette bought a lot across the street from Ord, where he built a two-story structure, with the bottom floor serving as a saloon. The building later was used as a schoolhouse and police station.

When the Pacific Electric railroad reached Orange County on July 4, 1904, the Long Beach papers reported that the Anaheim Bay land boom was on.[37] Of course, what the papers reported (fed by Ord and Stanton) and what actually was taking place was often not the same thing.

In truth, Bay City lot sales were slow. Competition was fierce from the other beach resort towns—Santa Monica, Ocean Park, Venice and Long Beach. It would get even tougher with the development of four more beach resorts—Huntington Beach, Newport Beach, Naples and Redondo Beach. Henry Huntington was a major investor in all four of these.

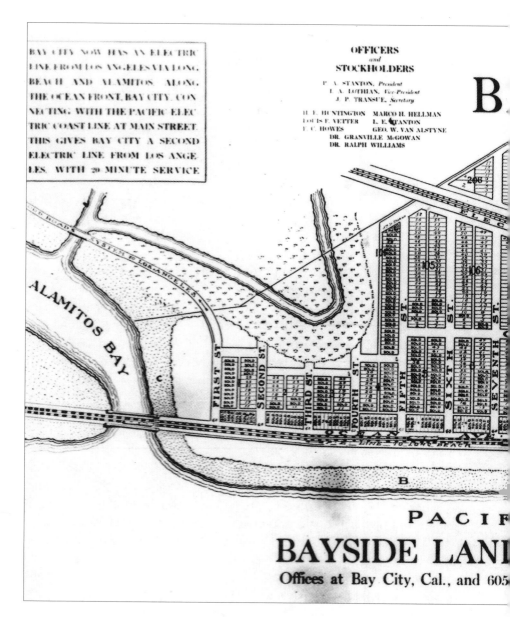

BAY CITY NOW HAS AN ELECTRIC LINE FROM LOS ANGELES VIA LONG BEACH AND ALAMITOS ALONG THE OCEAN FRONT. BAY CITY CONNECTING WITH THE PACIFIC ELECTRIC COAST LINE AT MAIN STREET. THIS GIVES BAY CITY A SECOND ELECTRIC LINE FROM LOS ANGELES WITH 20 MINUTE SERVICE

OFFICERS
and
STOCKHOLDERS

P. A. STANTON, *President*
L. A. LOTHIAN, *Vice-President*
J. P. TRANSUE, *Secretary*

H. E. HUNTINGTON   MARCO H. HELLMAN
LOUIS F. VETTER   L. E. STANTON
F. C. HOWES   GEO. W. VAN ALSTYNE
DR. GRANVILLE McGOWAN
DR. RALPH WILLIAMS

PACIF

BAYSIDE LAN

Offices at Bay City, Cal., and 605

The Pacific Electric entered Seal Beach in summer 1904 via Naples. In 1913, the PE opened a second line from Long Beach via Ocean Avenue.

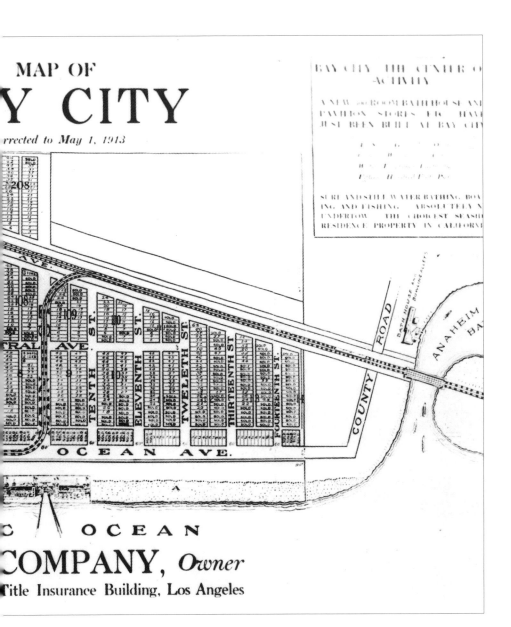

Huntington was free to do this because in December 1904, Hellman's group ended its involvement with the PE railroad. As per the May 1903 agreement, they sold their shares equally to Huntington and Harriman but maintained their interest in the profitable Los Angeles Railway and the Pacific Light and Electric subsidiary.[38]

As by-product of this last Pacific Electric stock sale, Harriman divested one of the Union Pacific's underperforming companies. The Wells Fargo express division was a solid moneymaker, but the banking side troubled Harriman. He made Hellman an attractive offer, which the banker accepted, and within a couple months, the Nevada Bank merged with Wells Fargo and became one of the nation's leading financial institutions.

By mid-1905, the Bayside Land Company was now managing Anaheim Landing. It also made improvements to the Fifth Street wharf where the Alamitos Bay ferry docked. Newspaper ads touted it as "a neat station for the accommodation of those living in the upper part of Bay City."[39]

A later ad mentioned a new boat landing on Anaheim Bay, capable of handling powerboats. In addition, space for a tent city and a recreation park for baseball, tennis and other outdoor activities had been set aside to be developed. (Like so many Bayside claims over the next twenty years, these proved to be untrue.)

Stanton and Ord planted stories in the newspaper every week, telling of the latest land sale, the newest house, store and hotel, restaurant and pavilion, concrete sidewalk and curb, bathhouses and free ferry service to Alamitos Bay.

Ord also advertised his own real estate business ("Bargains in Secondhand Houses and Lots") and reportedly attracted visitors through a fine collection of squirrels, coyotes and skunks—thirteen of them, as tame as kittens and perfectly harmless, although he kept them caged. (Again, whether these actually existed is unknown.)

But these papers also ran planted stories for the eighteen other Southern California beach resorts that were trying just as hard as the Bayside Land Company to attract visitors and potential buyers.

In mid-1904, the Bayside Land Company built a pavilion and bathhouse at the foot of Main Street, but those both burned down in June 1905.

Within days, the company vowed to rebuild the structures. One of those people impressed by the town's potential was there to reopen the new facilities. R.D. Richards moved his wife and family to town and, on August 1, 1905, reopened the bathhouse, bowling alleys and concessions. He would soon oversee construction of twenty cottages around Anaheim Bay.

The Bayside Land Company competed with other beach developments in places like Santa Monica, Venice, Redondo Beach and Naples. Some early ads spoke of a wharf near Fifth Street and Central, where potential buyers could ferry across Alamitos Bay.

This coincided with a construction boom at all coastal resorts that was accelerated by renewed tensions between Harriman and Huntington, growing partly out of an SP veto of a PE line to San Diego and a tricky boardroom maneuver by Harriman that gave him one more director of the PE board than Huntington. In July 1905, Henry Huntington personally bought the Redondo Beach Company and its railroad, thus making the latter railroad beyond the control of the SP. Harriman countered by purchasing the Southland's largest independent electric line, the Los Angeles–Pacific, which connected downtown to Santa Monica, Ocean Park and Venice—and a branch line to Redondo Beach. Harriman upgraded those lines, making it easier for the public to visit the western beach towns.

Among those who enjoyed Anaheim Landing's new facility and boat rental in 1906 were Los Alamitos residents Nina (left) and Una Watts. In 1930, Nina would open the Glide 'er Inn restaurant, helped by a loan from Una.

Beach resort revenues—whether from amusements or sales of lots—were fueled by the weekend traffic of trolley cars. When Abbott Kinney's new Venice of America resort opened in July 1905 and diverted business from other rival resorts, Huntington countered by approving more spending on his Redondo, Naples and Orange County properties, including Seal Beach, and lowered PE rates to all the resorts to be the same as those to Venice.

Longer piers, new bathhouses, bigger pavilions, deeper canals and wider boardwalks, especially in the bays and marshlands around the Long Beach area, were detailed in newspaper ads. The improvements at Bay City were duly noted.

In January 1906, the Bayside Land Company announced plans to build "the longest pier south of San Francisco…from 1,200 to 1,600 feet in length." (It wasn't the longest pier, but the claim looked good on paper.[40]) A block away at the corner of Main and Central would be a two-story, sixteen-room hotel, with three stores and a large dining room on the ground floor. Beginning in May, press releases proclaimed that over $28,000 was being spent on street cement work, that the bathhouse at Anaheim Landing was open, that the new bowling alleys were some of the fastest around and that Phil Stanton "has evolved a plan which is to make Bay City the best lighted city on the Southern California coast." But the spending (and marketing) for Seal Beach was dwarfed by the efforts for the other resorts.

But then, virtually all Southern California real estate development took a hit. The April 1906 San Francisco earthquake and fire diverted some building supplies and capital northward. But, more significantly, the Bank Panic of 1907 made investment money tough to come by for much of the next four years.

Still, the July 14, 1906 *Daily Herald* announced a number of Stanton actions, including the establishment of a tent city at Anaheim Landing.

Tent cities were common at all the Southern California beach resorts. They provided an affordable alternative to hotel rooms. Additional revenue was brought in by the rental of cooking utensils and other amenities.[41] The potential for large-scale tent cities was made evident at the August 1888 Grand Army of the Republic (GAR) gathering at Anaheim Landing.

While small in comparison to some (Coronado's Tent City was twenty-six blocks long), Stanton's tent community proved popular enough that in 1908 John Ord and three others announced the formation of the Bay City Improvement Association to build "Bungalow City." These, too, were located near Anaheim Landing, on Thirteenth Street.

By 1906, the Bayside Land Company had optioned Anaheim Landing, torn down the old warehouses and replaced them with a new bath house, a bowling alley and a grocery store.

Stanton wasn't around for much of this. He was too busy in Sacramento, where his political career benefited after *Los Angeles Times* publisher Harrison Gray Otis was replaced by his son-in-law Harry Chandler. Otis despised the Southern Pacific and its cronies, like Stanton. Chandler was more interested in real estate than newspapers, and for this the SP and Stanton were useful. Aided by the *Times*, Stanton's influence grew. By 1908 he became speaker of the assembly.

He used his influence to help Bay City. When the coastal landowners felt the Orange County supervisors weren't paying enough attention to the coastal towns—vis-à-vis law enforcement and road construction—Stanton introduced legislation in Sacramento to transfer what is now Seal Beach, Huntington Beach and Newport Beach into Los Angeles County. The proposal drew heated discussion, but the supervisors allocated money for road improvements and law enforcement, and the recession issue was dropped.

When California tried to implement strong anti-Japanese legislation, Stanton, urged by U.S. presidents Theodore Roosevelt and William Howard Taft, worked to sidetrack it and avoid antagonizing the Japanese government. Stanton took a lot of heat for this, but Taft remained grateful over the years.

The most significant legislation passed during Stanton's tenure as assembly leader was the direct primary law. Although watered down from what Progressives had originally proposed, its passage gave voters more say in the election of their governor and legislators.

Ironically, it ruined Stanton's chances of being governor in 1910. Even though heavily backed by the Southern Pacific, the *Times* and the party leaders, he placed a distant fourth in the Republican primary, far behind the Progressive candidate, Hiram Johnson.

Although this ended his career as an elected official, Stanton wasn't done with politics.

In 1911, the city of Anaheim bought a seventy-five-acre tract of land between Gilbert and Magnolia as the site for a sewer farm. The property was adjacent to land owned by Stanton, who was still a large landowner in the area, and the main north–south street had even been named after him (though most of it would later be changed to Beach Boulevard). Stanton organized the local farmers into incorporating as a city to thwart Anaheim's plans. To honor their advisor, the farmers named their new city after him. This was the third community formed by Stanton.

The following year, he, along with *Los Angeles Times* publisher Harrison Gray Otis, became leaders of the "Get Johnson" league, and after the Progressive Party imploded in 1912–13, they succeeded in helping remove their fellow Republican from office in 1914.

Even after leaving political office, Stanton was as energetic as ever. And now the stage was set for the biggest project of his life.

CHAPTER 4

SOUTH COAST IMPROVEMENTS AND THE JOY ZONE

By 1912, despite his many accomplishments, Philip A. Stanton had never made the big financial kill. He arrived too late for the 1880s real estate boom. The depression of the 1890s denied him a chance to be a player in building a sugar beet factory. The progressive movement steamroller ended his political career. The San Francisco Earthquake and Bank Panic of 1907—and competition from other beach resorts—had hampered his development of Bay City. All together, these factors had kept him from joining the top echelons of California's movers and shakers.

In 1912 Stanton planned to correct that injustice by making Bay City into a major beach resort.

The first "modern" beach resort—one with a "pleasure pier" intended for amusement and recreation, not commerce—was in Brighton, England, built in the early 1800s. The first pleasure pier in America was at Coney Island in Brooklyn, New York. Southern California's first pleasure pier was built in 1898 in Ocean Park, just south of Santa Monica, by Francis Ryan and Abbott Kinney. It augmented their Pacific Ocean Casino, a narrow 1.5-mile-wide "country club,"[42] which in ten years grew to include a restaurant, tennis courts, a golf course, a horse-racing track, a boardwalk, a plunge (a large swimming pavilion), a pier and almost two hundred beach cottages.

By 1902, spurred by the growth of electric railroads, Ocean Park had competition. A few miles north, Santa Monica promoters had built a huge bathhouse. A few miles south, the Beach Land Company was developing Playa Del Rey into a Venetian-style resort.

The Brighton Beach area of Terminal Island, financed by the Clarks, had its own pier and giant bathhouse and had assumed the mantle of the "Newport of the West," complete with Southern California's first yacht club.

In Long Beach, where the new Pacific Electric could bring thousands of visitors daily, Colonel Charles Drake's grand bathhouse with an indoor freshwater pool and a waterslide was soon followed by a popular boardwalk where independent concessionaires opened attractions like a merry-go-round and a Japanese garden. By mid-1904, this strip was already being advertised as the "Pike," named after the "$10 Million Pike," the famed mile-long midway at the 1904 St. Louis World's Fair.

The nation's first amusement park—as we now know it—was the White City Midway Plaisance at the 1893 Chicago World's Fair. White City was technically the electrically lit, white buildings occupying the fair's main court, but most attendees associated the name with the more popular mile-long midway—the Plaisance—which featured the world's first Ferris wheel, Scott Joplin playing ragtime music, exotic dancer Little Egypt, as well as some electrically powered rides.

The White City midway became the model for the nation's amusement parks—including Coney Island. Over the next ten years, White City parks opened all over the country, usually with two purposes for its major investors.

One was to motivate people to use the electric railways on weekends. Second was to attract people who would buy lots in these new developments, which were usually partially owned by the same men who owned the railroads.

While Long Beach's Pike brought some of the midway to California, it was Abbott Kinney who brought the full-scale amusement park to Southern California. In early 1904, Kinney split from his Ocean Park partners and began developing an even larger community of wide canals, gondolas, hotels, a large pier with an auditorium and a restaurant ship and a midway plaisance facing his canals. His "Venice of America" opened in July 1905, and its success motivated his former partners to expand their amusement area as well.

Ocean Park added a $150,000 indoor heated plunge and an amusement pier. Venice answered with a heated salt-water plunge *and* a new midway pier. Ocean Park countered with a six-thousand-seat auditorium and skating rink, which Venice saw and raised with a huge dance hall accommodating eight hundred couples, and introducing the sport of surfing to Southern California with daily shows by Hawaii's George Freeth.[43]

Not to be outdone, Long Beach converted its livery stable into a skating rink and constructed its own municipal pier and then went "all in" in June 1907 with a roller coaster, Ferris wheel and other rides and amusements.

Part of this was motivated by the announcement of two other Long Beach "Coney Islands." The first was the seven-hundred-acre Riverside Tract, west of the Pike, where some Venice developers proposed a combination of residential canals, commercial port and a large amusement area. That project eventually became the start of the all-commercial Port of Long Beach. But farther east, in early 1905, real estate agent A.M. Parsons purchased four hundred acres on the mud islands of Alamitos Bay, where he planned to develop another community of canals—this one to be called Naples—to feature upscale homes, pavilions, bathhouses and hunting clubs, as well as a Coney Island–type amusement area. His plan was sound enough to get Henry Huntington to commit $1.5 million dollars to the project.[44]

Huntington committed millions more to his Redondo Beach property. By 1909, the resort sported a three-story dance pavilion, restaurant and theater, as well as a new pier. This was all overshadowed by the company's opening of the world's largest indoor salt water plunge—including three heated pools and over one thousand changing rooms.

That same year, Kinney opened an aquarium at Venice, while Ocean Park, rebounding from a terrible fire, debuted its million-dollar amusement pier.

In 1911, Long Beach's new attractions included a merry-go-round built by Charles I.D. Looff, the nation's premier carousel builder who also opened many White City midways. Around 1910, Looff opened a factory in Long Beach that built carousels that were highlights of Venice, Ocean Park, Long Beach, Redondo and other West Coast amusement areas.

Over the next few years, the battle for the hearts, minds and dollars of weekend visitors intensified. Newspaper headlines touted each resort's latest attraction—dance halls, vaudeville theaters, ostrich farms, skating rinks and even infant incubators, where premature babies were displayed and cared for. But getting the most attention were roller coasters.

Venice had the "Race Thru the Clouds," ninety feet high with four thousand feet of track for each of its two parallel tracks, and when it opened on July 4, 1911, with only half the cars on line, the coaster carried 25,230 people from 8:30 a.m. to 1:15 a.m.

In 1913, Redondo Beach opened the 6,000-foot-long Lightning Racer, and Ocean Park trumpeted the arrival of the Ben Hur Racer (4,200 feet), a new racing roller coaster, a feat matched in Long Beach by the May 1, 1915

P.A. Stanton united all the beach property developers from Long Beach to Balboa into the South Coast Improvement Association. Stanton (seated, at end of table) was elected president of the new group at their first meeting in 1913.

opening of the Jackrabbit Racer (3,250 feet long) on the Silver Spray Pier, where you could look down through the tracks at the ocean water.

Although they didn't have the rides, Seal Beach's Orange County rivals—Huntington and Newport—had dance pavilions and piers and were more favored because of easier transportation to their resort areas.[45]

This was the competition that Phil Stanton and the Bayside Land Company faced when he returned to Southern California in 1910. Something had to be done. For all its hype, the Bayside Land Company had sold relatively few lots. And many of those "sold" lots had defaulted back to the company.

Stanton's investment partners were of little help. I.A. Lothian was now basically retired, as was Henry Huntington, who by 1910 had totally sold out his rail interests to the Southern Pacific and set about expanding his real estate empire and building what would become one of the world's great art collections and museums.[46]

Stanton organized the major land developers from Naples to Newport into the South Coast Improvement Association, which immediately arranged for hourly trains and reduced rates on the Pacific Electric.[47] In return, the South Coast promoters agreed to take out large ads in the

PAVILION AND BATH HOUSE TO BE BU

Resort center projected by the Bayside Land Co., an organization of Los An
"South Coast." The improvement will follow closely the construction of

AT BAY CITY AT ONCE.

d beach capitalists, for popular shore town on
d Pacific Electric Alamitos-Bay City line.

Top: The Guy M. Rush Co. ("subdivision specialists") took over Bay City's marketing in 1913 and re-branded the failed real estate development as the new amusement resort of Seal Beach. Architect Burnsides Sturges was hired to design twin pavilions, which resembled Atlantic City's famed Steel Pier.

Bottom: The west pier (on the left) housed a dancing area that was twice the size of the old pavilion, and downstairs was a billiard parlor, a bowling alley and stores. The bathhouse in the East pavilion had three hundred changing areas for bathers.

In July 1913, the Rush Company ran the first of seventy "seal-based" newspaper ads, drawn by noted illustrator Henry DeKruif. The top two ads showcase the name change to Seal Beach, and the fun watersports, including motorboating, that the resort offers.

Sunday papers over the next few years, extolling the beaches, the towns, the roads, the crowds, the improvements and the money (exaggerated, of course) being spent on improvements.

In October 1912, the Bay City promoters announced their most ambitious project—a $75,000 canal between Alamitos Bay and Anaheim Bay. This wasn't as crazy as some might think now. The sloughs of Alamitos Bay still reached the site of the old wharf near Fifth Street and Central Way. Much of the land north of Electric was below the high tide line that would often fill with long-lasting ponds after heavy rains. A canal would have made Bay City an island like Naples, given the Bayside Land Company even more waterfront land to sell and made it the "connecting link" in a navigable inland waterway of many miles.[48]

While the canal proposal died, another improvement did see fruition: the "popular dancing pavilion at the pier" would be "doubled in size" and "stores, bowling alley and other features" would be installed below

These Henry DeKruif illustrated ads highlight the opening of the new Pacific Electric coastal line to Long Beach and the completion of the Boulevard, which connected Central to the bridges across the wetlands to Naples.

the dancing floor. Designed by architect Burnsides Sturges, company press releases implied that the renovated pavilion's cupolas were inspired by Atlantic City's famed Steel Pier, which modestly billed itself as the "Showplace of the Nation."[49]

This may have been developed with the Guy M. Rush Company, a prominent Southern California real estate marketer. He (actually, his staff) wrote how-to manuals for real estate salesmen, pushing the Rush philosophy, which, in modern terms, was basically, "go big or go home."[50]

Rush and Stanton were definitely in business together by March 1913. One of Rush's first actions was to re-brand the town. Out was the real estate failure of Bay City. In was the "new" amusement resort of Seal Beach,[51] named for "the herd of 150–200 seals which could often be found in the vicinity."[52] The town's name change and new pavilions were officially christened with a barbecue, parade, festival and moonlight dance on July 17, 1913. Two thousand people were treated to tables piled high with barbecue beef, tubs filled with frijoles, buns, pickles and barrels of coffee.[53]

The "Seal Beach" brand was introduced and reinforced by a year-long campaign of clever newspaper ads depicting seals engaged in many leisure activities—bowling, billiards, motorboating, parading, surfing, spring cleaning and

many more. The seals were drawn by Henri G. DeKruif. DeKruif's first seal-based ad ran on July 9, 1913, beginning a campaign of seventy ads that would run until October 17, 1914.[54]

On September 8, 1913, the Rush Company's general manager, Robert B. Armstrong, hosted another gala, celebrating the Pacific Electric's second line to Seal Beach. This one paralleled the coast,[55] starting in downtown Long Beach, down Railroad Avenue (Broadway) through Belmont Shore and the Peninsula on Ocean Avenue. After crossing into Seal Beach, it continued down Ocean to Main Street and turned inland. At Electric, it joined the main line to Anaheim Landing and Newport Beach.[56] Locals called this the "Dinky Line."

The new line made it easier for Seal Beach kids to reach the Pike and Majestic Ballroom in Long Beach and simplified travel from downtown Long Beach to Huntington Beach and Balboa. But unfortunately, it resulted in little increased traffic to Seal Beach (and Anaheim Landing), and more importantly, it didn't help sell Seal Beach real estate.[57]

However, twenty unsold lots were put to good use in December 1913, when the Guy M. Rush and Bayside Land Companies offered twenty lots at half price for the construction of a school between Eleventh and Twelfth

The new name of "Seal Beach" was reinforced through "trick photography," which stuck groups of seals onto photos of the town's pier, as well as this 1915 shot showing a lady walking along the beach past the new pavilion and the relocated bathhouse.

Streets. (New schools were always good fodder for real estate promoters.) Previously, students had been attending classes in the Labourdette Building on Main Street, which had also doubled as a city hall and police station. Within the next month, voters would approve a $5,000 bond issue to build a three-classroom school at Eleventh and the State (Coast) Highway.[58] A key player in this process was R.D. Richards, who had been on the school board since 1909. By the fall of 1914, a frame building faced with brick was constructed, housing two classrooms, an office and a library,[59] and Richard's son, Milton, was one of the first students enrolled.

The Rush company purchased an additional 13.85 acres "on the ocean front" adjoining the east edge of the Bay City subdivision. This would include the Hellman "Parcel C" land from Fourteenth Street to Anaheim Landing.[60]

Stanton convinced the Orange County supervisors to fund a bridge over Anaheim Bay and a paved road between Seal Beach and Sunset Beach. This would be the first segment of what would become the Coast Highway.

Throughout 1914, two thousand feet of concrete sidewalk was poured on Ocean between Main and Second. The Guy M. Rush Company organized numerous excursions (by train and auto bus from Corona, Redlands, downtown, Pasadena, etc.) and special sales events. But it was to little avail. The country was in the middle of another recession, with unemployment reaching 25 percent and productivity declining 20 percent. By the end of 1914, the Rush Company was out of the picture, although general manager Robert Armstrong stayed on with the Bayside Land Company. But things remained tough. The world war continued to affect the economy, and more people were driving automobiles—and with few good roads, it was an ordeal to drive to Bay City, especially after a heavy rain. Also, the other resorts had something Seal Beach didn't have—amusement parks with huge exciting roller coasters and other attractions.

But opportunity presented itself in 1915 with the success of the San Francisco's Panama-Pacific International Exposition, which not only celebrated the opening of the Panama Canal but also showed the world that San Francisco had bounced back from the 1906 Earthquake and Fire.

Hydroskimming.

The latest in water sports which was demonstrated on the waters at Seal Beach by Georgia Smith. She says that it is easier than it looks.

At Seal Beach.

HYDROSKIMMING, A NEW SPORT, INTRODUCED HERE.

Seal Beach promoters publicized activities like motorboating, "sand scooters" and hydroskimming (an early version of wakeboarding) with photos featuring attractive ladies, usually aspiring movie stars. The image of Georgia Smith (left) hydroskimming in Anaheim Bay predates the credited first instance of water skiing by eight years and wakeboarding by over seventy years. The 1916 image of Mary Reeves (right) is one of the earliest reports of a non-Hawaiian performing "surf-board riding."

From February through December 1915, the exhibition wowed eighteen million visitors with its lush gardens, Moorish-inspired fountains and pastel-colored buildings. Two major attractions were the "Scintillator," a bank of moving colored searchlights that, in the foggy, misty nights, resembled the aurora borealis,[61] and the Zone, a seven-block amusement park area that followed the pattern of the 1893 Chicago's Midway Plaisance.

Even before the exhibition was halfway over, the fair's concessionaires were wondering what would happen when the exhibition ended. (Each ride and concession was essentially its own separate business, although sometimes financing was arranged with the fair's backers.) Fortunately, for Stanton, two of the fair's key backers were Hellmans. I.W. owned the Hellman Ranch, and his son, Marco, was on the board of directors of the exposition and the Bayside Land Company.

On July 15, 1915, Stanton and others incorporated the Jewel City Amusement Company with a capital stock of $500,000. Rumors swirled

Former president William Howard Taft stayed at P.A. Stanton's residence in mid-1915. With him in this photo (left to right) are J.B. Bushnell of Los Angeles, A.L. Havens, P.A. Stanton, John C. Ord, A.J. Spinner, H.M. Magie, Taft, H.M. Snow and J.H. May.

that the San Francisco fair's amusement area would move south, but before plans could be confirmed, Stanton had some details to deal with.

One way to differentiate his amusement zone from Long Beach was to have liquid amusements (i.e., alcohol). Long Beach was a dry city. So was Redondo Beach.

Stanton needed the town to incorporate and then have the city council approve the sale of liquor. On September 7, the Orange County supervisors received a petition signed by 526 residents of the Bay City community asking that they be allowed to vote on incorporation.

Opposition sprang up immediately. Resident Ira Patterson, a carpenter, declared that there were not 526 residents of the city, which was true. Another opponent was R.D. Richards, who had become the first president of the town's new chamber of commerce in 1912 and had developed a rift with Ord and Stanton. Richards was decidedly part of the "dry" faction, which was backed by a Long Beach group that voiced concerns about having "a wet town on the eastern border of Long Beach, one within easy reach by electric car." But proponents countered, with a wink and a nod, according to the *Los Angeles Times*, that this was just a simple matter of civic betterment.[62] The Orange County supervisors must have agreed, because they set an election for October 19.

Stanton let it be known that over a million dollars in improvements would begin soon after the election, including "a concrete promenade from Anaheim Landing to Alamitos Bay. A double bulkhead would protect ocean-front property."

The issue was never in doubt, and on October 19, 1915, Bay City residents overwhelmingly voted to incorporate by a vote of eighty-four to sixteen. The "Incorporation ticket" also won handily.[63]

The celebration barbecue began before the last votes were cast. The *Times* described the city's birth as amidst "a blaze of light, with dancing and feasting." Part of the lights were additional bonfires and fireworks provided by a movie crew from the Balboa Amusements Company in Long Beach. Director Bertram Bracken was shooting a film that needed a big assembly of people, so he used the city celebration to stage an election scene directly in front of the pavilion following the fireworks. In addition to the bonfires, the scene was further illuminated by many torches.[64]

Two weeks after that, on November 9, newspapers announced that Frank Burt, the director of concessions and admissions at the Panama-Pacific Exposition in San Francisco, had signed a contract to "manage a great new amusement resort at Seal Beach."[65] It would be "the rival of Venice" and would bring in many concessions from the amusement zone in San Francisco, including the two-mile-long roller coaster,[66] as well as "many of the classic fountains, statues and ornamental light standards" and the "great battery of scintillators…[whose] searchlights, playing on land and sea, are expected to attract much attention."

Burt was already an experienced and successful actor and amusement manager. He had managed one of the nation's largest chain of theaters and then became a manager of amusement parks. His success with Lakeside Park, Denver's White City amusement operation, led to his hiring in 1912 to manage the amusement zone at the San Francisco Exhibition. That phase of the operation turned a profit before it ever opened, further enhancing Burt's reputation.

Burt brought with him three trusted lieutenants. Two had been with Burt since Denver. Bert St. John supervised concessions and marketing, and Wayne Abbott managed the fireworks, scintillators and the Fountain of the Sun and even did aerial parachute drops from record-setting heights. Abbott's background made him one of the Joy Zone's most interesting characters.

When Seal Beach voted to incorporate in October 1915, it also elected town officers. Those selected were (counterclockwise from top left): A.M. Snow (treasurer), John C. Ord, Herman Eichorn, James Blagge, C.A. Little, Harry Magie and City Clerk A.L. Havens. Ord would become the town's first mayor, and in 1917, Blagge would become the first of many elected officials to be recalled.

His real name was Armstrong Wayne Hogbin, born in 1874 and the son of a U.S. Army Indian scout in Wyoming and Colorado. In his late teens, he was traveling with a Wild West show, often portraying a Cheyenne Indian and using the name Mad Wolf. By 1896, he was working as a balloonist and parachutist in the Rocky Mountain area and known professionally as Wayne Abbott. He was already married to his first wife, Annie, at this time, who was fifteen years older than him and had two children, ages ten and five, by a previous marriage. By some accounts, she was also a professional balloonist using the name Lady Inman. Other sources say she worked at an amusement park restaurant and her aerial experience was limited to their well-publicized marriage in the basket of his hot air balloon. During the recession of the mid-1890s, they struggled to find work, but finally in October 1897, he was hired at a Salt Lake resort as noted aeronaut "Professor Wayne Abbott." The loneliness of being away from her family and leaving her children with her parents, combined with the uncertainty of "carny

FRANK BURT

Frank Burt, who will be remembered as one of the leading officials of the P. P. I. E., is now in charge of Seal Beach; one of the leading beaches and amusement resorts in the South. Burt has done wonders in building this latest place of amusement, and the vast crowds that attended the opening on July 1st were ably handled and made comfortable. All due credit is due to the hard working efforts of Seal Beach, and it is sure to be a huge success.

In late 1915, Frank Burt was hired to manage the new Seal Beach amusement operations. He previously ran one of the nation's largest chains of vaudeville theaters and managed Denver's Lakeside Park and the amusements at San Francisco's Panama-Pacific Exhibition in 1915.

life," led Annie to attempt suicide via chloroform, but fortunately, Abbott found medical assistance to save her. They soon returned to Denver, where he found regular work at that city's Lakeside Park resort, where his act included hanging on a trapeze that sometimes hung from a balloon and sometimes would be sliding down a cable that ran from atop a tower to an anchorage far out in the lake. On the latter stunt, he would hold Roman candles as he descended. He also made dubious claims about world records for highest balloon ascension but did perform numerous verified record-setting parachute drops. [67]

At Lakeside Park, he met Frank Burt, who gave Abbott the additional duties of overseeing the park's fireworks show. Abbott led a charmed life—he survived two falls when his balloons burst prematurely and his parachute barely had time to open fully, once landing on a roof and another time on a trolley bus, smashing through the front window. He was also badly burned and almost killed when defective wiring set off an explosion in a fireworks factory. But he learned enough about fireworks to later patent a grenade approved for use by the army and also had several patents on parachute development.

Wayne taught his son Harry all his tricks, and by the time they arrived in Seal Beach, the sixteen-year-old was equally ingrained in the carny life and was, by this time, the veteran of many balloon trips and even rope walking. His real accomplishments and outlandish exaggerations would outdo those of his dad. [68]

Another San Francisco import, architect Edward Symmes oversaw the Moorish-Venetian look of the amusement area and drew the fantasized illustration which was used for this ad in a July 1916 issue of *Billboard* as well as on the new city's letterhead (see back cover).

Another of Burt's key hires was twenty-eight-year old architect Edward Symmes.

In November, the new city council approved the sale of alcohol, causing the *Los Angeles Times* to gush that the new town now "edges its way into the spotlight of Southern California's numerous 'watering places' and resorts where the bright lights gleam and care is thrown to the winds."[69]

The new council also stated it would establish license fees for jitney buses to operate in the town, another favor to the Pacific Electric Railway. The "unreliable operators" had stolen so much of the Pacific Electric's business that the latter had dropped their scheduled runs to basically once or twice a day. With the new line to downtown Long Beach and the action of the Seal Beach council, the Pacific Electric committed to running at least twenty trips per day on weekends.

In mid-January, Burt announced that the amusement area's architectural theme would be Spanish Gothic (sometimes also called Moorish)—like Playa del Rey, Venice, Redondo and the Panama-Pacific—and that "the present pavilion, dance hall and pier at Seal Beach would form the nucleus of the new resort." All architecture would be under the watch of Symmes, who also drew the ornate beach scene that would soon adorn the Seal Beach city letterhead. The scheduled opening day was May 1.

Already, nearly two hundred men were at work, many working on the nearly four thousand feet of concrete walk between the Main Street Pier and Anaheim Landing at a uniform width of thirty-eight feet. (This was named Seal Way and was closer to the beach than the current alley that bears the same name.) A few feet closer to the water was one mile of bulkhead in the Seal Beach sand, which was designed to prevent waves from reaching the amusement area.

The construction fever spread to Anaheim Landing, where H.H. Wilcox, the original builder of Hollywood, and the White City Amusements Company, under the direction of W.H. Labb, purchased the casino and leased more land from the I.W. Hellman Company. Labb had constructed the original Chicago White City and many other White City parks around the country. He had also built the Ben-Hur roller coaster at Ocean Park which had burnt down soon after its opening. Labb's park would include carousels, a "shoot the chutes" waterslide (an early version of a flume ride like Disneyland's Splash Mountain), a toboggan slide, a picnic plaza, a casino and a dancing pavilion. The investors also announced plans for five hundred three-bedroom cottages near the park.

Stanton and Burt apparently had no objections to this competition. Anything that attracted more people to Seal Beach—and helped sell lots—was good.

At times, press releases said over $1,000,000 would be spent on improvements. Other releases said $200,000. Despite the inconsistency, the big dollars got big headlines, and not just in the Bayside Land Company's new Seal Beach paper, the *Post* (which started publishing in March by R.F. Bowers, a "man who knows how to write, plug and boost with both feet"[70]), but in the *Press-Telegram*, the *Santa Ana Register*, the *Anaheim Bulletin* and all the Los Angeles papers—the *Express*, the *Herald*, the *Examiner* and the *Times*.

On March 5, David Combs and James Blyler, who had recently bought the Seal Beach Inn at Main and Central (where Hennessey's and the parking lot are now located), announced plans to begin construction on a downstairs cafe and dance hall they would call the Lodge. It would hold "tables for

Noted photographer Edward Cochems took most of the photographs that show Seal Beach as it looked from 1915 to 1920. Many photos were also used as postcards and sent all over the country. This was the main entrance to the pier and promenade. The Jewel City Café was in the pavilion to the right. Both pavilions were expanded for the Joy Zone construction.

200 and a free parking space across the street for your auto." They also announced that additional space would be added to the upper-floor hotel.

That same day, Burt announced plans for a $50,000 ice rink to take advantage of the ice skating craze "which has struck Southern California the past few weeks."

But as building progressed, people started noticing that what was being promised was not necessarily what was delivered. The ice rink and other attractions never came through. And when the Scintillators arrived from San Francisco on February 12, some said they appeared to be smaller replicas, not the original lamps. They were. At San Francisco, there were two major lighting attractions: the main Scintillators, which used forty-eight-inch projectors, and smaller thirteen-inch Scintillators used on the Tower of Jewels. For Seal Beach, Burt purchased forty-eight of the Tower of Jewel's thirteen-inch projectors.[71] Although smaller, they still worked, and soon the colored lenses constantly passing in front of the searchlights created a rainbow "scintillating" effect that could be seen for miles in all directions.

But locals were already getting nervous. On February 16, after some residents and the city council delayed returning title of the property along

A highlight of the San Francisco exposition was the Scintillators, spotlights fronted by rotating colored gels. The most famous Scintillators were rows of forty-eight-inch spotlights set on a barge in San Francisco Bay, each requiring one man to operate, but a smaller set of Scintillators projected light onto the exhibit's signature Tower of Jewels. It was these smaller Scintillators that were brought to Seal Beach. The lights could still be seen from ten to twelve miles away.

beachfront alleys back to the Bayside Land Company as promised, Judge John C. Ord resigned from the city council (board of trustees). Then in mid-March, liquor licenses for Blyler & Combs' new Seal Beach Inn and new bars to be operated by the Jewel City Amusement Co. and the Anaheim Landing Casino were withheld pending the filing of proper bonds.[72] These events—and the Bayside Land Company's history of marketing exaggerations and unfulfilled promises—made locals and workers nervous.

On May 12, carpenters working on the roller coaster went on strike, demanding to be paid in cash and not by Jewel Amusement Company checks.[73] The forty strikers were immediately fired and new workers hired. But another strike was beyond the company's control: a longshoremen's strike left parts of the coaster and other rides sitting off the coast for a few weeks.

Things were also messy at Anaheim Landing. Carnival operator W.H. Labb was arrested for passing "fictitious checks." Although his partner, H.H. Wilcox, continued construction, the ambitious improvements at the Landing were scaled back.[74]

Nervous city residents continued to delay transferring the property along beachfront alleyways back to the Bayside Land Company as promised for its expansion. Finally, on May 22, Phil Stanton declared to the council, "We have made Seal Beach, and we can break it!"

"This town has been asleep for ten years, and we are just awakening it from its deep slumbers," continued Stanton. "Whether it shall grow and develop depends on you people…unless other action than has been taken here tonight is indicated by your honorable body, we shall immediately suspend all our operations here."[75]

The trustees reconsidered and passed a motion acceptable to Stanton and his partners.

One thing going to plan was the introduction of aviation in Seal Beach. By mid-May 1916, the Jewel City company had constructed three hangars, probably tent structures, on the beach west of the pier, and aviators were beginning to fill them.[76]

Aviation wasn't new to the town. In February 1916, the Seal Beach pier was the finish line for a twenty-mile race beginning in Long Beach.[77] Later that year, when Long Beach residents expressed opposition to beach flights, a group of pilots, led by Harry Christofferson and Earl Daugherty, the winner of that February 1916 race, shifted their operations—and afternoon flights—to Seal Beach's new hangars. After a few weeks at Seal Beach, Daugherty left to train army pilots, but he was replaced by other barnstorming daredevils like Jay Boyd, Thor Polson, Joe Boquel and Clarence "Ollie" Prest.[78]

Even though the longshoremen's strike kept most of the big amusement rides from operating, Seal Beach opened over the Memorial Day weekend for a "semi-official" preview. The Scintillators, several oceanfront concessions and two high-class cafés earned good marks from local newspapers. The opening also had some unplanned thrills by aviator Jay Boyd. Due to the soft sand, his plane struggled to build up enough speed on the three-hundred-foot beach runway to get his plane the thirty feet in the air necessary to clear a pile driver by the pier. Sensing he wouldn't make it, Boyd angled his plane down the slope toward the surf and began to lift off. But a wheel caught one of the incoming waves, causing it to drop. As its wheels hit the sand, the plane stopped, sending Boyd over the steering wheel and twenty feet away in the surf. Fortunately, he was unhurt, and a few hours later, "the plucky aviator climbed into his machine and thrilled the audience with steep drops and swerving glides."[79]

The town's real estate agent, the Robert Armstrong Company (now conducting business under his own name), said even with some rides not in operation, over twenty-five thousand people had shown up on Memorial Day. On the following weekend, patrons arrived in "over one thousand automobiles," causing a policeman to be stationed at Main and Ocean to direct traffic, apparently for the first time. Seal Beach had also hired a second motorcycle policeman to control the motorists who were "speeding" into town on the recently completed (but still very narrow, crooked and dangerous) road from Long Beach via Naples, the Alamitos Bay marshes and Central Avenue.

The next few weeks saw a barrage of articles from the Bayside publicity department, including an eight-page section in the *Santa Ana Register*[80] highlighting the new amusement area's attractions.

The *Times* reported on June 13, 1916, that four aviators flying "passenger-carrying and demonstration aeroplanes" were already at the "most up-to-

Shown at left is the street entrance to the Joy Zone's racing coaster, The Derby. Although advertised as "brought down from the San Francisco Exhibition," only the cars, motors and chains made the trip south. The Derby's Figure-8 configuration was also shorter and different from San Francisco's L-shape. The coaster was damaged in a 1923 fire and used sparingly after that.

date and completely appointed [airplane] hangars on the Pacific Coast." In addition, a new company, operated by Malcolm and Allen Loughheep (later Lockheed), was "seriously considering locating their hangars in the town, with a view of establishing a hydro-aeroplane passenger-carrying business this summer, the first one of its kind in Southern California. They are also figuring on conducting a seaplane aviation school on the side."[81] The Jewel Amusement Company also hoped to establish a training school under the command of a U.S. Army officer at the facility. Beyond the hangars was an ammo building where the company's fireworks, skyrockets and other pyrotechnics were built and stored, under the supervision of Wayne Abbott.

On the beach side of Ocean, between Sixth and Eighth, was a parking lot. Behind it, facing the shore was a lattice-enclosed picnic area (big enough to seat five hundred) with vine-covered arbors and cool retreats offering a view of the ocean.

At the foot of Main Street was the main entryway to the pavilions, the pier and stairs to the beach and boardwalk. On the east side, the two-year-old bathhouse had been extended two hundred feet. The dance floor—"now one of the largest in California"—would permit eight hundred people at one time, and the bathhouse was expanded to one thousand changing rooms to accommodate three thousand bathers. The company noted that a plunge (an indoor swimming pool) would be built later.[82]

In the west pavilion, the upstairs bowling alley now housed an elegant two-story café chantant,[83] later called the Jewel City Café, run by J.W. Miller

Looking down the Seal Way promenade, the arcade begins beyond the pavilion and continues to Twelfth Street. Although plans called for the arcade and promenade to extend to Anaheim Landing, this never happened. Beyond the roller coaster is the sign for Tent City.

Here's another view of the east beach, showing the Bath-house Pavilion, the arcade and the beach bulkheads—low concrete walls intended to prevent the waves from reaching the Seal Way promenade. Attendees also found them convenient to use as seats.

In 1916, the pavilion bowling alley was converted to the Café Chantant, soon renamed the Jewel City Café. Guests could still use the pavilion's two rooftop gazebos and enjoy a view of the pier and beach. The dance floor was installed in 1917 and saw much use over the next fifteen years.

Above: The upstairs of the west pavilion housed the Jewel City Café. Downstairs were a number of small concessions, including the Rathskeller, a less expensive food area, and picnic grounds surrounded by latticework.

Left: One of the concessions beneath the pier in the Rathskeller area was this stand selling "original red hot" Coney Island hot dogs.

(formerly of New York and Denver's Lakeside Park). Miller's eatery could seat five hundred, and the center area featured a tank containing freshly caught fish and lobsters. Guests were given a net and the opportunity to catch their meals and have them cooked to order in one of the brick ovens, which cost $30,000 to construct. Each table also had its own percolator "for ladies who prefer to make their own coffee." The restaurant kept the pavilion's two rooftop gazebos, where guests could enjoy a 360-degree view of the pier, the beach and the other surrounding features. Underneath the pier were some small concessions and the Rathskeller ("the best food at popular prices").

South of the main entry, the "racing coaster" was still awaiting the giant chain, thanks to the longshoremen's strike. The final figure-eight layout was not as long as the L-shaped coaster in San Francisco, but the shorter Seal Beach version still had all the safety features of the San Francisco coaster, which was reportedly the very first to have its wheel flanges on the outside, so derailment was practically impossible. Trains were sent off simultaneously by a power starter, and there was a bona fide race between them, determined by differences of momentum due to inequality in load. It was noted that fat girls were of great assistance to victory.[84]

Riders exited the coaster past the pavilion changing rooms, onto Seal Way—the thirty-five-foot-wide "boardwalk." The ocean side of the walkway featured ornamental statues, fountains and light fixtures brought down from San Francisco. New concrete light posts, about ten feet tall, were topped with four standing seals, each facing a different direction, and a large light emanated from the center area behind their heads. The beach side of the walkway featured the "pleasure places," as the concessions were called.

Next to the pavilion was a small "Jungle Show" and beyond that the Ocean Wave, a candy and popcorn concession whose "Salt Water Taffy made the San Francisco Fair," or so claimed its owners, R.W. Kaneen and John J. Doyle.[85] They also served Christopher's Quality Ice Cream.

Professor Cairo the Palmist "descended from three generations of palmists." However, in San Francisco, he operated his Temple of Palmistry under the name of "Ali Rajah."[86]

Beyond Cairo's Temple to the end of the midway (Seal Way at about Twelfth Street) were a shooting gallery, boxball alley, a Kelly game,[87] Ahern's Nifty Shop, a public convenience station, a roller skating concession, and another San Francisco import: the Jesters' Palace, a funhouse whose crooked mirrors, moving staircases, cylinders and revolving discs had been very profitable in San Francisco;[88] and the Seal Way boardwalk ended, although company officials promised it would eventually extend to Anaheim Landing. It never did.

The Seal Way promenade was illuminated by lights decorated with concrete seals, each facing a different direction. In the front right foreground is the Temple of Palmistry run by Professor Cairo (known in San Francisco as Ali Rajah), and just past it is the ice cream, candy and salt water taffy concession called the Ocean Wave.

At the Landing, H.W. Wilcox's new two-story casino earned praise for its architecture and new refrigeration unit capable of turning out one thousand pounds of ice daily. Forgotten were the earlier claims to add a carousel, a shoot-the-chutes, a baseball park and five hundred three-room cottages.

However, a new firm, the Anaheim Amusement Company, announced plans to build a new moving picture theater, a high-grade restaurant and 140 to 200 new cottages. These new buildings would replace Richards' Bowling Alleys and Bath Houses. They were never built either.

Standing at the pier and looking up Main Street, a viewer could see that the west (left) side street was now anchored by the beautiful new brick building housing the Bayside Land Company and Jewel City Amusement Company offices. The building's curved front paralleled the radius of the trolley tracks of the Ocean Street line from Long Beach.

Just beyond the alley was the Seal Beach Pharmacy ("a full line of beach comforts in addition to drugs and cigars"), whose owner, C.A. Little, claimed to be "the oldest merchant in Seal Beach." Next to that was the Seal Confectionary (and ice cream parlor) and beyond that the Raymond Café, whose specialty, their huge front sign proudly noted, was lunch.

The Studio was the arcade's "Kelly game" at which players hurled balls at a moving row of hats or clay figures. Winners received a cigar or some other prize. Other arcade concessions included a shooting gallery, Ahern's Nifty Shop, a Jungle Show and by some reports, roller skating.

Battery-powered electriquettes were introduced at the Venice and Santa Monica boardwalks in 1914 but became best known at the 1915 San Diego and San Francisco Panama Expositions. They came in two models—a three-wheeler that carried two people and a four wheeler designed for four. The vehicles, which could move at four miles per hour, cost $1.00 an hour or $7.50 for the day.

No sooner had the Pacific Electric laid tracks to Seal Beach, more and more visitors started making their trips to the beach resorts by car. This put Seal Beach at a disadvantage because there were few good roads leading to town. Still, enough drivers made the trip that parking lots were built off Ocean Avenue.

Patrons at the Seal Beach Pharmacy (left) could buy drugs, ice, Kodak film and Coca Cola or use a scale to weigh themselves. Beyond it were a confectionary, a café, the Tourist Hotel and the notorious Tower Café and Seal Beach Hotel.

Saddled between some vacant lots was the Canary Cottage Café and beyond that the brick-constructed Tourist Hotel. At the end of the block (at Central) was the Lodge Café, whose parking lot was across Main Street and next to a building owned by town plumber Walter Stortz. Ten years before, Stortz had come to the Los Angeles area after being told by his doctor that he didn't have long to live. He visited the beaches around Bay City, determined to enjoy his few remaining days. After some time resting on the sand, swimming, basking in the sun and eating shellfish, he recovered, and in less than one year, he went to work. As there was no local plumber, he was soon in great demand and opened a shop, which would remain a fixture for years at 142 Main Street.[89] The rest of the east side of the street was virtually vacant.

Newspaper ads proudly noted the qualities of other businesses in town: O.O. Richardson's Grocery ("the nearest grocery to the beach"); Henry Anderson's Dry Goods ("specialty in beach apparel" and "the things you want most when you come to the beach"); Seal Beach Furniture Company, operated by M.M. Litten, formerly of Santa Ana (which rented out "low-priced furniture to resort visitors and even tents to those strong for outdoor life"); Seal Beach Dye Works ("French Dye and Steam Cleaning" for hats, suits). The dye works also had a branch office up Main Street close to the Seal Beach Pool Hall (Bauman & Wilcox, proprietors, "second block on Main Street").

Near the junction of Main and Electric was A.B. Snow's Lumber Company at Sixth and Electric. Snow, whose family also had a yard in San Pedro, urged residents, "Don't Haul Your Lumber Sixteen Miles."

Just down Ocean Avenue from the Bayside Company's new office was Charles McAllister's Royal Dairy ("the best ice cream made or delivered in Seal Beach"). McAllister was also an agent for the Huntington Beach Ice and Cold Storage Company.

The day before the official opening, to prime the publicity pump, Burt staged an auto parade that snaked its way through Southland cities, including Long Beach, Compton and Fullerton before finally making its way to Seal Beach, where the town had increased its police force from two to six to handle the eagerly anticipated crowds.[90]

Finally, on July 1, the Joy Zone opened. At 10:00 a.m., with bands blaring, Governor Robinson in Sacramento pressed a button that electronically "opened" the new resort's midway. "Thousands of people flocked to the bathing beach, Hawaiian surfboards (weighing around 100 pounds) were taken out, and the mile and a half long promenade was crowded with spectators," all wishing to enjoy the newest "Coney Island of the Pacific."

None of the other local "Coney Islands of the Pacific" rolled over for Seal Beach's big opening. That same weekend, Venice staged a bullfight, Ocean Park hosted an amateur swim meet and Long Beach featured bands, the Pacific Coast Tennis Championships, a boat race and an assortment of track and swimming competitions for all levels. All claimed "their busiest Sunday of the year."

Still, over the first weekend, a reported forty thousand visitors enjoyed the attractions of the Joy Zone—the rides, concessions, restaurants, bands and a variety of daredevil acts, which included hot-air balloonist Wayne Abbott, who, when he wasn't running the Scintillators and nightly fireworks show at the end of the pier, would drift over the ocean and drop by parachute into the sea. Over the next few weeks, stunt pilots like Joe Boquel did spiral loops and dives, figure-eight slides and upside-down flights—sometimes at night illuminated by flares on the wings and the Scintillator lights. The daredevil antics were not limited to males. In mid-July, Georgia "Tiny" Broadwick, who three years earlier was the first women to parachute from an airplane (and was also the first person ever to do a planned freefall jump) exited an airplane at some three thousand feet of elevation and parachuted safely to the beach. Not all locals approved of women taking part in such aerial activities. When Lillian Bonna ("a pretty Los Angeles miss") was about to

Aerial races and stunts over Seal Beach go back to 1913. Noted Long Beach pilot Earl Daugherty (above left) appeared in an air race over Seal Beach in February 1916. After training pilots for World War I, he returned to the area and did many stunt-flying exhibitions over Seal Beach. Georgia "Tiny" Broadwick (right), the first woman to parachute from an airplane, was one of the earliest daredevil headliners at the new Joy Zone resort in July 1916.

take a "joyride" (well-publicized, naturally) as a guest on Boquel's plane, she was prevented by Seal Beach marshal Cornelius Neuschwanger, who said, "There was no use for a girl to risk her life flying in that thing."[91] Despite protests from Bonna and other women, Neuschwanger stuck to his guns, and Boquel taxied off for his next show without his passenger.

The marshal apparently didn't have issues with women partaking in activities at sea level. All the newspapers posted stories (the same exact one, as a matter of fact) about the Hawaiian activity of surfboard riding as performed by "Miss Mary Reeves, a young society girl of the Jewel City." The *Times* added that devotees of the sport now number "scores." (Within a month, it would be up to "hundreds.") Although the legendary Duke Kahanamoku performed surfing exhibitions at Corona Del Mar in 1912, and George Freeth did a surfing exhibition at the opening of the

Wayne Abbott (shown above standing on wing) came to Seal Beach in 1916 to run the Joy Zone's Fireworks Display and do a weekly balloon ascension and parachute jump. He set several world records for highest parachute drop, including some from the airplane of Long Beach pilot Earl Daugherty. Abbott's son Harry, who also worked at Seal Beach, later became a daredevil, a stunt pilot and, incredibly, the commander of the Nationalist Chinese Air Force.

new Huntington Beach pier in 1914, Miss Reeves's ride on the local waves is one of the earliest recorded instances of surfing by an Orange County local, or at least a non-Hawaiian.[92] Beyond dispute is the evidence that nobody publicized the new sport of surfboard riding more than the Seal Beach proprietors.

Throughout the summer, Stanton and Burt pulled out all the stops— string ensembles, the Venetian Orchestra, the Anaheim Elks orchestra, the Glendale Band, the electriquette wheelchairs brought from the San Francisco Exposition[93] and "Sunset Dinners" every Tuesday night at the Jewel City Café.

Wayne Abbott even swore he saw a massive sea serpent out beyond the pier, "a great deal like the Derby coaster in outline," while operating the Scintillators and fireworks show one night. Abbott surmised it must have been frightened away by the explosions of the giant aerial bombs, which were part of the grand finale of the national salute.[94]

Almost immediately after the July opening, café owners petitioned to extend the closing time from 12:30 to 2:00 a.m. to capture the patronage of the Los Angeles "café goers" and "lovers of the night life" who "will not travel the long distance to Seal Beach unless they can stay until the small hours of the morning."

Opposing the small-hour drinking were Methodists from Long Beach and Santa Ana. Reverend Henry Rasmus of Long Beach's First Methodist Church equated Seal Beach with "Tia Juana" and called it "the plague spot at our doors" and a "monster which was slowly but surely sapping the purity of the girlhood and boyhood of surrounding cities."[95] Not unexpectedly, Rasmus's comments didn't hurt attendance or change any behavior.

Beach resort promoters tried anything to attract a crowd—including baseball games. In summer 1916, the Jewel City Amusement Company announced it had formed a team and would play games when it could be arranged. The team took multiple photos (above), but whether they ever played a game is unknown.

Within a couple weeks, residents complained about a late-night, after-hours "orgy" by café workers at Anaheim Landing who partied a little too heartily from 2:00 a.m. to 5:00 a.m. one night.

On the same day, the Consolidated Lumber Company of Los Angeles filed a lien against the Jewel Amusement Company, claiming it was still owed half of a $9,000 lumber bill for the construction of the coaster.[96] Undeterred by these challenges, Burt and his crew continued their marketing onslaught.

Early August saw the swimming and diving performances of Miss Aileen Allen and her California Mermaids. August 19 was Movie Day, when "nearly 2,000 movie actors descended on Seal Beach. Participating studios were Universal, Signal, Chaplin, Horsley's, Morosco, L-K-G, Fine Arts, Selig, Keystone and a large group from the nearby Balboa studios in Long Beach. A special event was an all night dance held in the dance pavilion managed by Guy F. Mills."

That same week, Burt announced that Seal Beach would field a "fast amateur baseball team" and bring the best teams of Southern California to play Sunday games at the resort. The manager of the champion Pacific Electric team said he looked forward to playing the team after they "properly organized." Although the team took some nifty team photos, the author couldn't determine if they ever "organized."[97]

The following week saw the arrival of Workman's Carnival Shows, "with ten tented attractions" camped on the sands north of the pavilions and picnic area.[98]

And duly reported, of course, were the numerous "near-death" falls and dives of parachutists Wayne Abbott, Tiny Broadwick, balloonists Billie

Because it was easier to get publicity photos in newspapers if the shot included attractive girls, beach resorts organized bathing beauty pageants. Venice held the first in 1915. Shown above are the contestants in the 1917 Seal Beach Screen Beauty Bathers Pageant (the first bathing beauties competition in Orange County).

Little and J.J. Edelman and aviators like George Edelman and Joe Boquel, all of whom managed to pick themselves up and do it all over again at their next scheduled performance. Boquel was game for just about any kind of publicity and even participated in a race on the sands between his plane and a new Chalmer six-cylinder automobile.

Despite the late start, the labor strikes and mechanics' liens, the 1916 season showed promise for the Bayside Land Company. The company said it was committed to spending another $15,000 for more concessions, but first the issue of closing times had to be dealt with—it needed to be 2:00 a.m.

Mayor James H. Blagge, who had previously lived in Venice, was opposed and wanted to keep it at 12:30 a.m. But his methods—he would ignore community petitions, and if he didn't like the way a council meeting was going, he would arbitrarily adjourn it—had caused a large number to seek his recall.[99] John C. Ord, who five months earlier had resigned from the council, now campaigned to replace Blagge. After Blagge reportedly criticized Ord's age, the latter challenged the mayor to race "sixteen miles to Anaheim, each man to have a fifty-pound anvil strapped to him."

The Bayside Company backed Ord, saying its new $15,000 investment was contingent upon his election. So on April 21, 1917, by a vote of 133 to 87, Mayor Blagge became the first—but by no means the last—Seal Beach council member to be recalled. (Two others faced recall later that same year.) Ord was elected in Blagge's place with 127 votes. All but 17 of the 240 registered voters cast their ballots.

In between the politics, the town had time for fun. On March 27, 1917, the chamber of commerce sponsored a Snowball Dance using specially treated snowballs shipped in from Chicago and immediately "placed in refrigeration plants to retain their rotundity and solidity" for the battle that would take place at the dance hall. The dance became a local tradition for many years.[100]

The new resort opened its 1917 season on Memorial Day weekend with an Allies Day Celebration, an acknowledgment that on April 6, 1917, the United States had declared war on Germany. Beachgoers responded to the patriotism even more so on July 4, when over 100,000 reportedly enjoyed the Seal Beach activities.

Besides patriotism, the town's reputation grew because it proactively courted the still-new moving picture industry. The first Southern California studios had been established in Silver Lake only seven years before—and since then had sprouted up in Santa Monica, Culver City and Hollywood. Among the biggest of all was the Balboa Amusement Company in Long Beach. But many films were still shot on location, especially those set at a beach or amusement park. With Santa Monica, Venice and the Long Beach Pike becoming too crowded, film companies began using Orange County more frequently. Balboa Pier and Laguna and Santiago Canyon saw most of the action, but Anaheim Landing and Seal Beach were used on occasion. The Joy Zone cafés also became a regular hangout for stars like Fatty Arbuckle, Buster Keaton and Jackie Saunders who either worked at the Balboa Studios in Long Beach or, like Theda Bara, lived on the Long Beach shoreline.

Frank Burt recognized the PR value in movie tie-ins. After the success of Seal Beach's first Movie Day in August 1916, Burt allowed a Mack Sennett crew to shoot footage of Joe Boquel doing loop-to-loops, which were used in *Her Circus Night*.[101] A few days later, the Morosco Company director William Desmond Taylor sent a stuntman and a car off a Seal Beach road into Alamitos Bay.

Newsreel companies were also welcome. In June 1917, the Mutual Weekly newsreel shot the motorcycle daredevils training at the resort, not only for stunts but also as potential dispatch carriers in war conditions. A month later, the Hearst-Pathe weekly newsreel showcased some "spectacular motorcycle races" with a daredevil motorcycle show by movie stuntmen.[102] Hopefully, it included footage of "Sailor" Martin wowing the crowd as he rode around the Derby's coaster tracks on his motorcycle.

One of those who saw this stunt was young Harry Wayne Abbott. The next day, he borrowed a motorcycle and repeated the trick—for free. A few days later, he road the coaster tracks on his bicycle. On occasion, young Abbott placed that same bicycle on the pier's railing and rode it all the way to the end, where he then jumped it into the ocean.[103]

Burt also utilized the tried-and-true attraction of beautiful yet scantily clad women competing in bathing suit competitions. The "bathing beauties" craze swept the nation in 1915, thanks to producer Mack Sennett, who recognized that publicity photos got more play in newspapers if they included an attractive woman displaying some uncovered leg above the knee. Eschewing subtlety, Sennett placed women in bathing suits throughout his films (and publicity photos). The public response led to beach resorts holding their own bathing beauty competitions. Venice held its first bathing beauty parade in 1915. Within a couple years, it was drawing almost 200,000 spectators.

On June 24, 1917, Seal Beach held Orange County's first "bathing beauty" event, a diving competition, and then followed that up in July with the 1917 Seal Beach Bathing Girls Parade featuring over forty studio starlets.[104]

The 1918 parade, which was filmed by Burt, featured over fifty starlets attired in "the latest sea-going gowns." Over thirty-five thousand spectators reportedly attended the competition, which was officiated by Fatty Arbuckle and judged by Mayor Ord, P.A. Stanton and the wives of four company officials. The finished product, *The Seal Beach Bathing and Fashion Parade*, was playing local theaters by late August.[105] The top three finishers were Jane Starr of the Arbuckle Studios, eighteen-year-old Bebe Daniels (already a co-star in many Harold Lloyd films) and Peggy Aruth of the Douglas Fairbanks Studios.

In early 1918, when frequent Arbuckle co-star Buster Keaton was drafted and about to be sent to France, Paramount and Arbuckle threw him a going-away party at the Jewel City Café.[106]

All of these doings were dutifully reported in the town's second newspaper, the *Seal Beach Wave*, which was started by A.W. Armstrong in June 1917. Armstrong had edited papers in Alhambra and South Pasadena before he ventured out on his own with the *Wave*. In 1921, he bought out the older *Post* from the Bayside Land Company and combined the two publications.

By 1917, Seal Beach was connected by a gravel road to Huntington Beach. Motorists could stop for gas at the new station opened at Main and Coast Highway by Donovan Lawhead. Or they might stop to spend a couple days at the expanded Tent City, where a family of four could rent a tent for around ten dollars a week, plus an additional two dollars for cooking utensils.[107]

Despite the "successes" of the 1916–18 seasons, the Joy Zone was a business failure. The aerial photos of 1921 and 1923 show most of the town's lots still vacant. Without revenue from land sales, it was tougher for the Bayside investors to justify spending more on the amusement area. The boardwalk to Anaheim Landing was never completed, and some key concessionaires left for greener pastures, as did key company officials. Bert St. John left to become the general manager of Clune's Auditorium, the largest vaudeville movie house in downtown Los Angeles, which, under the financing of William Clark Jr., would become the first home of the Los Angeles Philharmonic.

By 1918, the aerial shows and fireworks were cut back as well, causing Wayne Abbott to seek additional work. In the late 1917 draft registration for World War I, Wayne listed his occupation as "self-employed, inventor." The latter may have come about through his arrangement with two Pasadena businessmen to form the American Trench Gun Company to make guns, mortars, grenades, ammunition and other materials, including a hand grenade and a mortar tube made of paper invented by Abbott. The latter invention was approved by the government just as World War I ended. During this time, Wayne also made significant improvements in parachute technology. After the war, Abbott became head of amusements for the Long Beach Chamber of Commerce and scheduled special-occasion air shows over the Pike. He and his son Harry Wayne, now just out of the Navy's submarine service, did parachute and occasional wing-walking exhibitions with Earl Daugherty. At the 1919 Armistice Day celebration, young Harry broke his father's world record for highest parachute leap. Months later, they performed together in a dueling parachute drop.[108] Harry even did some occasional stunt work in

Even by the summer of 1917, 60 percent of the lots on Main Street were vacant and unsold. Two vacant lots are covered by a billboard (right) that promotes the upcoming "Screen Beauty Bather's Parade," which also capitalized on the movies "bathing beauties" craze that was very popular at the time.

Hollywood films, doubling for Harold Lloyd and others. In mid-1921, the Abbotts led a troupe of barnstorming daredevils (Abbott's Demon Aviators) on a tour of the western states that lasted "eight or nine months."[109]

In San Jose in 1922, they were seen by a Chinese representative, who asked Wayne if he would be willing to train pilots for Dr. Sun Yat-Sen's revolution to form a Democratic government in China. Although agreeing to do some aerial shows in China, Wayne declined to help with the training. Harry, however, accepted, and in August 1922, Harry and his wife headed to Shanghai, China, to train new pilots for the Chinese Nationalist Army. Harry was originally the number-two man in the Chinese Aviation Bureau, but when the commanding general died on a bombing mission, Harry Wayne Abbott, formerly of Seal Beach, was appointed commander-in-chief of the Republic of China Air Force. One of his other jobs was to also build the planes his pilots flew. Harry led his pilots in a few battles. After his contract ended in mid-1924 and he planned to return home, he found that inflation had made all the cash the Chinese nationalists gave him virtually worthless, and he had to perform exhibitions in Hong Kong and other areas to earn the cash to return.[110]

When finally back in the States, Harry and his father both settled in Northern California. Harry became a noted test pilot and parachute

Despite the hype, the Joy Zone—and the Bayside Land Company—was never a financial success. It was even less so after a 1923 fire destroyed the southern half of the Seal Way concession area. As this 1921 photo shows, most of the lots in Seal Beach were still vacant.

engineer but still did occasional stunt flying exhibitions. It was on one such event in August 1930 that his midget racer went out of control and crashed, killing him.

Although Wayne agreed to organize Seal Beach's July 4th aerial celebration in 1928, he had basically retired from the aviation business at this point. However, he revived his old Wild West Show character of the Cheyenne chief Mad Wolf, and started working with other groups of Indians to put on shows at county fairs while in full Plains Indian regalia. He even played Indian parts in some Hollywood western films. Chief Mad Wolf's fame was such that General Motors hired Abbott to promote the Pontiac line of cars by touring the country and delivering lectures on Native American life. Family members recall that part of his salary included receiving a new Pontiac each year, until he was killed in an auto crash in Wyoming in 1933.[111]

World War I ended in November 1918, but the celebration did not last long. The New Year transitioned with a killer influenza epidemic that closed schools, theaters, dance halls and carnival areas. By the time it abated in February 1919, all the world war soldiers were returning home and foreign competitors were flooding the markets with their products. A worldwide recession began.

In 1919, Burt tried new ways of bringing business to the seaside resort—including more motorcycle races (attracting over two thousand motorcyclists), auto races with cars driven by screen sirens like Fay Tincher and airplane gymnastics put on by aviators of the Cecil B. DeMille organization and the Scream Club of Los Angeles, which was "largely composed of photoplay [movie industry] people." The club staged a second event in June 1919, which featured "airplane and flivver flights, and stunts to last from afternoon to moonlight dancing." Also included were aquatic sports with Mack Sennett's diving beauties and "a galaxy of peaches from all parts." Later that summer, the resort hosted a water carnival, featuring races pitting sail and motorboat entries from the rival South Coast and Newport Yacht clubs, as well as AAU-certified swimming and diving competitions.

The town hosted another bathing girls event, but it was smaller and held in the Jewel City Café.

All these made great entertainment, but still no one was buying lots, forcing Stanton to float yet a third rebranding of Seal Beach: that of a town "exclusively of people connected with motion picture productions."[112] Stanton, of course, claimed to have several companies already interested, but nothing more was heard of this plan after its initial printing.

To make matters worse, Prohibition became the law of the land, making the sale and transportation of alcohol illegal as of January 1920.

The joy had gone out of the Joy Zone.

CHAPTER 5

THE NOT-SO-ROARING '20s AND PROHIBITION

The Eighteenth Amendment and the Volstead Act removed Seal Beach's main attraction: being a legal "wet" resort.

Frank Burt returned to San Francisco to become the general manager of a new movie studio being built there.[113]

Perhaps Stanton wasn't concerned about his declining business at this time. In 1922, the fifty-four-year-old bachelor took the former Grace O'Sullivan, a forty-five-year-old "Whittier socialite," as his wife. For their honeymoon, they traveled east, stopping in Washington to visit former President William Howard Taft, who was now Chief Justice of the Supreme Court.[114]

The Joy Zone still got some business, and company press releases continued to present a rosy picture. Releases noted concerts every Sunday featuring the Elks Band of Anaheim while stating that Seal Beach was "a favorite camping place for auto parties which numbered in the hundreds." Press materials also claimed, "This has been the greatest year Tent City has ever known."

Enough people moved to town that the Bay City School—a brick, three-classroom structure where Principal Howard Harper and teachers Blanche Lopresti and Elizabeth Polk were getting ready to expand.

A 1920 state survey referred to the "crowded condition" alleviated by the addition of two new classrooms[115] and noted the appointments: "Venetian blinds, indirect electric lighting, furnace heat and ventilation, graduated seats, drinking fountains and inside toilets." It also noted interestingly enough: "A few Japanese children are enrolled here but present no problems. In common with the other beach communities the pupils in the school are transient, and the community interest is mediocre."[116]

By 1929, Police Chief A.G. Johnson had formed the Seal Beach Junior Police "to protect little children at all times and to see that vacant property was not vandalized." They also kept tabs on misbehavior when movies were shown in the room at the back of Patterson's Store on Main Street.

By October 1921, a schoolroom was set aside as a branch of the new Orange County Free Library, which soon sported 275 books of its own, used by 174 cardholders. New school principal Earl DuLaney was the branch custodian, ably assisted by his school faculty of Laura Stroud, Elizabeth Steele, Blanche Glass and Frances Rider. A second branch was set up at city hall, with Miss Sarah Dyson custodian of the facility, which was open Tuesdays, Thursdays and Saturdays from 2:00 p.m. to 4:30 p.m.

Movies were still made in the area on occasion—most notably, two biblical epics. For his 1923 version of *The Ten Commandments*, legendary director Cecil B. DeMille set much of his famous crossing of the Red Sea sequence on the peninsula surf just south of town. On June 13, 1923, DeMille's Israelites traveled six hundred strong from Hollywood on the red cars of the Pacific Electric and joined up with four hundred horses, two hundred head of cattle and two boxcars of camels. Arriving a little late were two regiments of U.S. Cavalry from Arizona, who would pilot the chariots. In just over a week of

Anaheim Landing and Seal Beach hosted films starring Douglas Fairbanks, Rudolph Valentino, Fredric March, Fatty Arbuckle and others. Probably the best-known film shot here was Cecil B. DeMille's 1923 version of *The Ten Commandments*, which used Anaheim Landing for some of the crossing of the Red Sea sequence. Most of the biblical scenes of the film were shot near San Luis Obispo.

shooting, DeMille captured the pursuit of the Israelites and the engulfing of the pharoah's wheeled elite in the Red Sea on a scale and spectacle never before seen on screen—although most of the sequence was shot at the Nipomo dunes near San Luis Obispo, and the parting of the sea needed help from wind machines and gelatin back at the studio's special effects room.[117]

Anaheim Landing again stood in for the Near East in several scenes of *The Wanderer*, a 1926 retelling of the Prodigal Son parable by director Raoul Walsh that featured some Babylonian orgies shot at a castle constructed at a cost of $25,000 by forty-two Paramount craftsmen. A number of palace façades were built around Anaheim Bay for the movie, which starred William Collier, Greta Nissen, Tyrone Power Sr., Wallace Beery and Hawaiian surf legend Duke Kahanamoku (who presumably took time to check out the local waves between takes).[118]

Anaheim Landing starred in more than biblical epics. The wharf stood in for New York in Douglas Fairbanks's 1919 film, *When the Clouds Roll By*; the Baja California coast in 1922's *Moran of the Lady Letty* (starring a miscast Rudolph Valentino); the docks of Portsmouth, England in 1922's *To Have and To Hold*; and the Greek islands in the 1919 *The Temple of Venus*, which also gave bit parts to a herd of local sea lions.

However, by the late 1920s, the only movies in evidence usually were the ones shown at the Coast Theater, until it closed in 1930. After that, they were shown in the room behind Patterson's Grocery Store[119] near the corner of Main and Central. These were mainly silent films, mostly westerns, to the dismay of the girls.[120] Police chief Andy Johnson had started a junior police department, with one of its main responsibilities being to keep order at the movies.

The movies' desertion of the Long Beach area was largely due to the discovery of oil in Signal Hill in 1921, just six months after it was found in Huntington Beach. The Signal Hill field was the largest discovered in the United States up to that time. Oil wells sprouted up on either side of the Newport-Inglewood anticline from the Huntington Beach Mesa northwest through Landing Hill and Signal Hill, up to Baldwin Hills. The oil made a lot of money for some local residents and the local economy, but the thousands of derricks dotting the hills and the wetlands were unsightly and smelly, and tourists and movie production deserted the area.

The discovery of oil gave temporary hope to the Bayside Land Company, which suspended land sales "where there are more than five lots adjoining each other."[121] But the lots were back on the market by June 1920—at prices as low as $600.[122]

Ironically, the Huntington Beach Company—initially started by Phil Stanton and even recently on the edge of bankruptcy—was now flush with money. By 1923, Huntington Beach had over 230 wells and Signal Hill nearly 300. Huntington's population grew to six thousand. Even more came to Signal Hill and Long Beach, where that field was producing 20 percent of the world's oil. Within a few years, the Seal Beach field[123]—although nowhere as big as the other two—was also producing oil for the Hellman and J.W. Bixby heirs.

But with no wells of their own to produce revenue, Seal Beach residents voted to ban drilling and the construction of the smelly, unsightly derricks within the city. That didn't stop the nearby oil fields, many run by future billionaire J. Paul Getty, from becoming the town's largest employer, bringing in many newcomers.

Among the newcomers were Jesse and Cora John, who moved from Kansas with their three children: their son, Wayne, and daughters Marcile and five-year-old Virginia. Jesse would become a town councilman (who would naturally face a recall, in 1927, but he survived), and Virginia would marry Francis Haley and become the mother of surfing legends Jack and Mike Haley. Virginia recalled driving west in a big, brand-new Model T Ford, making the "hard trip" across the desert and over mountains. Their car had "special shades that we rolled down at night while my mother and sister and I would sleep inside the car," she said. "My father and brother would sleep outside in a tent."[124] Even at the age of ninety, she could remember her first image of the town, driving past all "those eucalyptus trees on Seal Beach Boulevard—all the way up into Los Alamitos."

The Johns attended the Methodist church, which was soon joined by a Catholic church. Prior to this, good Catholics hadn't been totally abandoned. Nuns from the Sisters of the Immaculate Heart had conducted Sunday school classes, but in 1921, a mission church was formed from St. Matthew's Church in Long Beach. Some of the first services were held in a grain warehouse behind the drugstore on Main at Electric. When the parish of St. Anne's was formed, with Reverend Austin Fleming as the first pastor, a site was purchased at 317–319 Tenth Street by a few parishioners, aided by a $1,000 donation to the Catholic Extension Mission Society by a generous Chicago woman who requested that the parish be dedicated to St. Anne. Father Fleming, acting as priest and carpenter, erected the new church aided by Elmer Hughes, the foreman of the Hellman Ranch and a future mayor of Seal Beach. To raise additional money, Father Fleming provided the music for parish socials on the pier, earning the name the "Fiddling Priest." By the 1930s, St. Anne's had almost one hundred parishioners, and in August 1937, several hundred additional Catholics from Los Alamitos, Sunset Beach and Long Beach, as well as over thirty priests and monsignors, and Los Angeles Archbishop Joseph Cantwell, helped dedicate the handsome new St. Anne's Church at Tenth and Electric.[125]

Virginia John remembered much interaction between the faiths. She said, "The Catholics had a bazaar every year that we went to and they'd come to our church turkey dinners."

The churches had their work cut out for them because the oil boom attracted the fast buck crowd, and many of the oil workers—especially the single ones—sought out the gamblers, prostitutes and bootleggers. Huntington Beach did its best to discourage these vices, but the laws of science and human nature dictated that a vacuum be filled. The sand-bottom coves of Anaheim Landing and Alamitos Bay became a favorite for rum-running smugglers eager to service this demand. Naturally, the federal authorities were eager to shut this business down. But it was difficult.

With profits generally around 700 percent,[126] the opportunities attracted the attention of local organized crime syndicates. (For most of the 1920s, the larger East Coast groups, their hands full with protecting their own turf, left Southern California alone.) Three groups are known for sure to have operated around the Seal Beach–Alamitos Bay area. The City Hall Gang (so named because of its very strong influence at Los Angeles City Hall and thus the harbor) was led by Marvin "Doc" Schoulweiler and LA gambling kingpin Milton "Farmer" Page. Getting a larger and larger foothold were the Black Hand Sicilians (with their New York and Chicago roots) working under Frank Ardizonne and Jack Dragna.[127] Loosely connected to this last group, but still independent, was the operation of Tony and Frank Cornero. Tony had worked on ships as a teenager and developed an extensive network of connections and a fleet of very fast speedboats and well-maintained trucks. Both Schouweiler and Cornero were called the "king of rumrunners" by government officials and newspapers, but Cornero's maritime savvy was such that he was also called the "Admiral," a name made even more famous when he operated the gambling ships *Lux* and *Rex*.[128]

Large booze-laden ships, usually from Canada, made their way toward an American city and anchored fifty or more miles off shore. In Southern California, these "mother ships" (sometimes carrying as much as sixty thousand cases of booze valued at over $1 million[129]) formed a "Rum Row" in locations ranging from the Channel Islands to the Cortes Banks and Ensenada.

Liquor was moved closer to shore (but outside the twelve-mile limit)[130] on intermediate-sized ships, which would then transfer their cargo, often on dark, moonless nights, to speedboats, sometimes using the new short-wave radios, sometimes just wireless telegraph keys. The speedboats carried the illegal booze to trucks waiting on the beaches and, in some cases, at the piers. Southern California harbor officials estimated that five thousand cases a night were illegally offloaded during the mid-1920s. Although authorities monitored the mother ships, it was assumed that for every case of liquor intercepted, another thousand were landed successfully.

The smugglers' speedboats were faster than anything the feds had, plus the latter had to cover one hundred miles of coastline and remote coves from Malibu to Laguna. Among the most active were Alamitos Bay, Anaheim Bay and Seal Beach.

In June 1922, the Tower Café on Main Street was raided and shut down when authorities took issue with the proprietors' definition of "near beer."[131]

By the end of the year, newspapers called Seal Beach "Southern California's wettest spot…the Mecca for thirsty souls from Los Angeles and Long Beach." Prohibition officers cited the town as a thorn in their side, and several raids were aborted because of "a well-developed system where offending beach café proprietors have been tipped off."[132]

Cornero bribed officials in Laguna Beach and Seal Beach. At the latter, his crews safely unloaded tons of illegal liquor in the bay coves and sometimes brazenly at the pier itself. The bribes were passed on by a rumrunner tossing a wad of cash into the rear seat of a police vehicle, usually parked at the Tower Café or Seal Inn and then split with superiors also "on the in." The bribes were said to have reached $25,000.[133]

Needless to say, the character of some of the Seal Beach police force was questionable. One Seal Beach motorcycle officer was indicted in June 1927 along with Tony Cornero and his brother, Frank. Another former police chief who was fired when a recall changed the council majority in 1927 was arrested a few months later for robbing a bank in Pasadena at gunpoint.

But just in case the bribes weren't effective enough, for additional security, one rum-running group reportedly used a plane at the Seal Beach Airport (then just a dirt strip) to scout the area and let syndicate boats know when it was safe to land.[134]

The rumrunners had to watch out for more than the feds. Other gangsters made quite a haul hijacking rum that had just been smuggled in. After being hijacked a few times, Cornero set a trap and ended up in a shootout near Alamitos Bay with a rival group led by Milton "Farmer" Page, the king of Los Angeles gambling.[135]

Booze off-loaded under the Seal Beach pier was quickly hauled up and transported to waiting cars and trucks, or taken to one of the Main Street cafes offering a drink to go with its appetizer and main course of gambling and girls. One report says a pipeline, four feet in diameter, ran from the cellar of an Anaheim Landing cottage 180 feet out into Anaheim Bay where rumrunners would drop over the sides sacks of hooch which were then pulled through the pipe into the house's basement.[136]

Longtime Seal Beach resident Ray Gise remembered the gun-carrying hoodlums as "nice guys if you didn't cross them."[137] Others remember a heavy trade in fishing at the end of the pier, with the catch not always being fish. Secondhand reports spoke of a room underneath the pier (in some versions, it was underneath an Ocean Avenue house) where boys were hired to fill flasks with recently landed whiskey—five dollars for filling one bottle. The flasks were put in coffins. A county hearse backed onto the pier, and the coffins were loaded into the hearse for transportation to their final resting place at some Southern California speakeasy.[138]

The overwhelmed county and federal authorities had some victories. On April 22, 1923, Orange County sheriff Sam Jernigan led a Saturday night raid that resulted in thirty arrests and 250 gallons of illegal alcohol being confiscated. Jernigan told the *Times*, "We got reports that nearly everybody in Seal Beach was bootlegging. The reports were exaggerated…but we found a good many who were." The arrested included four prominent men: a football player, automobile dealer, oil man and real estate man. Not all arrested went willingly. As officers began searching cars, some of those drivers of cars containing liquor tried to escape by driving through fences and yards.[139]

A week later, the feds staged another late Saturday night raid, this time hitting the Jewel Café and the Seal Inn. Six people were arrested and twenty gallons of booze confiscated, including two bottles hidden inside a piano.[140]

In July 1923, after an "exciting chase and gun battle" at midnight, feds captured a fishing boat off Anaheim Landing carrying one hundred cases of bootleg liquor.[141] In late November, the *St. Andrew*, a sixty-five-foot fishing boat went aground near present Surfside, while unloading rum.[142]

In a 1932 raid, Orange County authorities surprised bootleggers who had backed their car onto the pier and were unloading liquor from a speedboat. Apparently, the surprise was kept that way because Seal Beach authorities (long suspected of tipping off the bootleggers to raids) were not let in on the raid's details. Still, the rumrunners hopped in their car and sped away, but without $6,000 in liquor that was still stacked on the pier.[143]

In July 1925, the *Times* reported that a "raiding party" of twenty county deputy officers dropped in unannounced at Captain's Inn in Seal Beach, where five hundred customers were enjoying gambling, a little bootleg liquor and some music (which incidentally was broadcast live every night on local radio station KFON). Some of the five hundred fled at the arrival of the badged party crashers, but the band played on, waiters kept serving and customers jeered and hooted at the officers as they checked under the tables for illegally stowed liquor, prompting one flapper to taunt "You're not looking for liquor—you're looking at my legs." All were taken to the Seal Beach jail. Ultimately, fifteen men were arrested for gambling, twenty-seven on liquor charges and twelve women as "social vagrants."[144]

"Social vagrancy" was not unknown in town. As early as December 1918, the Orange County district attorney had successfully charged "Doc" Smith (owner of the Seal Inn and Seal Café), Tower Café proprietor Louis J. White and the Tower Café building's owner, the Bayside Land Company, for allowing the places to be used for "lewdness and solicitation of prostitution." The ladies of both cafés would meet gentlemen while dancing and adjourn afterward to the Seal Inn, where they could "really party."[145]

Depending on which faction was in power, the town council sometimes took action against the offenders. The owner of the Captain's Inn was summoned to explain why his city café license shouldn't be revoked. George Parry, whose Parry's Café drew unwanted attention from prohibition enforcement authorities, faced similar questioning. At various times, the council conditions required Parry's to pay for a Seal Beach policeman to be inside at all times and ordered all curtains be removed so the activities inside were visible to all. This latter order was overturned by a judge, and soon after, the café curtains and the "pro-business" faction on the council were reinstalled.[146]

The pro-business faction loved the publicity the town garnered by a number of live radio broadcasts on Long Beach station KFON ("Where Your Ship Comes In"). In addition to the Captain's Inn Orchestra's nightly broadcast (from 6:30 to 7:00 p.m. in 1925 and 1926), by February 1927, the Parry's Cafe Orchestra was hosting a weekly show on Sunday nights from 7:00 to 7:45.[147] Sensing a good thing, the town's chamber of commerce began producing its own show on the station—with business leaders A.W. Armstrong and W.D. Miller welcoming various guests who promoted the town's interests.

By the mid-1920s, the amusement area was an eyesore. Things weren't helped when a fire broke out in the concession area of the Joy Zone area on August 31, 1923. Although Long Beach firemen arrived quickly enough to confine the damage to the south part of the coaster and the concession area, thirteen minor concessions, including the shooting gallery and fortuneteller's headquarters, were "wiped out," with damages estimated between $35,000 and $50,000.[148]

The rum, the raciness and the run-down Joy Zone made the town less attractive to "good family folk" and more attractive to men looking for female companionship. Some of the town's residents did not take sordid behavior lying down. In the fall of 1923, after a recall election resulted in the Stanton-backed "liberal" elements gaining control of the board (and promptly ousting the city attorney and other staff put in place by the previous conservative majority), Mayor R.D. Richards, now part of the minority and targeted for recall by the new majority, took his case to the people—at least the female people of the town. He addressed the recently formed Woman's Improvement Club on the need to clean up the town's image.[149] The women's group decided a good place to start was a campaign against Sunday dancing. This drew fierce opposition from the Bayside Land Company. The little money it did make came from the rents on buildings where dancing was held.

To force a compromise allowing Sunday dancing, Stanton's group said if one of its operations was closed, it would close them all—and on a Sunday in late December 1923, the Bayside Land Company closed all the Joy Zone amusements (including the roller coaster) and its concessions.[150]

But in January 1924, the council, either tired of company bullying or afraid of the wrath of the local women, surprisingly and unanimously approved an ordinance banning Sunday dancing. Ultimately, this had little effect. It was just another law to be broken and more council members to be recalled—and Seal Beach had plenty of experience at the latter.

Between the introduction of the recall process in the early 1900s and 1929, only Watts, with eleven recall elections, endured more recall campaigns than Seal Beach's eight. But apparently Seal Beach, the younger town, indulged its recalls with a unique "enthusiasm and abandon." One study noted that the towns were not that disreputable or inefficient, but it was more that the side that was "out" found the recall process a convenient way to quickly regain power. In 1926 and 1927, the town suffered three recall campaigns, each targeting whatever three-member majority existed at the time. While these were always battles over the degree to which Seal Beach would be "an open or a closed town" (regarding drinking and gambling), they were usually portrayed by one side as a battle between "pro-business" progressivism and spendthrift decadence (the extravagance once even being detailed as wasting money on glorified, over-manned police departments).[151]

Perhaps the new regulations did attract some families to visit. Future president Richard Nixon visited the beach in the late 1920s with a visiting uncle from Ohio. Nixon later said, "He did not have a swimsuit, and so we had to rent one from a concession stand at Seal Beach. The only one we could get that fit him was an old-fashioned, grotesque-looking knee-length model. I was somewhat embarrassed when other people on the beach laughed at him."[152]

The new regulations didn't last long. By April pro-business (i.e., Bayside Land Company–backed) candidates regained control of the city council and modified the restrictions on Sunday dancing. They also made it easier for cafés to stay open later. Ironically, the controversy helped bring business to town, as the headlines made groups aware of Seal Beach's big dance floors and cafés likely to have booze. Groups like the American Legion, the Scioto Club of Fullerton, the Orange County Firemen's Association and even the Orange County Peace Officers Association booked the dance pavilions. The local Catholics, now led by Father Raley, even got a permit to host a fundraising dance at the closed-at-the-time Parry's Café. And as the negative consequences of Prohibition became more visible, even the dry faction became more receptive to activities once frowned upon. In June 1930, the American Legion and promoter Robert Taylor even got the unanimous approval of the council to host a fundraising dance marathon at the old pavilion.[153]

But cafés and entertainment were no longer the main businesses in town. In January 1924, the Los Angeles Gas & Electric Company constructed a new power plant off First Street where Alamitos Bay emptied into the ocean. The Seal Beach site was chosen because of its water free from sewage and seaweed, its firm ground beneath and its proximity to fuel supply and customers.

If visitors to the resort didn't have bathing suits of their own, they could rent them.

The plant officially opened on May 31, 1925, with 48,000-horsepower capacity that would soon be expanded to 288,000 horsepower, almost ten times that of the company's other plant. A large cooling tower 375 feet high redirected much of the heat and gases from the six boilers before the water was released back into the stream and ocean.

The tower, visible for miles, became a landmark for local sailors (and rumrunners). The plant's whistle became part of Seal Beach's daily life, blowing at 8:00 a.m. at the start of the morning shift, at noon for lunch, at 5:00 p.m. for the end of the workday and finally at 9:00 p.m., which unofficially signaled the nightly curfew for any kid under sixteen years of age.

A more notable achievement occurred in March 1925 with the completion of a paved coastal highway connecting Long Beach to Newport. The next year, it was extended to Laguna (and thus San Juan Capistrano). The new road was formally opened on October 9, with a parade from Long Beach and a formal ribbon cutting by Mary Pickford and Douglas Fairbanks. Each coastal town sponsored a float and selected a young girl to represent the town. Eleven-year-old Norma Barraclough, daughter of a town police officer, was Miss Seal Beach.[154]

More aquatic transportation was the goal of many Long Beach officials (and the owners of the East Naples Land Company) who wanted

The Los Angeles Power & Electric plant opened in May 1925 with a 375-foot-high cooling tower, which became a beacon for local sailors (and rumrunners). After the 1933 earthquake caused cracks in the structure, a smaller tower was built.

to develop Alamitos Bay into one of the area's premier yacht harbors. To do so would require re-routing and constructing a separate channel for the San Gabriel River and dredging much of the bay's sloughs. The process was further muddied by the confusing jurisdictions and conflicting agendas of Long Beach, Seal Beach and both counties. To solve the problem, the state legislature passed a bill that would allow Long Beach to annex its smaller neighbor. Because of opposition from Stanton, the governor vetoed the bill, delaying extensive development of the bay.[155]

The Alamitos Marina issue raised its head again in January 1929 when state senator Frank Merriam of Long Beach introduced another bill to allow annexations across county lines. This one seemed to have more support, especially from the businessmen of Seal Beach, led by banker and chamber president Walter Miller. The initiative gained strong support from Los Angeles County supervisors and rapidly made its way through the legislature. By late March, it was awaiting only a signature by the governor, but Orange County and Phillip A. Stanton were again pushing back. After July, little was heard of the effort.[156]

North of town, Fred H. Bixby had assumed management of the Hellman Ranch and other Hellman properties in California. Bixby's assistant

The 1926 celebration of the final link of Coast Highway from Long
Beach to San Juan Capistrano included a parade and a young girl
from each of the nine communities along the route. Above, four young
ladies stand before the Sunset Beach float. Miss Seal Beach, Norma
Barraclough, daughter of a Seal Beach policeman, stands on the far right.

manager on the Hellman property was Elmer Hughes, and the foreman was
Hubert Tyler. Hughes would serve on the Seal Beach council for eighteen
years, and Tyler stayed on as Hellman foreman for forty-three years. Bixby
had ranch hands plant a grove of gum trees (eucalyptus) on the north side
of Landing Hill to be used as fuel. Some of the ranch hands spent months
cutting and cording the wood from this gum grove.

Some tenant farmers, including the remaining Belgians who mostly lived
north of Westminster Road, still grew sugar beets, but by 1925 Orange
County agriculture was changing. A series of challenges—bugs, foreign
competition, higher profits from other crops and ultimately the Great
Depression—forced farmers to adapt. By 1925, sugar beet acreage was
half that of 1916, and four of the county's five beet factories had closed.
But revenues for other farm crops increased. In 1930, citrus, walnuts,
lima beans, peppers, tomatoes and boysenberries, along with livestock,
collectively yielded more than $51 million. Five years later, it was just
$30 million. Fortunately, the two main farms in Seal Beach—the Bixby
Ranch and the Hellman Ranch—had oil revenues so ranch employees
kept working.

Tenant farmers replaced beets with beans and more alfalfa for the growing
number of dairy farms to the north in northern Los Alamitos, Cypress and

Artesia.[157] Dairy and poultry, only 3 percent of the county revenue in 1930, would grow to 40 percent by the mid-1950s.[158]

During World War I, a number of Japanese farming families—Abe, Tanemachi, Kaneko, Endo, Kawanami, Kawasaki, Yasuda, Hirao and a few others—began leasing Hellman land east of Bay Boulevard. Some grew beets but more grew produce—celery, strawberries, chili peppers, etc.—that they could sell at the markets in Los Angeles. Florence Tyler, wife of the ranch foreman, remembers that they grew beautiful flowers as well. The Japanese formed a Seal Beach Farmers Association, and every morning one of them hauled the picked crops to the farmers' produce market in Los Angeles.[159]

George Abe, who lived here as a young boy and teenager, remembers the accommodations as primitive. "Our house was lined inside; it was papered, but just with wallpaper. No insulation, no heating. In the wintertime, you froze; in the summertime, you roasted. Most of the houses in those days didn't have insulation. And there was no such thing as central heating." The family got their water from an old well that he says "went back to Indian days. It was called Skunk Springs."[160]

Mine Yabuki Kaneko, who mothered seven children while working in the fields, recalled that the Hellman tenants were fortunate enough to have electricity at this time. The Kanekos even had a Japanese-style bathtub behind their house.

Abe's house, located on the present naval weapons station, was built on a mound full of clamshells. He used to plow up Indian artifacts there all the time.

Most of the farmers—the Japanese, Belgian and even Fred Bixby—hired Mexican laborers, sometimes as many as ten, to help work the farm. Abe said some returned every night to the Mexican *colonias* in Stanton or near Wintersburg, while others lived nearby in shacks, usually made out of two-by-fours and not lined. Kaneko said they also hired Filipino and even some single Japanese men as farm workers.

During the week, a few of the younger Japanese children attended public elementary schools in Seal Beach, but most went to Huntington Beach and Garden Grove. On weekends, they were sent to Japanese schools in Long Beach and Garden Grove.

By now, motorized tractors and trucks had replaced all the horse-drawn wagons in the fields and dirt roads.

After the crops were picked, Fred Bixby brought in large herds of beef cattle from his ranches in Arizona and Northern California (the huge Cojo-

Jalama near Santa Barbara and Hellman's Nacimiento) to roam the shorn fields and feed off the remnants.

Some town leaders tried to get the Hellmans and Bixby to open their land for residential use. Bixby had no intentions of breaking up his beloved ranch, not as long as he had oil wells for his cattle to rub up against. The Hellmans, all of whom now lived in San Francisco, were also disinclined, although they did allow some land to be annexed to provide for better and wider roads.

After his marriage, Phil Stanton made Seal Beach his official residence, but not for long. Some reports say his wife didn't like Seal Beach. For sure, his relations with the city got worse.[161] In 1928, he moved to west Anaheim, to a new "13-room house surrounded by five landscaped acres" and fifteen acres of citrus on Manchester Avenue at Brookhurst. That home is now the site of Fairmount High School and on the national register of historical places.

With the deaths of Henry Huntington in 1927 and I.O. Lothian in 1928, the Bayside Land Company lost its two primary investors, and their heirs did not wish to sink more money into the debt-laden company. In 1930, the entire company was put up for sale. A newspaper ad listed: "4,000 feet of ACTUAL OCEAN FRONTAGE—including pier, bulkheading, bath house, dance hall and other buildings—also approximately SIX HUNDRED UNSOLD LOTS AND FIFTEEN ACRES UNSUBDIVED." This means that nearly three-fourths of the eight hundred town lots originally laid out in 1903 were still unsold.[162]

While the company may have given up on Seal Beach, the locals hadn't. They voted to buy the water system from the Bayside Land Company, to put in a complete sewer system and to pave the roads between Seventh and Anaheim Landing, and in January 1929, they approved a $50,000 bond issue to build a city hall so they could stop renting Pete Labourdette's building. In 1923, the rent for the two-story structure had gone up from fifteen dollars a month to twenty-five dollars. Six architects submitted plans and nine sites were considered before the corner of Eighth and Central was selected.[163] The new building was formally opened for city business in October of the same year.

Seal Beach also formed its own fire department—not that it really had any choice. After the August 1923 fire that badly damaged the coaster and arcade areas and might have "destroyed the entire town" were it not for the help of the Long Beach Fire Department, the council accepted Fire Chief Combs's recommendation to purchase a used Seagraves fire truck for $600 and contracted with "Mr. Chronicle of the Seal Beach Garage" to keep and maintain the truck at $10 a month for storage and $5 for "care and driver."[164]

In 1929, the city bought a five-hundred-gallon-per-minute American La France Fire Pumper, which would be manned by a more formal volunteer department with John Reese as fire chief and painter and part-time city employee Sperry Knighton as his aide—when Knighton wasn't using parts from the old Seal Beach roller coaster and the PE Railroad to build one of the world's first successful turbines to produce energy from wind.[165] The firemen and their wives held dances to raise funds for helmets, coats, boots and other necessities.[166] In 1934, the city allowed the firefighters to choose their own leader. Knighton was selected fire chief, a post he held until his retirement in June 1966.

By the end of the decade, Main Street was not only offering illegal booze but games of chance and bookmaking as well. Gambling wasn't new to Seal Beach. In August 1917, Orange County deputies busted a Joy Zone concessionaire for operating Wheel of Fortune "Games of Chance."[167] Gambling became widespread at all beach resorts in 1927, when summer attendance dropped dramatically after the introduction of air conditioning into area movie theaters. Gambling *per se* was illegal, but tango (a variation of bingo and also introduced around 1927) was presumably legal because players rolled balls to determine the numbers selected—thus making it a game of skill. It quickly became a mainstay of all the beach areas. A *Los Angeles Times* article stated that a tango parlor could pay off its labor costs within two hours and the rest of the day would be all profit.

By 1933, there were at least five Main Street gambling establishments offering legally licensed "tango" and "chip" games—the latter a variation of roulette. Even gas stations on Main Street and stores at Anaheim Landing had slot machines near the front. But by the mid-1930s three active Main Street gambling establishments were providing casino-style action: the Inter-City Athletic and Social Club, the Bees and the B&P.[168] Running all three was Ballard Barron.

Barron was born in East Texas in the early 1890s and was soon a "night clerk" at hotels in Wichita Falls, Dallas and El Paso and associating with well-known Texas gamblers and crime figures. One was Lester "Benny Binion," who had amassed quite the criminal record in Dallas before building the Horseshoe Club in Las Vegas[169] and later remembered Barron as a "real good shark card player."[170] Another associate was Jake Freedman, who would build the Sands in Vegas and tried to entice Barron as a partner. Barron and Freedman "started gambling in Texas by going into an alley after a football or baseball game and spreading out a blanket and shooting nickels and dimes and dollars, trying to catch suckers."[171]

Around 1920, Barron followed his sister from Texas to Anaheim. By 1928, he was in the Seal Beach Directory, listing his profession as "oil worker." The next year it was "real estate." In 1930, the directory shows him as the manager of the Seal Inn, but in reality he was the "kingpin "of Seal Beach gambling. He first operated out of Ballard's Chip Parlor[172] before opening the aforementioned larger clubs. Barron was short, "tough as hell" and carried a gun under his suit jacket.[173] But he was also a gentleman who helped out local charities and youth organizations.[174] Although arrested many times for gambling, he was rarely convicted by local juries.

In late 1933 and early 1934, tango, bingo, keno and other "games of chance" had been banned in Los Angeles County and Orange County. But in February 1934, Seal Beach alone confirmed they were legal in their town. As a test case, the Orange County district attorney and sheriff led repeated raids on five of the town's Main Street gaming parlors, which, in addition to Barron's Chip Parlor, included Larry's Tango Parlor, the Seal Beach Amusement Company and the Mirror. Over twenty owners, managers, operators and checkers were arrested. As misdemeanors, the cases were tried in Seal Beach, where in each case a jury acquitted the owners and employees.[175]

When this recurring practice was noted by the Orange County district attorney, along with the suggestion that gambling be made a felony and tried elsewhere, twenty-nine Seal Beach businessmen and the chamber of commerce requested that the county attorney stay out of the town's business.[176]

The February 1936 Orange County Grand Jury annual report singled out Seal Beach for especially harsh criticism, saying, "Gambling is openly carried on at Seal Beach, with the knowledge of peace officers, but because public sentiment seems to favor it, convictions are impossible."[177]

Locals were not welcome at the Seal Inn, according to Virginia Haley. Her father, Jessie told her "that hotel was for big-time gambling. The people in the black suits and fedora hats."[178]

Ray Gise, an assistant manager at the Seal Inn when quite young, said Barron discouraged locals in his gambling joints because he did not want local wives angered at him over their husbands' diminished paychecks. If his employees ever skipped town owing debts, Barron would cover them.[179] Most of Barron's employees lived in the Seal Inn, whose proprietor, Mildred Blankenship, also served bootleg liquor and had a stable of "ladies" who could help the gentlemen gamblers have a good time.[180]

Blankenship wasn't the town's only employer of ladies of questionable virtue. In 1933, Jane Dray, who operated out of a "tourist hotel," was arrested for running a house of prostitution and "forcing" young women, at least one of them a minor, into "lives of shame."[181] Locals recall another bordello operating on Ocean Avenue.

The town's activities attracted a rough crowd that didn't always settle differences through diplomacy. In early 1936, gunshots shattered the late-night downtown hubbub. Seal Beach police officer Glenn (no first name was in the newspaper article) rushed from the police station to see twenty-five-year old Tommy Walker Craemer, a victim of two gunshots, stumble out of an alley holding a gun. When Glenn challenged him, Craemer fired off two shots at the officer. Both missed, but Glenn's shot put a third bullet into the hoodlum.

A few weeks later, Craemer "enlisted the aid of prominent Long Beach persons" to provide testimony that would help him avoid being sent to state prison.[182] The prominent Long Beach person might have been Ballard Barron, who had married and was living in Naples by this time.

There was also gambling offshore. On June 28, 1928, the first gambling ships anchored off the coastline of Seal Beach (or Long Beach, depending on which historical society is doing the bragging). Perhaps the rum-running made gamblers more aware of maritime laws, but someone realized there were no federal laws against gambling. Gamblers converted old schooners and barkentines into casinos and anchored them outside the three-mile limit where state, county and city jurisdictions ended. The first gambling ship was the former lumber schooner *Johanna Smith*, which was "moored off Seal Beach" according to the *Los Angeles Times* (and the Los Angeles district attorney's office as well). This ship's investors all had connections to Los Angeles' "City Hall gang." Among the most prominent was Marvin "Doc" Shouweiler (rumrunner king), gambling kingpin Milton "Farmer" Page and Guy McAfee, who also happened to conveniently be the head of the Los Angeles Police Department Vice Squad.[183]

Long Beach officials prevented water taxis from transporting people to the ships, but the courts stopped this. Then they uncovered an old anti-piracy law that allowed any ship not following its licensed activity to be seized. The gambling ships were licensed for "coastal trade" and permanently anchored ships were not "coastal." To comply with the law, in November, the gamblers sent out a second ship, the *Monfalcone*.[184] Every so often, the two ships would switch positions, thus ostensibly engaging in coastal trade.[185] On the *Monfalcone*, the "City Hall syndicate" had new partners: Italians under the direction of rising LA crime boss Jack Dragna.

The usually anchored ships were successful. The *Long Beach Sun* did a twelve-part series analyzing the income. Conservatively assuming a $5 gambling loss per person, it estimated that the syndicate owners were netting $54,000 a week from their floating casinos.[186]

For legal reasons, gambling ships often anchored off Seal Beach, sometimes straddling the Orange County line. At least four gambling ships were co-owned by gamblers with Seal Beach connections, including the very first, the *Johanna Smith* (opened 1928, burned in 1930), and the *Rose Isle*. After a 1932 murder on the *Rose Isle*, the owners renamed her the *Johanna Smith II* and within a week were up and gambling again.

While not crazy about the gambling, state officials were more alarmed by the ship's ancillary activities—money laundering, extortion, pickpocketing, pandering and other prostitution preliminaries, and they were especially concerned about people accidentally encountering bullets. They tried to ban water taxis from transporting citizens to a place of illegal activity. The gamblers countered by anchoring a fishing barge (a ship with no propeller) at a reef about halfway between the wharves and the gambling ships. Taxis then merely transported well-dressed people to these fishing barges.

In April 1930, the *Monfalcone* was profiled by the *Los Angeles Times*. Five speed boats left every half hour from Long Beach, carrying over two hundred people to the ship. Customers could dine or dance, but most played roulette, craps or blackjack.[187] Relationships between the ship's owners, some of whom had been rum-running rivals just a few years before, ran fairly smooth, but the profits caught the interest of mobsters affiliated with East Coast interests. On more than a few occasions, the ship's cashiers' cages were hijacked, with persuasion by gunfire sometimes being employed, although frequently patrons at the gaming tables were not aware of what happened.[188]

The following September, while anchored off Seal Beach, the *Monfalcone* somehow caught fire. Its three hundred stylishly dressed guests were all calmly rescued by water taxis and other boats that put out from Seal Beach while crowds gathered along the shores from Huntington Beach to Seal Beach to watch the blazing ship slowly burn and sink. The next morning, divers went down to retrieve the ship's safes, but both were found open and empty, leaving a reported $50,000 in silver, currency and checks unaccounted for.[189]

To replace the *Monfalcone*, the ship's owners purchased and converted (for $100,000) an old passenger ship, which was re-christened as the *Rose Isle*. One of its owners was William Gleason of Seal Beach (sometimes Long Beach), who also acted as the ship's manager. It opened for business in mid-October 1930, after thousands of invitations had been mailed offering free parking, free water taxi service and a free dinner and an evening of fun on the ship's three decks. The fun included reclining and enjoying the stars on the boat deck, a stroll on the four-hundred-foot-long promenade, elegant dining on the promenade deck or an exploration of the "A" Deck, which featured "delightful diversions...of such unusual interest and fascination that any attempt to describe its charm and appeal would fail miserably." These "diversions" were also known as roulette, craps and slot machines.

The Olympics came to Los Angeles in 1932, and the rowing events were held at Long Beach's Marine Stadium. To accommodate the crowds' need for additional sport, a third gambling ship, the *Monte Carlo*, opened on May 7, 1932,[190] and joined the *Johanna Smith* and *Rose Isle* off Seal Beach and Long Beach. Police records show that on July 9, 1932, the local water taxis ferried 4,486 patrons to the three ships: 1,240 to the *Rose Isle*, 1,510 to the *Johanna Smith* and 1,736 to the newly opened *Monte Carlo*.

Such attendance continued to draw the attention and harassment of local authorities[191] and the underworld. Very soon after this, another gaming war with Chicago connections broke out, this one resulting in the burning of the *Johanna Smith* and the shooting death of a dealer aboard the *Rose Isle*.[192] The shooting not only slowed business aboard the latter but also drew too much attention to its owners, who sold out to the *Johanna Smith*'s owners. Within a week, it was renamed the *Johanna Smith II* and back in business off

The *Monte Carlo*, considered the classiest gambling ship, opened for business in time for the 1932 Olympic games. In 1934, it was shut down in a combined effort by Los Angeles and Orange County officials, but a Seal Beach judge determined they had no legal jurisdiction, and all charges were dropped and all equipment returned.

Seal Beach, still managed by William Gleason of Seal Beach and Clarence Blazier of Long Beach.

In May 1934—simultaneous with his attack on the Seal Beach Main Street tango parlors—Orange County district attorney S.B. Kaufmann and his Los Angeles counterpart raided the *Monte Carlo*. Eight water taxi owners were arrested, as were two of the ship's owners and eight dealers. Los Angeles County would prosecute the water taxi owners, and Orange County the rest. But defense attorney Jonah Jones earned his money on this case. He obtained a restraining order prohibiting interference with the water taxis or gambling ships, pending outcome of the trial. Then he "convinced" Seal Beach justice Fred Smith to rule that the *Monte Carlo* was beyond the three-mile limit and outside the jurisdiction and all its gambling equipment be returned. And finally, a month later, Jones convinced a Seal Beach jury of nine men and three women to issue a blanket acquittal of all the charges.[193]

Ballard Barron had financial interests in some of the gambling ships. One was the SS *Caliente*, which was operating off the shores of Long Beach and Seal Beach as early as 1937. Its other owners included Marion Hicks, a contractor and car dealer from Long Beach, two bookmakers and a realtor from Long Beach, and at least three from Seal Beach — Barron and George Parry, who owned Parry's Main Street "café" together, and the aforementioned William Gleason. The *Caliente* had a very sophisticated casino set up and offered free meals to lure visitors to the ship. It operated without problems for a year until a man was found dead on the upper deck with a bullet hole in his head. The ship changed its name back to its original *Mount Baker* for a while and then to the *Show-Boat* (sometimes spelled *Sho-Boat*) and was parked off Seal Beach/Long Beach near the *Tango* when state attorney general and future governor Earl Warren organized his famous August 1939 raid of four gambling ships (including Tony Cornero's original *Rex*), which basically ended the gambling ship era. Although Cornero received most of the publicity for his photogenic nine-day "Battle of Santa Monica," the *Show-Boat* also fought off authorities with a fire hose at one time and technically held out longer.[194] This standoff, and the recall of Los Angeles mayor Frank Shaw, marked a major escalation in the war with the gamblers, and most of those connected with the gambling ships soon moved their operations to Las Vegas.

CHAPTER 6

POPS CRAWFORD'S AIRPORT AND THE EARTHQUAKE

Joy Zone general manager Frank Burt developed a keen interest in aviation during his days at Lakeside Park in Denver. It was here he met Wayne Abbott, the former Wild West Show Indian who had become a featured aeronaut (balloonist) as early as 1896.

Burt used well-publicized aerial stunts at Lakeside Park and then at the Panama-Pacific Exposition in San Francisco, and his aviation plans for Seal Beach, with its three hangars on the beach, were bigger. The summer of 1916 saw nonstop balloonists, parachutists and, most of all, stunt flyers.

In August 1917, Clarence O. Prest, a daredevil motorcycle racer turned pilot (the "Demon Aviator"), used a dirt strip at the Coast Highway and the County Road (Bay Boulevard) to stage a three-weekend exhibition. On the first and third weekends, Prest attacked mock forts (one at the end of the pier) with a simulated aerial bombardment.[195] On the intervening weekend, on August 12, 1917, he attempted to set a new world's altitude record, reaching an incredible height of 18,100 feet with a makeshift oxygen system while a reported thirty-five thousand spectators gasped below. Only the lack of having his altimeter certified when he landed (National Aviation Society officials certified it before take-off, but after a two-hour delay, they'd given up waiting and gone home) kept it out of the official record books.[196]

Even as the Joy Zone declined, Seal Beach's seaside aviation thrived, providing stunts and flight lessons. One of those who learned to fly was Wayne Abbott's son, Harry, who when not parachuting or doing other stunts, learned flying in his spare time. When the United States entered World War

II, he went to San Pedro, lied about his age and volunteered for the Navy as a submariner. But soon after returning from the war, in November 1919, as part of the one-year Armistice Day celebration, Earl Daugherty took Harry Wayne Abbott into the sky, where he jumped out and parachuted 8,200 feet to the ground, which broke his father's world record.[197] Daugherty was busy at Seal Beach that year. In August, he and Clarence "Ace" Bragunier conducted an hour-long aerial "stunt exhibition."[198] A month later, Daugherty and Wesley May engaged in "death-defying, hair-raising feats" amid a "flock of planes in mid-air." Daugherty and May's "death defying feats" included both of them "wing walking" at the same time. While one of them hung from the lower right wing, the other one stood on his head atop the upper left wing.[199] The following year, Daugherty opened Long Beach's new aviation field (now the Long Beach Airport), and air shows moved away from the seashores. However, local aviation was kept alive at the dirt strip on the coast highway.

As noted earlier, Prohibition bootleggers reportedly used this runway to house a scout plane, which aided them in their quest for the perfect liquor landing spot. By late 1927, pilot and airplane builder William F. Crawford was operating a legitimate thirty-acre airstrip just above Anaheim Landing. The property was three thousand by five hundred feet.

Crawford and his brother Harvey grew up around Tacoma, Washington, where their father introduced them to hot air ballooning. Harvey got an early contract (1910) for delivering mail by air, and William helped him build the plane for it. After Harvey moved to Los Angeles for the 1912 Dominguez Air Meet, William followed, and they set up a factory to build airplanes at the Venice Airport around 1915. Although they continued to collaborate, William set up a separate operation at the new Long Beach airport around 1922 and was still there in August 1927 when he survived a near fatal crash. Soon after, the *Los Angeles Times* reported that Crawford had organized the Crawford Motor and Airplane Manufactory "to operate an airplane field and school on the I.W. Hellman Ranch, north of Seal Beach… and the manufacture of modern airplanes and motors."[200] Six weeks later, Crawford announced his new company, with its almost completed plant and 2,500-foot-long oiled runway, would employ thirty people immediately and sixty people within a year at the site, which he said he had been trying to obtain for the past six years. Initially, Crawford's operation was large enough to produce twelve planes a month.[201]

Crawford also had a deep interest in gliding. While serious American gliding is credited as starting in 1928 near Cape Cod, Crawford and other

In 1927, aviator William F. Crawford constructed a hangar and 2,500-foot runaway (oiled, not paved) at the corner of Bay Boulevard and the Coast Highway to manufacture airplanes and motorized gliders like the one behind him.

Californians were doing it before then at Daugherty Field and at Seal Beach. Perhaps it was the ocean breezes, better for gliding, that prompted his move to Seal Beach.

Crawford was said to be the first man to install a motor in a glider. The plane could take off in one-fifth the distance of a normal plane, climb to ten thousand feet and land at fifteen miles per hour in less than sixty feet. He also designed a small airplane with folding wings that could still fly forty to fifty miles an hour.

In December 1928, the *Times* reported of another of his innovations: an airplane equipped for refrigeration, to be used to transport shrimp from Chihuahua, Mexico, where it cost ten cents a pound, to Los Angeles, where it normally costs sixty cents a pound.[202] When a Mexican syndicate placed an order totaling $250,000 in the project, Crawford's thirty-acre facility proved "inadequate for the volume of business" so he enlarged the plant to make it capable of building thirty-six airplanes a month and lengthened the runway to four thousand feet.[203] Either flaws in the idea or the October 1929 stock market crash doomed this project.

In 1928, 1929 and 1930 Crawford advertised regularly in *Popular Mechanics*, offering services and blueprints in construction of engines, propellers, gliders and blueprints for ice sleds. His ads also pitched how-to books, including *Simple Aerodynamics and the Practical Airplane*. The ads noted that Crawford made propellers for Harley-Davidson, Indian and Heath-Henderson motorcycles.

Popular Aviation ran a substantial article on Crawford's gliding operations, which mainly consisted of a school training ten students a day. The school's instructors, including Crawford's son, L.R. Crawford, were successfully putting "embryo fliers…into the air in any time from twenty minutes to two hours" in the first open glider ever built. A smaller glider could attain a height of four thousand feet and land at a speed of five to fifteen miles per hour. A larger glider with a forty-horsepower engine could reach ten thousand feet and land at ten to fifteen miles per hour.[204]

Crawford pursued regular flight as well and established the nation's second recognized aerial racecourse in 1931. The straight course started at his airfield and went east over the wetlands.

One of Crawford's protégés was Long Beach native Clyde Schlieper, who began hanging around Crawford and other Long Beach aviators when he was eight years old. In 1929, at the age of sixteen, he was at Seal Beach learning how to make and fly Crawford's gliders. After a few months of training, Schlieper landed Crawford's large glider on the roof deck of a motorboat speeding forty-five miles per hour in Long Beach harbor. After resting for a few minutes, Schlieper took off again and returned to Seal Beach.[205] Under the eye of John Tremayne, another instructor at the field, it only took eight hours for Schlieper to learn how to fly in an OX-5 Waco.[206]

C.W. Hitchcock learned in even less time. On June 5, 1930, Hitchcock took off on his first flight in a training glider equipped with a three-cylinder motor for takeoffs. He stayed aloft until he went over the Grapevine and Tejon Pass and landed at Kern County Airport in Bakersfield, where he was grounded by federal authorities for flying without a license.

Soon after ,the Seal Beach police commissioned another Crawford Field pilot, E.E. Smith, as that town's first air patrol officer. He patrolled the beaches watching for bathers in distress and also enforced rules prohibiting low flying over the beaches.

By 1932, the airport, now sometimes called Seal Beach Airport,[207] was housing John Roulstone's "flying school, charter service and repair station,"[208] a passenger service operated by Wes Carroll and another by aviator Howard Bear, who gave beach-goers short airplane rides for a penny per passenger pound.

Orange County pioneer aviator Eddie Martin said aviators from all over Southern California would fly into Crawford Field to spend a day at the beach. Charles Lindbergh and Amelia Earhart were said to have flown through there.

Others just wanted breakfast or lunch at the hot dog stand just across the Coast Highway, operated by Jim Arnerich and Nina Bennis. Arnerich had been in the area since 1929, having worked at the Bear Café in Anaheim Landing.

Bennis was no stranger to the area either. Although originally from Kansas, she had grown up in Los Alamitos with her younger sister, Una, and her mother, Bertha, who soon after coming to California had married James Watts, the first barber and constable in the new town by the sugar factory.[209]

As children Nina and Una had visited Anaheim Landing many times. When Nina grew older she married Karl Bennis, who would soon be the sugar factory's Number two man, behind Gus Strodthof who married Nina's sister, Una.[210]

After suffering lung damage during a Sugar Factory fire in 1921, Karl Bennis spent more and more time in the dry air of Temecula. When he moved there permanently in 1930, Nina did not move with him. They had grown apart, especially after they got into a car accident, which left her unable to have children. The split was amicable.

To support herself, Nina found work as the Los Alamitos census taker in 1930 but began to spend more time in Seal Beach, where she met Arnerich. By 1931, the pair had moved in together and opened a hot dog stand by the airport. Una helped out with a loan of either $200 or $1,000 (details in her stories frequently changed, according to her nephew).

One day as a plane or glider landed, a wheel popped off and started rolling across the highway. As it reached the restaurant parking lot, one of the patrons reportedly yelled out "Glide 'er in!" and the name stuck. The story may be apocryphal, but the name was in the 1931 county directory.[211] An old photo from that same year shows a big sign stating: "GLIDE'ER INN" and "EAT Fish, Steaks, Sandwiches Tamales, Clam Chowder, Chili PRIVATE BOOTHS."

The stand was soon providing meals and snacks in wicker baskets for the pilots who began using the inn as a sort of lodge hall. Clark Gable and many other celebrities ate there, with most of them signing the restaurant's logbook.

The restaurant's future lay in the balance in July 1934, when sixteen thousand acres of the combined "Bixby, Bryant, Hellman and Stanton Ranches" were

The Glide 'er Inn opened in 1930 across from Crawford Airport and became a popular stop for pilots and locals alike. When the Navy took over Anaheim Landing in 1944, the inn moved to a location at Sixteenth Street (currently Mahe). The inn also brought the T-34 Trainer airplane on its roof but placed it atop a taller base

offered to the Navy for use as a massive Navy Base. This would include most of the land that makes up present-day Seal Beach, Surfside, Sunset Beach and Huntington Harbor. Although endorsed by area business groups, the idea never received serious consideration at this time, but it would.[212]

When the postwar Depression hit, Seal Beach's Tent City remained busy as a reasonably priced alternative to hotels. In 1919, among its newer tenants were Everett and Jessie Reed, just arrived from Arizona. By 1931, Jessie was managing the site's approximately forty cottages,[213] while the Orange County directory lists her husband, Everett, as the "Constable" of Tent City. He apparently also delivered ice.

The Glide 'er Inn had loyal customers and loyal staff, shown here with founders and owners Nina Watts Bennis (second from right) and Jim Arnerich (far right).

The Bayside Land Company still owned the Tent City and almost all of the town's many vacant lots. You could stand on Twelfth Street and have an open view to Main Street.[214]

One of the buildings in the middle of the first block on Main Street was a two-story brick building. The bottom floor was a grocery store run by Hans and Dagmar Schmidt, and above it was the Tourist Hotel, where the Schmidts leased a room. Because it was the Depression, the Schmidts let people run up bills—some never paid—but somehow the pair eked out a living. Their daughter, Marge Ordway, remembers that to help provide food, her father always had a garden, plus he dug up clams for sale. Between these various sources, she said, "We did alright."[215]

They weren't the only gardeners in town. Russ Carley recalled a community garden on a big plot of land at the Coast Highway and Bolsa that helped during the toughest Depression days.[216] He said, "We all took care of it, and we would go over and take what we needed. Nobody took more than they needed."

Despite differences with the city government over the oil wells, the Hellman Ranch folk also helped out the locals, letting them glean from the lima bean fields what the big harvesters missed. Harriett Carley noted, "I

used to go over there and take all the lima beans I could carry. But I swore that once we had some money I would never eat lima beans again."[217]

In early 1933, unable to afford the hotel rate, Hans and Dagmar Schmidt moved into a more affordable cottage a block away on Central and Eigth. The move was fortuitous.

March 10, 1933, was a calm Friday afternoon. Some residents were preparing for dinner, others for afternoon mass at St. Anne's. Marge Ordway, who by now was living on Eighth near Central, remembers her father heading to First Street to pick up a friend before an American Legion meeting. On the counter were some bean sprouts he had just bought so they could make chop suey. The kitchen and bathroom in their recently rented cottage had no cupboards so everything was on shelves.

Suddenly, at 5:55 p.m., the earth began shaking. A 6.4-magnitude earthquake, centered southeast of Long Beach, shook the area violently.

Ordway remembers cans flying all over as her mother tried to get her out of the kitchen through the back door. "Three times she tried to shove me out that back door, and the earthquake was so strong I couldn't get out." Finally, she pushed her out, but not before some of the cans flying off the shelf hit her in the head and face. She finally got outside in time to see the two-story brick building they had formerly lived in fall down "like a deck of cards."[218]

Russ Carley also remembers his mother struggling to get out of the house. "The quake jammed the door. The chimney started falling apart, and there were bricks falling from the air." Mrs. Carley finally made it, but "it was a terrible experience."

At the barbershop next to the American Legion Hall, Police Chief James Zoeter had just left when the quake hit. Unable to get out the door, the barber jumped through the front plate-glass window to escape being trapped. "He was cut up pretty bad, but he was alive," remembers Marge Ordway.[219]

Top: The 1933 Long Beach earthquake caused an estimated $250,000 damage to Seal Beach, most to brick buildings like the power plant, the Tourist Hotel on Main Street and the elementary school. The latter two had to be demolished.

Bottom: Seal Beach suffered $260,000 in damage from the earthquake but got off light compared to neighboring Long Beach. To help those displaced as well as relief workers, U.S. Army mess crews provided emergency food and shelter across from city hall for over a week.

The nearby city hall was slightly damaged. The drugstore lost its entire front. Scared residents ran into St. Anne's Church, but the pastor said they were safer outside and yelled at teenagers to get out from underneath the power lines. As aftershocks continued to rock the area, fears of a tsunami spread around, and many families sought the "high ground" of Landing Hill. Some set up tents and spent the night, which was still interrupted by aftershocks—thirty-one of them before midnight. This was too much for Hans Schmidt, who "piled his family into their Star Durant automobile and took them to relatives in Los Angeles, fighting traffic from 9:00 p.m. to 3:00 a.m."

The next day's *Times* reported an estimated $260,000 in damage to the town. Most was at the power plant, but the school also suffered, and a high-diving platform/barge in the Amusement area snapped its lines. Officials were worried it would drift into the Alamitos Bay bridge, which itself was "wrenched" by the temblor. Part of the Jewel City Café fell down as well.

In the following days, with residents without water, gas and food, Mayor Elmer Hughes organized the police, fire and citizens into an extensive relief organization. An emergency refugee camp was set up across from city hall with tents for those with no place to go, including many from Long Beach. Food was brought in by state and county agencies from Los Angeles, and Mayor Hughes brought in bottled water from the Bixby Ranch. Over five hundred were fed in the morning and at lunch and over one thousand at dinner. Within a day or two, the National Guard arrived to help the beleaguered citizenry, although it was too late to stop some of the looting, done by outsiders and local youths alike.

The earthquake demolished much of the Seal Beach school, and the board organized plans to rebuild it.[220] But in a June election, the townsfolk voted down a bond. Times were already tough enough in the Depression.[221] But by the end of the year, thanks to a state bond (and federal monies), funds became available to repair schools damaged in the earthquake. The old brick structure was replaced with a new, larger, reinforced concrete one. After a couple years, the school got its third name, changing from Seal Beach Elementary to Mary Zoeter Elementary.

During the Depression, governments—federal, state and local—were seeking ways of raising additional revenue. Roosevelt promoted the repeal of Prohibition as a way to increase local tax revenues. In 1931, the Nevada legislature legalized casino gambling. In 1933, California gambling interests succeeded in getting parimutuel betting on horse races approved by voters. Backers of new tracks like Santa Anita, Bay Meadows and Del Mar quickly got their projects in order.

Colonel John S. Berger, a promoter with experience at Baltimore's Pimlico Track, proposed a $250,000 horse race track "off Seventeenth Street and Los Alamitos Street."[222] This could mean the property behind Anaheim Landing as Bay Boulevard was the road to Los Alamitos or also just off Westminster Road, which is an extension of Seventeenth Street if you're coming from Santa Ana.

Promising jobs for one thousand, Berger's Orange County Jockey Club had many supporters, including Thomas Talbert, former chairman of the board of supervisors; Hugh T. O'Connor, secretary of the Los Alamitos Chamber of Commerce; Seal Beach banker W.D. Miller; and Mayor Elmer Hughes.

These men said that opinion in their sections was practically unanimous for the racecourse. Apparently it wasn't unanimous enough. Church-related groups convinced county officials that Seal Beach already had enough gambling as it was.

CHAPTER 7

SURF SIDE COLONY

In 1905, John C. Ord, through his Ord Land Company, filed a complicated suit against, among others, the Alamitos Land Company over property on the peninsula across from Anaheim Landing.[223] Ord had filed a federal claim on the land, saying it had originally been an island and thus was excluded from the original Rancho Los Alamitos grant. He prevailed in the suit.[224]

As Anaheim Bay grew more popular and cottages became unavailable, the Ord Land Company, which was actually run by Philip A. Stanton, sold lots across the inlet "on the peninsula." But sales were slow until an automobile bridge was put across the inlet, parallel to the PE tracks. Streets in East Seal Beach went as high as Twenty-fourth Street in a two-block-wide strip on the inland side of the Pacific Electric tracks, which ran right behind the cottages.

Soon after the opening of the Coast Highway in the late 1920s, the Ord Land Company optioned the property beyond Twenty-fourth Street to the Phillips and Hambaugh Realty and Construction Company of Los Angeles. This firm built the Surf Side Colony, a name intended to capitalize on the recent opening of the exclusive Malibu Colony north of Santa Monica.[225] At the same time, Phillips and Hambaugh began construction on a beachside resort in Oxnard called Mandalay, which, like the Surf Side Colony, would offer cottages on a lease-to-buy plan.[226] Initially, three rows of beach cottages—A row, B row and C row—were constructed on the ocean side of the highway, with D and E rows of houses to be added later on the east side. The company also blocked direct ocean access to the "East Seal Beach"

The Surf Side Colony was developed in mid-1929 in the buzz surrounding the new Malibu Film Colony. Beach cottages were offered through a "lease with an option to buy" program. The 1929 stock market crash caused the original developers to default.

By the time of this 1931 aerial photo, the peninsula side of Anaheim Landing was quite populated. But the builders of the Surf Side Colony, who bought the land on the ocean side of the railroad tracks, constructed a fence that prevented the peninsula residents from accessing the ocean. The residents filed a lawsuit that lasted for a number of years.

homes on the peninsula, for which forty residents took the company to court in 1930.

The Surf Side Colony started well, but the October 1929 stock market crash stymied it. M. Penn Phillips acquired R. Hambaugh's interest in late 1929, but by 1931, the development had been taken over by Los Angeles Underwriters, Inc., who, of course, advertised that the colony laid claim "to the most rapid growth of any subdivision in Southern California" (from 19 homes to 163 in just over a year) and that the D and E Row subdivision would open soon, as would a tunnel passing beneath the PE tracks and highway to facilitate easy transit back and forth.[227] (The tunnel also was reportedly convenient for rumrunners.)[228] Sales did not pick up, and by 1934, the property had reverted to the Ord Land Company.

Throughout the 1930s, the colony (now more frequently spelled Surfside) sported a permanent population around one hundred, although it housed around 150 homes.[229] The regulars frequented the peninsula beaches and the Commissary (a combination café, soda fountain and gathering place serving "hamburgers, malts and some of the best buttermilk pancakes ever")[230] and kids played hide and seek under the pilings of the A row houses (when they weren't being threatened by waves). By the late 1930s, there were also a couple good nearby restaurants, Sam's Seafood ("clam-shaped drinks, tropical waterfalls, and Polynesian dancers—who could ask for anything more?") and the Dunes ("best Mexican food ever!").[231] Surfside mothers could also count on the weekly visits from the vegetable truck man, the two milkmen (Adohr and Golden State) and the Helms Bakery Truck.

Like Anaheim Landing, Surfside remained an isolated pocket where life seemed perfect. This began to change with the construction of the first Seal Beach jetty in the mid-1930s. With the breakwater obstructing the current from the southwest, incoming waves no longer had enough power to push sand back onto the nearby shore, causing beach erosion. The issue would become far more drastic when the Navy took over the Landing in World War II and significantly extended the breakwaters.

CHAPTER 8

THE BAY AND
A NEW PIER

As a young girl, Joan Stegman, whose grandparents owned the Willard Hotel on Twelfth Street, visited Seal Beach often in the mid-1920s and early '30s. Her initial memories of the town were mainly dismal ones of the crumbling pier and collapsing pavilions. The roller coaster looked like a skeleton of some prehistoric monster, and the concession shops were long gone. High tides had broken up the concrete boardwalk, and jagged pieces, some three to five feet tall, protruded from the sand at odd angles. "It looked as if an army had erected a barrier to protect the town from the invaders from the sea."

But as a teenager, Stegman started walking to Anaheim Landing, which she soon discovered was "the place to be…the gathering place for local people and summer people. Some who had houses around the bay and some from town."

Seal Beach kids visited other beaches as well. They'd take the Red Car south to dance at the Huntington or Balboa Pavilions or head west to Long Beach. They might go with siblings or friends to the dances at the Pike. Take the streetcar for a nickel and get into the dance for a dime. Or go to a show and get a candy bar, all for a quarter.

But if you stayed in town, you had two options. The ocean was okay, but you had to go around the shell of the roller coaster, which was closed down around 1929[232]—not that local kids didn't enjoy the occasional, if somewhat forbidden, ride on it. Hop over the fence and rock one of the cars back and forth enough to get it over one hump and as far up the next hump as you could, then jump in and "ride down as many bumps as we had pushed it up."[233]

Even during the heyday of the Joy Zone, the Bay, with the Anaheim Landing Bath-house and Bowling Alley, was the favorite swimming spot for locals.

But generally, local kids preferred the "Bay." Nobody had sunscreen. They'd paint their cheeks and noses with zinc oxide. "We looked like a band of warring Indians," laughed Stegman. They would swim, dive, splash, sunbathe and play until they heard the nine o'clock whistle from the power plant.

The Bay was also a source for money. Fred and Paul Krenwinkle, sometimes helped by sister Annabelle, used to dig for fishing bait that they'd sell, sometimes to P.A. Stanton. "He loved cockles," said Fred.[234]

On windy days, local kids looked for coins on the beach where breezes exposed quarters, nickels and dimes. Or they'd crawl under the boardwalk or bathhouse and find coins that had fallen between the gaps in the planks.[235]

If parents neglected to pack a lunch for their children, there was always Ruth Meissner's store by the trestle or Irene and Carl Templeton's restaurant, which served hamburgers and hot dogs for ten cents apiece. There was another hamburger stand between Kupferle's bathhouse and Louis White's store and bowling alley.

Low tide would find some dads rowing up the bay to fish, harvest razorback clams or cockles or catch a leopard shark or a croaker. If they fished in the surf, they usually caught corvina or surf perch.

Some local youths fished off the wharf while the Red Car clattered over the nearby trestle on its run to Newport Beach. If the train's passengers looked out, they might see swimmers—some on surfing mats rented from Stangeland's concession.[236]

The swimmers might drift out with the tide in a group, tossing a big ball as they drifted toward the train bridge. As they neared the bridge, one would grab the dangling rope and everybody else would grab somebody's heel and see how many could hang on.

Sometimes kids would float on "windbags," muslin sacks about six feet long and not quite half as wide. Kids would run along the beach filling their bag with air and quickly tie it off. They were good for a number of rides on the waves until they needed refilling.

When kids heard the trains coming, they'd race to get under the tracks and listen to the roar of the train passing directly overhead.

Some adventurous youths, like Stegman, even climbed the trestle. "If they didn't catch us and if it was high tide, the bravest ones would jump in [to the water]."[237]

All agree that the best diver by far was lifeguard Earl Whittington, who, along with his brothers Jack and Ned, had been watching the beach since the mid-1920s. Earl was especially remembered by the town's girls, including Joan Stegman. "He was over six feet and had this beautiful tan. He would often go to the very top of the bridge and do a swan dive that was quite beautiful. Everybody would stop what they were doing when Earl went to the top."

Many residents lived year round at the Landing. Ruth and Fred Meissner came to town in 1921 from the Imperial Valley. Fred found work on the oil rigs, and Ruth opened a shop near the bridge and train trestle to Sunset Beach, selling cakes and other goodies to motormen and conductors. They lived in a simple tent cottage at Anaheim Landing. It had no bathtub "but who cared," she asked, "when you could just jump into the bay?" Over time, they bought lots and built apartments, eventually constructing the Green Lantern, with a larger store for Ruth and six to eight apartments.[238]

Many cottages were rented to the same families every summer. George Brown's dad always rented #7 at the end of the pier—two bedrooms, partitions about seven feet high, a living room with a couch and dining room table and a kitchen—all for seventy-five dollars a month.

Patt Gray, whose family spent many summers at Anaheim Landing, vividly recalled, "Our green cabin was in the front row facing the sand. There was a brown shingle two-story building with changing rooms above, below was a bowling alley/snack counter." She also recalled a Monopoly game that started at the beginning of each summer and lasted the season. "It was held on the picnic tables next to the bath house."[239]

The children of the summer visitors hated to go home and more than one said they almost had to be dragged away from the beach at the end of the summer. But most of those same visitors returned the next summer. "It was like greeting old friends," said Stegman.

Some summer visitors ended up staying full time. Earl Shea's parents met on the dance floor at the Jewel City Café in the early 1920s. They married and moved to Downey but frequently visited Earl's grandmother in Seal Beach. Finally, in 1937, the Sheas moved to Seal Beach, and Earl enrolled in the eighth grade class, which now numbered eleven girls and ten boys. Like all Seal Beach students, Earl attended Huntington Beach High School. He played sports, but during his sophomore and junior year, Earl worked part time at the Anaheim Landing bowling alley, setting pins by hand and cleaning the alleys and bowling balls.

The bowling alley wasn't the only recreation in town. In the late 1920s, the Seal Beach merchants sponsored a team in the Long Beach City baseball league.[240] In the 1930s, the team played in the SoCal InterCity Baseball League.[241]

Larry Howard managed a fast-pitch softball team that played in the Huntington Beach League in the 1940s and sometimes three other leagues at the same time, usually playing their home games on a field where McGaugh School is now located.

Visiting teams and Sunday Drivers now had more places to eat when in town, as the Glide 'er Inn was no longer the only eatery on the Coast Highway. In 1937, brothers Sam and George Arvanitis, who owned a bait shop near Surfside, opened Sam's Seafood Grotto and let patrons pick their fish out of the pool of water next to the café. It drew enough crowds that in late 1941, Sam's opened its four-hundred-seat Neptune Room with the music of Arthur Gibson and his Orchestra.

Another restaurant on the highway was Dovalis's 101 Ranch House ("west of the Seal Beach Airport") near Fifteenth Street. It opened in June 1940 and featured a menu of "delicious barbecued meats" and seafood dinners.

Closer to the Long Beach border was Vivian Laird's Garden of Allah. After divorcing an oil roustabout in the mid-1920s, Laird settled in Long Beach with $2,500. In 1929, she opened a restaurant in Naples called the Garden of Allah.

The restaurant became so popular that Laird relocated, as early as 1938, to bigger quarters in Seal Beach at Eighth Street and Coast Highway. It

Belgian-born doctor Homer DeSadeleer was a Seal Beach fixture for over forty years, and he delivered nearly four thousand babies. His office at 119 Main Street was also where lifeguards took anyone who had been injured on the beaches.

billed itself as "the swankiest nite spot this side of Hollywood with excellent food and entertainment and dancing till 2."

In 1939, future *Star Trek* star DeForest Kelley, arrived in Long Beach from Atlanta, Georgia. After visting the Garden of Allah he wrote home of its glamour, exotic partying, drinks and music. "There were Mediterranean and Asian faces, and Catholic girls with Beauty Marks."[242]

One performer was bandleader Peggy Gilbert, who played sometimes with her all-girl Dixieland band and sometimes with a mixed group.[243] Another was pianist Freddy Slack ("Beat Me Daddy Eight to the Bar").

One didn't even have to be at the club to enjoy it. The "Danceable Melodies of Raymond Jasper and his Five Counts of Rhythm" were broadcast from the Garden of Allah from 10:45 to 11:00 p.m. nightly on KFOX Radio (1260 AM). By mid-1940 Jasper's airtime had been moved up to run from 9:30 to 9:45.[244]

Food, dining and dancing weren't the club's only attractions. In September 1941, authorities busted a gambling den in the garage behind the club. Ten dealers and workers were arrested, including Ballard Barron, ending the evening's fun for the eighty customers playing roulette, blackjack and craps.[245]

There were respectable businesses in town. One was the growing medical practice of one of Seal Beach's most revered figures, Dr. Homer DeSadeleer, who had assumed more and more of the duties of the town's longtime physician, Dr. Ernest Greene, whose office was right above the California State Bank.

DeSadeleer was born in 1912 in central Belgium and came to Seal Beach in 1925 when his dad became one of the many Belgian farmers growing sugar beets on the Fred Bixby and Hellman Ranch properties. After getting a degree in medicine at Loyola Marymount and some internships at local hospitals, DeSadeleer returned to Seal Beach in 1938 to open a small general practice specializing in obstetrics at 119 Main Street, in what formerly had been an old gambling hall (although in Seal Beach, you might probably ask, "What hadn't?"). Over the years, DeSadeleer built up a loyal and large following. His office was also almost an unofficial lifeguard station for all the people who got cut up on rocks or by barnacles on the pier timbers or injured in the water. Described by one longtime patient as "like a Norman Rockwell painting come to life," DeSadeleer delivered over four thousand local babies during his career.

As if the Depression economy wasn't bad enough, nature was equally tough on the area in the 1930s. Floods in 1934 and 1938 had left the area stranded for days a time. Fortunately, by this time the lower stage of the San Gabriel River had been channeled, and the concrete and gravel rock channel walls directed much of the floodwaters and silt directly to the ocean.

Getting the channel and jetty built had not been easy. It mainly benefitted Long Beach (and the East Naples Land Company which owned most of the undeveloped land around Alamitos Bay), so Seal Beach (and especially Philip A. Stanton) tried to leverage that to get help with some desperately needed items. Because a number of people, including children, had been killed while crossing the Pacific Electric trestle over the entrance to Alamitos Bay, the town wanted a new bridge that would allow trains, autos and pedestrians to cross. It also wanted long jetties to carry the waters of the straightened San Gabriel (and the wastewaters of the Los Angeles Gas & Electric power plant) far enough out to sea so as to not affect Seal Beach's beachfront. The town held out for over six months, but in July 1931, Long Beach and Los Angeles County agreed to fund and construct these items. The new channel turned the wetlands northwest of Central and Fifth to dry land and made it available for development by its owners, the East Naples Land Company and the Hellman Company. The former's land was now isolated from its main activities by the concrete walls of the straightened San Gabriel River, so in 1938, it leased the Seal Beach land to Captain Russell Grotemat. He not only built himself a nice home there with a great view of the developing Alamitos Bay Marina, but he also started placing trailers on the land and leasing those out. This was the beginning of the Seal Beach Trailer Park.

Next on the to-do list was the run-down amusement area and pier. In March 1935, city leaders announced plans to remove the old roller coaster, construct a new pier and convert the lands into an open beach playground. Unfortunately, the city didn't have the consent of the Bayside Land Company.[246]

But that issue became moot in July 1935 when a freak storm washed out a forty-foot section of the pier, marooning sixteen persons near where the Scintillators used to light up the night. A Coast Guard cutter anchored two hundred feet off the splintered pilings of the wooden structure used its searchlight to guide a dory through the pilings to rescue the sixteen.[247]

With the collapse of the pier, Stanton gave in. On August 31, 1935, one of the largest foreclosure sales recorded up to that time in Orange County took place, when $295,246.56 worth of Bayside Land Company property was awarded to Security First National Bank of Los Angeles at an auction on the Orange County courthouse steps.[248] This included the entire oceanfront and nine hundred lots throughout town.[249] In July 1936, the bank announced it would demolish the former Joy Zone area and develop a swanky new subdivision with lots between Seal Way and Ocean Avenue widened from twenty-five feet to fifty-eight, and a one-story height limit would be imposed. While neither of these happened, aerial photos show that by November, the roller coaster and the rest of the old Joy Zone had been removed. However, the pier, still owned by Stanton, remained.

By December, other old buildings joined the list of the razed and demolished—the Tower Café and John C. Ord's structure at Main and Electric. Over the years, it had been the town's bank, Wells Fargo office and the Bayside Land Company's real estate office—and always active. In the early 1930s, while approaching the age of ninety, Ord once again ran for mayor and was supported by Bayside Land Company–backed Citizens Safety Committee, which had also filed a petition for (big surprise) recall against Mayor John Bragg. After a stroke in 1935, to show he was still active, Ord posed for a newspaper article showing him learning how to use a typewriter to conduct his daily business.[250] Just over a year later, he passed away at the age of ninety-four.

In 1935, the bankrupt Bayside Land Company's assets were sold at auction and the ruins of the Joy Zone and roller coaster soon removed. In 1939, much of the property was purchased by Phillip C. Norton, who began building the Seaside Colony tract around Ocean and Thirteenth. These homes were marketed to the area's growing number of defense workers.

By 1937, housewives had additional shopping choices. Yeagers (at Fifth and the Coast Highway) was selling Russet potatoes at ten pounds for fifteen cents, a solid head of lettuce for a nickel and sirloin steaks at twenty-five cents per pound.

On a fall Friday night in the late 1930s, locals might have headed east to watch "Cap" Scheue's Huntington Beach Oilers football team, which featured some very talented Seal Beach athletes, including end Jim Stangeland (who, as a coach, would later lead Long Beach City College to three national championships and marry Betty McGaugh, the daughter of Zoeter School principal John J. McGaugh).

All this was duly recorded in the *Seal Beach Post & Wave*, even though it had been going through many ownership changes. In 1932, A.W. Armstrong sold a half interest to Robert Deu Pree and then in 1936 sold out the rest to William and Mildred Banninger. The Banningers bought out Deu Pree's share a year later, and Armstrong returned as editor. Frank Fowler purchased the paper in 1939, and he kept it into the mid-1940s.

In October 1938, contractor Phillip C. Norton acquired much of the former Bayside property and began building the Seaside Colony, a new tract near Thirteenth Street.[251] By this time, Stanton, motivated by a potentially costly condemnation suit filed by the city in 1937, had deeded the pier to the city, which had already obtained a Federal Public Works Administration (PWA) grant for $49,000 and a $60,000 loan to rebuild it as a municipally owned pier. Residents then passed a bond for an additional $100,000 to fully fund the project.[252]

The man responsible for the PWA, President Franklin Roosevelt, made a brief appearance in Seal Beach on July 16, 1938, as he motorcaded from Los Angeles to San Diego via downtown Long Beach. As the entourage crossed into Seal Beach by the old power plant, the cars stopped and Orange County officials greeted the president. The parade then continued down the Coast Highway to San Diego, where Roosevelt boarded the USS *Houston* for some weeks of fishing off the Galapagos Islands.[253]

The new pier was celebrated with three days of festivities beginning on May 19, 1939, involving 1,800 Boy Scouts, a contest of high school bands, fishing and kayak competitions, a beauty contest and aerial circus. This festival would continue on for many years as Beachcomber Days. Much of its success was due to help from members of the Seal Beach Lions Club, which had formed a few months earlier in January. Among its first members were John "Frosty" Felts, Neil Franklin, Charles Irvine, J.C. Putnam, A.W. Stegen and George and Sam Arvanitis.

The decade ended with Seal Beach making national headlines three times in less than a month. The week of September 17–24, 1939, brought a severe heat wave, which closed businesses and schools and sent hundreds of thousands of Southern Californians to the beaches. In the middle of the week, the nation's newspapers carried a tongue-in-cheek article stating, "Seal Beach, which boasts about its wonderful fishing, hosted a fishing contest in which the winning catch, by city clerk F.W. Hickman, weighed just nine ounces."

More serious headlines ran a few days later. On Sunday, September 24, a "sudden" storm from Mexico dropped a record-setting 5.42 inches of rain one day and then unleashed hurricane-force winds the next. A funnel cloud formed near Newport and began moving up the coast, destroying the Sunset Beach boardwalk, and then clipped Anaheim Landing, ripping two doors off the old bowling alley and damaging several of the cottage homes.[254] Seal Beach police chief Al Scaife said waves of over thirty feet swept over Seal Way, but fortunately no homes were there at the time. Overall, Seal

In October 1939, two Seal Beach airport pilots Wes Carroll and Clyde Schlieper set a world's record for longest flight. Their refuelings took place in the Mojave Desert and at Seal Beach airport, by hauling up gas from speeding cars below. Long Beach radio station KFON did live reports every day from the Seal Beach site.

Beach got off easy, but elsewhere, the storm took forty-five lives on land and another forty-eight at sea.

Less than a week later, the town made national headlines again with the coverage of aviators Wes Carroll and Clyde Schlieper's month-long attempt to break the endurance flight record which at that time was just seven days.

To fund their venture, the pilots had hired a manager to secure some sponsorships. The Kay Jewelry Store of Long Beach agreed to sponsor them, but only if they broke the record. In addition, they would receive $100 for each day they flew after breaking the record. To raise additional funds, Carroll said they endorsed everything from "seasick pills to cigarettes."[255] The plane was redesigned as a seaplane so additional gas could be stored in the pontoons. With the extra tanks, the plane could hold ninety gallons, enough for twenty-two hours of flying.

On September 29, Carroll and Schlieper departed from Long Beach Marine Stadium in a Piper Cub dubbed the Spirit of Kay. The plane was refueled by flying low over an automobile speeding along the runway, usually at Rosamond Dry Lake (now Edwards Air Force Base) but on occasion at Seal Beach. The aviators dropped a line with a hook on it and pulled a three-gallon can of gasoline up into the plane. Pulling up enough cans to fill the ninety-gallon tanks was quite time-consuming and required a lot of circling of the airports. Their food was hauled up in similar fashion.[256]

The plane was equipped with instruments for night flying and a radio set for communication and listening to entertainment, such as live coverage on Long Beach radio station KLON, which aired regular live reports from Seal Beach airport, where crowds gathered to watch the refueling. Newsreel camera crews also sat on the ground, getting footage of the pilots as they did their refueling.

Eventually, the pair flew nonstop for thirty days (726 hours). When they landed back at Marine Stadium on October 29, they had to be helped from the aircraft and held up as they spoke with the press.

Other headlines were quickly replaced by less celebratory ones. The Pacific Electric Railroad pulled out its tracks on the Ocean Avenue Bridge, ending direct train service to downtown Long Beach and Belmont Shore. The end of service caused a small storm of protest among the locals, but this was soon forgotten as World War II began to dominate the headlines.

CHAPTER 9

WORLD WAR II

B y the late 1930s, the U.S. government was preparing for war. The Pacific Fleet, based in San Diego, was ordered to Pearl Harbor, and Congress approved funding to build dozens of new military posts on the Pacific coast. A new navy shipyard was built in Long Beach, and many aircraft plants were built in Southern California, such as Lockheed and Vega near Burbank, North-American and Northrop in the South Bay area and Vultee in Downey. Douglas, the largest of the companies, had three plants—in Santa Monica, Westchester and the biggest one in Long Beach, which was announced in 1939, broke ground in November 1940 and opened for business on October 17, 1941.

The workers at these new facilities needed places to live, and thanks to federal incentives for low-income defense workers, Philip Norton's new Seaside Colony off Thirteenth Street and Ocean offered them. Seaside Colony featured twenty-seven homes of 817 square feet with detached garages in a variety of designs—"modified modern, farmhouse simplicity, corner windowed cottages, and comfortable Cape Cods. The homes offered dual floor furnace, overhead garage doors, large service porches with automatic hot water heaters." The full price was $3,675, and only $275 was necessary for a down payment. Federal Housing Authority (FHA) loans required only 5 percent down.

By mid-February, six homes had been sold. The expected increased number of children motivated the passage of a $40,000 bond issue to build additional elementary school classrooms and recreation areas.

Others thought the military's expansion would expand aviation in Seal Beach as well. Three Long Beach men announced they would raise $200,000 to take over Seal Beach Airport, develop a seaplane landing area and build an additional ninety-eight- by- one-hundred-foot hangar and research areas. But nothing more was heard about this idea.[257]

The growing tension overseas affected Seal Beach in other ways. In early 1940, physician Homer DeSadeleer returned for a visit to his native Belgium. While Belgium was technically neutral, that detail was of little interest to the Germans, who attacked in May 1940. DeSadeleer got out of Europe "by the skin of his teeth" and managed to return to Seal Beach.[258]

One not so lucky was former Seal Beach Airport instructor John Roulstone. After the war began in 1939, the twenty-eight-year-old volunteered to join the British air force, but in August 1941, he and seven Canadian pilots were killed when their trans-Oceanic transport crashed on takeoff in England.[259]

The Douglas expansion at the Long Beach airport forced the Navy Reserve Air unit there to find a new home. The Reserves were already using 160 acres near Los Alamitos as a touch-and-go field, and much more open land was available near there. In February 1941, the U.S. Navy announced plans for a 1,300-acre reserve air base just south of that town. It would be the first of five military bases built in Orange County in World War II. The runways were completed in November, and barracks were slated to be finished the following month. The base was active even before the new year, although it wasn't formally commissioned until May 1942.

The day after the December 7, 1941, attack on Pearl Harbor, authorities ordered a complete nighttime blackout of lights—streets, auto and home. Radio stations, which could be used as directional aids, were ordered to limit their hours. And four regiments of troops from Camp MacArthur at San Pedro were assigned to protect the new defense factories with searchlight batteries around these facilities.

Searchlights were also placed at the Los Alamitos Sugar Factory, near the Douglas and other aircraft factories, as well as in Cypress and along the beach. A huge mounted gun unit was put in place at the Bolsa Chica Gun Club. A battery was also set up at the Seal Beach Airport, directly across from the Glide 'er Inn, and the army rented the end of the new Seal Beach pier for spotting duties.

Most of these batteries were already in place on the night of February 25, 1942, and more alert than usual. That morning's headlines blared "SUBMARINE SHELLS SOUTHLAND OIL FIELD!" The night before, a Japanese submarine surfaced and shelled an oil facility twelve miles north of Santa Barbara but fortunately did minimal damage.

At 1:44 a.m., Signal Corps radar picked up an unidentified object 120 miles off the coast and tracked it to three miles off Los Angeles Airport. Sirens wailed, and searchlights combed through the clear black skies. Thinking this was only a single scout plane, pursuit planes stayed on the ground, ready to ascend once the main Japanese attack force was located.

At 2:43, an unidentified plane was reported between Long Beach and Seal Beach, and the local sky lit up with crisscrossed searchlight beams. At 3:33, artillery units fired on unidentified planes over Artesia and headed to Long Beach and then out to sea. At 3:25 came a report of planes over the Long Beach Douglas plant. Similar reports came in at 4:03 and again at 4:13. Most observers noted three planes in a V formation, although some said two. Flying at reports of six thousand to nine thousand feet, they were apparently too high for the thirty-seven-millimeter guns that were in place.

Those were the last reports of the evening. But few went back to sleep that night.[260]

By now the military had already begun the forced evacuation of Japanese from the coastal areas. Raids had already taken place on February 15 and 24. By March 1, nine thousand Japanese Americans had been relocated, two thousand from Orange County. Many were farmers from the Bixby and Hellman ranches. Local Japanese were taken to Westminster and loaded on Pacific Electric trains and taken to Santa Anita for initial processing.

Even though their fathers had already been taken and they themselves were awaiting relocation, Japanese Americans like Aiko Tanamachi Endo continued to live life as normally as possible at their Hellman Ranch home. She recalled this incident from early 1942.

Naturally, we didn't prepare the land again to plant vegetables; we just tried to finish up and harvest what was there. We had time on our hands until we actually had to evacuate. My brother took one of the Kaneko boys fishing at Anaheim Landing below the bridge. Some mother that was driving past saw that they were Orientals, and they reported the boys to the police, saying that they might be trying to blow up the bridge. I remember my brother coming home that day, laughing, and saying that the chief of police came over to check up on them. The chief saw Tom and said, "Oh, it's you, Tom. Somebody said that there was a couple of Japanese trying to blow up the bridge, so I had to check it out." [laughter]

A few days after the above incident, Endo and her family were shipped to Poston, Arizona, where they rejoined his father.

The military considered the Seal Beach power plant a potential enemy target. The annual Holiday Carnival of Lights competition along the Orange County Coast Highway was cancelled. But with some creativity, life went on. Vivian Laird advertised that even though her club was "dark" outside, everything was bright and cheery inside where Max Fiddler and his musicians played until two o'clock every morning.[261]

Gas was rationed, as was meat. The Glide 'er Inn and other restaurants complained about meat rationing, which only allowed six ounces per meal.

But local women stepped up when the War Productions Board asked that used silk and nylon stockings be donated to the cause. The reprocessed silk was valuable for powder bags because the silk burned instantly, while nylons were melted down and remade into very tough and durable thread for war use. The bin at Frosty Felts store on Main Street was soon overflowing.[262]

Up in Los Alamitos, the Navy was already announcing plans to enlarge its new station by an additional 715 acres, to accommodate the training of thirty thousand pilots. An additional quarter-mile-wide bottom strip was taken from the Fred Bixby Ranch—and he was not happy about it. The Navy also took some of his acreage southwest of his Rancho Los Alamitos home—to make into a hospital—at Seventh and Bellflower.

The Seal Beach airfield was taken over by the Navy as an outlying airfield for use by the naval pilots to practice touch and go landings. It was one of many OLFs used by Alamitos pilots, along with Fullerton, Anaheim, Haster Farm, Horse Farm, East Long Beach (actually Meadowlark Airport in Huntington Beach) and Mile Square in Fountain Valley.

In June 1942, Earl Shea became a lifeguard, joining the Whittington Brothers. As senior lifeguard Earl Whittington usually kept the prime Anaheim Bay assignment for himself. His brother Dick manned the first street area near Ray Bay, leaving Shea with left-of-the-pier duty.

Another new lifeguard that year was Lloyd Murray, who recalled the city's unique hiring system. There were no tests of one's swimming abilities or conditioning. The lifeguard applicant would "go up to the city hall and talk to the chief of police. And if he wants to hire you, he hires you."

Both Murray and Shea finished out the summer but were then drafted. Slightly older than Murray and Shea was Francis Haley, who was already a chief petty officer in the Navy when the Japanese attacked. He volunteered to be a diver and would soon earn a commendation for his underwater work salvaging ships sunk at Pearl Harbor on December 7.

Many of the kids who weren't lifeguards earned money at Stangeland's Umbrella Stands, renting out umbrellas and surf mats (three-by-four-and-a-half-foot pads made of a rubber-like canvas and with cylinders running along the edges front to back). The concessions were owned by Gerhardt Stangeland, who operated "stands" at Dolphin Street and at First, Eighth and Tenth Streets. Kids could earn up to $2.50 a day plus tips for an eight-hour shift (plus free use of the surf mats). Such fortunes were quickly spent on necessities like comic books, sodas, candy and the occasional trip to the Pike in Long Beach.[263]

For adults, the local oil rigs still supplied many jobs, but now so did the expanded defense factories Long Beach shipyards. Sensing an opportunity, the chamber of commerce printed sixty thousand four-page fliers, encouraging area defense workers to live in Seal Beach. Soon, most of the town's homes —and even the cottages at Anaheim Landing—were all occupied.

The new residents meant more voters—and a smaller percentage dependent on income derived from gambling. This changed the town's dynamic. In May 1942, Jessie Reed, who had been running the town's Tent City for the past eleven years, defeated a twelve-year incumbent for a spot on the city council. Reed's promise to keep gambling out of Seal Beach resonated with a council majority, who elected her as mayor, making her the first woman ever to hold that office in Orange County.[264]

"Our people do not want public card houses, or gambling or bars…and I am going to do my best to keep them out," she said in an article that received nationwide attention.

Perhaps it was the shortage of meat and other rationed items, or maybe the increased heat on gambling places, but in mid-1943, Vivian Laird closed down the Garden of Allah (and asked the city to refund the balance of her business license for that year). In early 1944, she sold the building and business to two Long Beach businessmen, George E. Stucken and Earl S. Raines, the latter a successful Long Beach bookmaker. Business at the Garden was still slow, so Raines installed a shuffleboard court in 1948 and switched to a hot jazz lineup, but it appears his focus was on his bookmaking activities.[265]

But the biggest local news happened in mid-January 1944 when the Navy announced it would build a five-thousand-acre Weapons and Net Depot at Anaheim Landing.[266] Three hundred homes would be removed and a new harbor reconfigured and dredged. And over one thousand acres of the Hellman Ranch, most formerly farmed by the evacuated Japanese, would be converted to ammunition storage.

In January 1944, the U.S. Navy announced plans to take over Anaheim Landing and the surrounding area to the north to store ammunition and anti-submarine nets and the buoys that supported them. Over three hundred cottages from both sides of the bay had to be moved or demolished, the channel re-dredged, the port enlarged and two long jetties constructed.

On March 28, six large construction companies began demolition and new construction simultaneously. "Pops" Crawford's airfield was dismantled, as was the Landing's casino and bowling alley. The Airport Administration building was moved to the corner of Eighth and Central, across from the Seal Beach City Hall. After some time, it became the Red Cross.[267]

There were few objections. Hopefully, the Navy would bring jobs and more money to town.

The Glide 'er Inn also relocated a few blocks north (west) to a location on the Coast Highway at Sixteenth Street. It still retained much of the original ambience. Outside, the T-34 flight trainer was placed even higher on the new building's roof. Inside were high-backed booths with dozens of model planes hanging overhead. Aviation memorabilia covered the walls, ceiling fans looked like propellers and the "world's largest hand-carved propeller" decorated the bar. A sign was mounted beside the sit-down counter: "All aviators are requested to sign our pilots' register." And stars like Gene Kelly,

The Net and Ammunition Depot was built in 1944 to house Naval ammunition and the anti-submarine nets and the buoys that supported them. This photo from 1955 depicts the marines who are guarding the pile of buoys that were stacked along PCH for years.

Joan Crawford and Victor Mature—who were on their way to Newport or Laguna (or the nearest local gambling spot)—still dropped in to enjoy some food during the drive.

Overall, 225 homes were ultimately moved. Many were replanted in Seal Beach and other communities, but some of the cottages did not meet post-earthquake building requirements and were abandoned.

Over the next six months, sixty-five buildings were constructed, as were thirty-five miles of paved roads and fifty miles of railroad track to serve the sixty-nine magazines that were strategically isolated to prevent a chance explosion affecting a neighboring magazine. Heavy earthen blankets covered each magazine, and a mile-long earthen barricade bordered the freight car area.

A 1,200-foot-long dock was constructed and two new breakwaters—one 3,526 feet long and the other a 2,300 foot extension of the existing 1,211-foot jetty—now protected the channel's new 600-foot-wide entrance. The jetties were built of rock shipped in from the same Riverside quarry that supplied rocks for the Long Beach breakwaters and jetties. Both the Coast Highway and Pacific Electric Railroad were rerouted north and the old bridges and trestles removed.

The new station was expected to eventually number two thousand sailors, forty-three officers and five hundred civilian employees.[268] Still, not everything on the site was used for new naval purposes. Some reminders of the old days persisted. On March 1, 1945, one thousand acres of barley grown on the station was declared surplus by the Navy and put up for bid.

The end of the war was the biggest but not the only milestone of 1945. The year was also the end of another era as Phil Stanton faded from the scene. His last years were not unproductive. In 1930, he supported the successful gubernatorial campaign of James Rolph Jr. and was appointed to the State Highway Commission. He remained a walnut grower at his west Anaheim ranch, and in February 1941, his Jonathan Club colleagues in Los Angeles honored him as one of its twenty-five longest-serving members.

In mid-1943, Stanton returned to his home in Seal Beach. Quite feeble, he liked to sit in his upstairs bedroom and look out over the ocean.[269] His house was still the biggest in town, apropos of his being the man with biggest ideas, the biggest ambitions. But, perhaps symbolically, it sat alone on the west side, which, like most of the town, had still not developed.

On September 9, 1945, the force behind Seal Beach's founding and its first twenty years passed away at his oceanfront home after an illness of several months.

CHAPTER 10

SEAL BEACH CONFIDENTIAL

WILLIAM ROBERTSON AND THE POKER WARS

By war's end, Seal Beach was a town of almost 3,000. The biggest employers in town were the Weapons Station, which still employed 350 civilians, the Los Angeles Bureau of Power and Lighting (later the DWP), and the Dow Chemical Company's Iodine Division plant. Far more residents were employed in Long Beach, especially at the shipyards and other defense-related plants and in the nearby oil fields.

Thousands of veterans used the GI Bill to get a college education, some at Long Beach State College, which opened its doors in 1949.

On Main Street, John Nescher had taken over Walter Stortz's properties (across from present Hennessey's) and built John's Food King market. Jerry Brockman, a pharmacist from Belmont Shores, opened Brock's Drug Store at the corner of Electric and Main.

Before the summers, some college students applied to be Seal Beach lifeguards. The "department" was at first still under the guidance of Earl Whittington, who had relocated to a lifeguard station at Tenth Street, still working from 9:00 a.m. to sunset. But growth meant the need for more lifeguards, and it wasn't long before seven lifeguard towers dotted the beaches. Lloyd Murray had returned from the Navy, and being a veteran, he was immediately rehired—and just as immediately out of work come Labor Day when the summer season ended. But within a few years, he would run the department. Although some hires were forced on him—friends of the city officials, a Masonic Lodge connection through the mayor, etc.—Murray usually hired guys who fit his ideal of professionalism: strong swimmers,

After the war, new lifeguard chief Lloyd Murray required lifeguards to meet minimum swimming and strength requirements and be able to "back you up when you were dealing with a group of drunk party-ers." *From left to right*: Lloyd Murray, Harry Schurch, Tim McElrath, Paul Chaife, Chuck Hasley and Ron "Chi" Kredell.

reliable and smart. An early hire was Ron Kredell, always called "Chi" because he was from Chicago. Murray liked him because he was a good swimmer and had a reputation as the toughest kid in town—a good person to have on your team when dealing with guys who have been drinking too much wine around the fire ring.

Kredell joined with Murray, Dick Thomas and Jack Haley to form the core of a unit that oozed cool. More and more young men applied for the summer lifeguard positions, including Rich Chew, Tim and Dan Dorsey, Bob Polis, Paul Chaife, Harry Schurch, Tim McElrath, Mike Haley and others.

On Thursday, November 22, 1945, the night before Thanksgiving, Main Street was decorated with colorful bunting to welcome the opening of the new Beach Theatre on Main Street near the Coast Highway. Manager Oscar C. Johnson gushed over the seven-hundred-seat venue with its lush

The seven-hundred-seat Bay Theatre first opened its doors on November 22, 1945 (Thanksgiving night), as the Beach Theatre. Previously, movies in town were shown in the back room of Patterson's store near Central, although there are articles that say a Coast Theater closed in mid-1930.

When the Beach Theatre opened in November 1945, the *Post & Wave* noted, "There is hardly a family in Seal Beach that does not plan to attend the opening movie." The double bill for that opening night was *Out of This World*, starring Eddie Bracken and Veronica Lake, and the comedy-thriller *The Phantom of 42nd Street*.

red carpets and dark red plush seats.[270] The debut double bill featured Eddie Bracken and Veronica Lake in *Out of This World* and *The Phantom of Forty-Second Street* with Dave O'Brian and Kay Aldridge. Admission was fifty cents or thirty-five cents if you were under twelve.[271] On weekends and vacations, kids would line up to see just how far a dollar could take them. Once inside for the double feature (and cartoon), the big decision was popcorn and a soda or pig out on the

GALA OPENING TONITE!

YOUR NEW ULTRA-MODERN

BAY THEATRE SEAL BEACH

FORMERLY THE BEACH THEATRE

FOX WEST COAST THEATRES

Proudly turn over to you—its patrons—this modern-ized and revitalized theatre with its rich new hang-ings and luxurious appointments.

- New RCA Sound Equipment
- New Ventilation System
- Newly Acoustically Treated

- New Projection Equipment
- New Screen
- New from Side-walk to Screen

Box Office Opens Daily 5:45 P. M.
Sat., Sunday & Holidays From 12:45 P. M.

Adults 80c
Jrs. & Servicemen—35c
Children—14c
(Incl. tax)

'Swank' IS THE WORD FOR IT

and here's our opening feature!

John Payne
Maureen O'Hara
"SENTIMENTAL JOURNEY"

Veronica Lake
Sonny Tufts—Pat Phelan
"MISS SUSIE SLAGLE'S"

Changes of Program Every Sun., Tues. and Fri.

The Beach Theatre encountered difficulties, and in June 1946, it was acquired by the huge Fox West Coast Theatres operation, closed for three weeks to undergo some major refurbishments and reopened three weeks later as the Bay Theatre.

almost unlimited choices of nickel candy—Charms, Juicy Fruits, Juju Bes, Fruit Drops and Milk Duds, to name a few.

For whatever reason, the new movie palace encountered problems, and a June 1946 newspaper ad read, "Fox West Coast Theaters Announced the Addition of the Beach Theatre to Their Group."[272] Three weeks later, on July 17, the movie-house reopened, now called the Bay Theatre.[273] The films were *Sentimental Journey* and *Miss Susie Slagles*.[274]

So many local kids flocked to the Saturday matinees that the local Lions Club paid for a new bike rack in front of the theater.[275] After the movies, teens might hit Taxi Burger next door, power down a "suicide" coke at Brock's Drugs or head to the pier, where Seal Beach Burgers sat in front of the old Bayside Land Company Building and was one of the first places to offer "Diced Cream," pre-cut cubes of ice cream ("no slicing, no scooping"). Purists might head down to Dolphin Street to grab a burger at Dave's Place, run by Dave Stangeland.

Three weeks later, Tony Cornero reneged on his 1938 deal with the state and opened a new gambling ship, the *Lux*, which was to open for business off the Seal Beach/Long Beach coast at 5:00 p.m. on August 7, 1946. The day before, Navy veteran Jimmy Slyter, a nineteen-year-old "veteran of 10 Pacific engagements" and one failed attempt to swim from Catalina to Seal Beach, decided that he wanted to swim out and see Tony Cornero's gambling ship. Three friends were supposed to stay with him in a dory, but they apparently lost track of him. A Coast Guard search was launched but no more word is heard of Slyter.[276] Perhaps news about Slyter was pushed aside for the publicity for Cornero's new gambling ship operation. In the first three hours of operation, the *Lux* took aboard 3,600 customers, but within a couple weeks, under state pressure, his ships were out of business again.

Two months later, there was more activity at the Seal Beach pier, where U.S. senator from Idaho Glen Taylor, a former cowboy and singer in a country band, saddled his horse at the west end of the Seal Beach pier and began a horseback ride across country. Taylor's stunt was designed to attract attention to U.S. foreign policy, which Taylor felt was too trusting of the Soviets. While attracting attention, he made good time—after four days, he was already in Phoenix.

When Taylor left town headed for the Santa Ana Canyon, local newspapers—which now also included the *Seal Beach News* from publishers Hammond Hart and John K. Blystone—didn't lack for things to write about, not with the emergence of one of Seal Beach's most colorful (and infamous, to some) characters, William L. Robertson, the town's new gambling czar. Robertson filled the void created by Ballard Barron's departure to Las Vegas in late 1941.

Earlier that year, an old Texas friend of Barron's, R.E. Griffith, who owned a chain of movie theaters, went to Vegas with the idea of opening two theaters. He stayed at the newly opened El Rancho, the first hotel-casino on the strip just outside the city limits. Griffith forgot about the theaters and decided that Vegas needed an even bigger hotel/casino. He and his architect nephew William Moore would build the Last Frontier hotel, and to manage the casino operations, Griffith recruited his old Texas friend Barron, offering him control of the gaming room.

Barron may have also been concerned about events in Southern California. Fletcher Bowron's reform administration in Los Angeles had forced many high-profile gamblers, some of them associates of Barron like gambling ship co-owners Milton "Farmer" Page, "Tutor" Scherer and Marion Hicks, to relocate to Las Vegas. In addition, mobsters Ben Siegel and Mickey Cohen were trying to earn a bigger cut of the Southern California bookmaking action for their East Coast backers (which included Lucky Luciano and Meyer Lansky). People Barron worked with were getting punched, pistol-whipped and shot at.[277] Then in July 1940, a fire destroyed Barron's longtime base of operations, the Seal Hotel and the downstairs Seal Café. He no longer lived there, having moved five years earlier to Naples, where he may have been involved with some Second Street gambling operations.

Whatever the reasons, Barron was in Las Vegas by 1942, and it worked out well for him. For most of the 1940s, the Last Frontier was considered the classiest gambling casino in Las Vegas. Barron also managed the Silver Slipper casino and was a respected figure in town. (His wife, Bea, even led the drive for a new library.)[278]

Barron's departure didn't take all the gambling away from Main Street. At the Garden of Allah, even though the new owner, Long Beach bookmaker Earl Raines, had installed a shuffleboard court in 1948 and switched to a hot jazz lineup, it appears his primary focus was still on his bookmaking activities.[279]

Barron's vacated position as the town's gambling czar was quickly assumed by former Los Angeles Police Department detective lieutenant William L. Robertson. Robertson grew up on a New Mexico ranch and, in the 1920s, migrated to Los Angeles and became a cop. By the mid-1930s, he ran the LAPD's hotel squad, overseeing hotels that rented rooms by the hour as well as swanky hotels with big bars that had liquor issues. He was also known as being a guy who could deliver campaign donations from the liquor and hotel industries.

A 1940 LAPD hearing revealed that from 1936 to 1939, at least $197,500 in unexplained assets entered Robertson's bank account. LAPD records showed that most came from Seal Beach gambling clubs owned or managed by Barron.[280]

After answering some initial queries, Robertson resigned from the department.[281] When asked at the 1950 Senate Hearings Into Organized Crime (the Kefauver hearings) to explain such a large amount of money in his bank account, Robertson credited it to the frugality of he and his wife and good investments.[282] When asked later as to why he resigned, Robertson said he had bad sinuses and the Los Angles smog really irritated him.

By the early 1940s, Robertson was not only enjoying the smog-free air of Seal Beach but also reportedly running at least one "bingo" parlor at the corner of Main and Central and probably more. In 1943, he bought the town's newspaper, the *Post & Wave* and began ingratiating himself with the community—or at least key parts of it.

Robertson's associates included many well-known Los Angeles gambling figures, among them Phil Tapper, Southern California's biggest bookmaker, and Jimmy Utley, who together owned a piece of one of Seal Beach's Main Street parlors for "bridgo," a form of bingo.[283]

An unconfirmed but logical story from Robertson's police days might explain some of his juice. During a raid of a hotel-based brothel, Robertson recognized some out-of-town mobsters. Under "intense questioning," the mobsters revealed they were sent by East Coast interests to execute a hit on a rival Los Angeles crime boss. Robertson warned the intended target of his predicament before he released the out-of-town boys. A few weeks later, after the gangland dispute was resolved, the grateful (and still alive) Los Angeles boss reportedly let Robertson have very favorable access to the race wire he operated.[284] The wire meant profits, which could be used to buy votes and public officials.

Over the next decade, Robertson's methods polarized the community. Some liked him, especially the one hundred or so he employed at his various enterprises, and the players on the teams and groups he sponsored and offered financial support. But if schmoozing didn't work, Robertson was not averse to coarser methods.

After Jessie Reed, the first female mayor of Seal Beach, took on the gambling interests, Robertson's paper, the *Post & Wave*, printed an article implying that Mayor Reed was running a brothel at her Tent City operation. The tact was successful enough that she resigned as mayor after two anti-gambling councilmembers were successfully recalled in 1944, and three, including her, were recalled in 1947.

Walter Hanzlik, a school board member and a chamber of commerce president, said that after opposing "the gambling czar," his local business dropped to zero, eventually forcing him to leave town.

Virginia Haley was treasurer of the Seal Beach PTA when Robertson "came to the school carnival and insisted I take a check for $1000.00 so all of his employees could be members of the PTA." When Haley tried to return the check, Robertson declined, all the while telling Haley and those around her "all the good things he'd done for the people in town." Haley finally dropped the uncashed check off at his office.

A Good Government League was formed in 1947—with many of its members coming from the new merchants who had moved into town after the war. They too were smeared in flyers circulated by Robertson's group, and the 1947 recalls—in which Reed, who had been re-elected in 1946, and Mayor Louis Jaeckel were removed—were as ugly as any before them.

Unfazed, Brockman and other merchants revived the chamber of commerce and led the campaign for a Main Street populated by productive, family-friendly establishments. The group quickly grew, and over fifty members participated in its first Father-Son Night and Thanksgiving Dinner.[285]

With the town's growth, Robertson could see small-time gambling on Main Street was a losing hand, but he had another play. Because it involved skill at discarding, courts ruled that draw poker was not a game of chance. By 1946, Gardena had six legal draw poker casinos that were taking business from Seal Beach. By 1948, Robertson convinced a Seal Beach council majority that the citizens who were tired of gambling on Main Street wouldn't mind a small "draw poker zone" on the State Highway near the Long Beach boundary. Nor would the citizenry object to licenses being limited to "non-profit" organizations at an annual fee of $10,000.

His proposed poker zone was reclaimed land resulting from the straightening of the San Gabriel River and thus owned by the state. Glide 'er Inn co-owner Jimmy Arnerich had already obtained a ten-year lease on this parcel and had begun construction on a $125,000 "restaurant" in some old World War II Quonset huts he had moved into this new zone.

With the council's approval of the poker zone and the awarding of the nonprofit license to Arnerich, Robertson was "brought in" to manage the new poker parlor, which was called the Airport Club, probably an homage to Arnerich's Glide 'er Inn/Seal Beach Airport history.

In October 1948, public outrage over the sweetheart arrangement caused the council to backtrack. But the following April, the initiative was back, slightly reworded and limited to just one nonprofit per three thousand population (the town's population was, coincidentally, just over three thousand). The fee was also increased to $20,000. A public reading of the measure was waived, deemed unnecessary since all the council members knew it. Through political skill and strategic promises, Robertson was able to get the Airport Club opened.

Local residents were again outraged, and in April 1950 elections, anti-gambling candidates received 60 percent of the vote. But that vote was split among seven candidates and allowed the three pro-gambling candidates to sustain their council majority.

Although set up as a nonprofit operation to benefit local charities, the club's partners were definitely profit-motivated. Cornelius Klausnick, a former Los

Angeles bookie, was now in Vegas as one of the Desert Inn's eleven owning partners (although he may have been a front for Mickey Cohen's minor interest). Ray Faust was the slot machine king of Orange County. Subsequent investigation by the state attorney general's office showed that during the period from June 9, 1950, to October 1, 1950, the Airport Club—through sixty tables of draw poker and its two-hundred-seat bingo game—took in revenues of $1,148,000, but only $44,000 was declared as profit and only $900 was given to local charities and social groups, including the Lions Club, churches, Boy Scout groups and the Red Cross.

In May 1951, the city council confirmed draw poker's legality with a new ordinance permitting any games not specifically prohibited by state law[286] and reconfirmed the limiting of all legal gambling in town to the twenty-three-acre location already occupied by the Airport Club. Both the council and Robertson couldn't understand the fuss—gambling was removed from Main Street and the one location was a provable economic boon to the community.

In October 1952, anti-gambling forces forced a referendum on the issue. This push was led by Admiral John McKinney, the former weapons station commander. Local voters were mailed pamphlets that featured testimony from Robertson and others before the Kefauver Committee.

The town turned out in record numbers, and the anti-gambling measure passed by seventy votes. The Airport Club would have to cease actions when its license expired in May 1953. Also voted in was an anti-gambling majority on the council.

Almost immediately, Robertson financed a referendum and recall, and local papers couldn't resist the puns: "Could a pair of democratic elections beat a full house of poker patrons?"[287]

Perhaps coincidentally (or perhaps not), the weekend before the second election, the Airport Club was raided by Orange County authorities, and Robertson, some employees and taxi drivers were arrested for conspiracy to bring citizens to his establishment for the purpose of gambling.

Out on bail the next day, Robertson remained defiant, saying, "My place here pumps about $40,000 a year into the city treasury every year," about $37,000 of it in permits and fees. He also pointed out that his club employed 141 people—almost all from Seal Beach, and most of them women—who collectively took home $10,000 a week "not counting tips."

Robertson said, "I give more to Seal Beach youth and charitable groups than all the clubs in Gardena give to Gardena combined." He also claimed to have the majority on his side, but they'd been "too confident" at the last election.

But on election day, April 14, the gambling opponents once again held the better hand. More residents voted, and the margin was smaller, but by a vote of 843–811, voters confirmed the end of legal gambling in Seal Beach.

Despite some last-minute maneuverings, on May 20, 1953, the Airport Club closed its doors. Robertson did fund two more recalls and referendums, but voters turned both down in September 1953 and April 1955.

The result was probably inevitable. Many pro-gambling residents had moved out of town (fifteen dealers alone followed Ballard Barron to Las Vegas.) These were more than replaced by families whose incomes were not dependent on Robertson's activities. As skillful as Robertson was, ultimately he couldn't control growth.

And after the end of World War II, Seal Beach, like almost all of Southern California, was growing. The war had exposed over a million soldiers to the Southern California climate. An even bigger factor was the growth of defense-related jobs, led by aircraft manufacturing and shipbuilding. By 1943, prime aircraft-related jobs employed 250,000 people in Los Angeles County alone, and one quarter of those people had arrived in the last four years.

With the end of wartime restrictions, many builders went back to the old way, building four or five houses at a time, at most forty a year. But some builders wanted to build entire communities, utilizing lighter materials and assembly-line methods developed during the war.

Across the nation, large projects happened. The most famous was the 17,500 homes of Levittown, New York: eight-hundred-square-foot homes constructed using assembly-line techniques perfected during the building of military housing during the war. In California, Fritz Burns teamed with Henry Kaiser to build Panorama City, a totally planned community of 3,500 homes and schools, parks and commercial areas—all laid out before one house was built.[288]

Onerous inheritance and property taxes led to large tracts being built in the Long Beach area. In 1947, the heirs of Susannah Bixby Bryant sold land to builder Lloyd Whaley, who built his Los Altos tract of homes.

About the same time, the Clark heirs (owners of the Los Alamitos Sugar Company and sugar factory) decided to sell off their large chunk of undeveloped land north of Long Beach to three builders: Louis Boyar, Ben Weingart and Mark Taper, who in 1950 began construction on seventeen thousand homes in what would become Lakewood (most were eight hundred to one thousand square feet on fifty- by- one-hundred-foot lots).

What these developments had in common was open space and proximity to jobs. Seal Beach was surrounded by plenty of open space, most owned by the heirs of I.W. Hellman, who were disinclined to help Seal Beach because of the city's ban on oil drilling.

But the success of Levittown and Lakewood—and even more locally, Los Altos, Lakewood Plaza and Ross Cortese's Lakewood Rancho Estates (both located just west of El Dorado Park in Long Beach)—changed everything, especially by dramatically increasing the assessed property value of nearby undeveloped land. The onerous taxes combined with the potential profits from subdivision motivated the Hellmans to reconsider developing the "Hill."

The Hellmans made a proposal: if voters would approve de-annexing seventy-three acres north of the Coast Highway to remove it from the city's prohibition of oil drilling, the Hellmans would open the land from the Coast Highway to the crest of the Hill for development.

Residents approved this de-annexation in April 1953. Six months later, the Ajax Construction Company of South Gate announced a 1,000-home subdivision to be called Marina Heights (sometimes also called Marina Highlands) on which groundbreaking would begin shortly after the first of the year. The plan included a "modern business section" on PCH running from Bolsa to Eleventh, 950 single-family homes and 50 multiple-unit residences. The three-bedroom homes would start at $11,500, and individual lots would be available at the top of the hill for custom homes.

Unfortunately, that project fell through, but in February 1954, the land was sold to the Lakewood Park Company, the builders of Lakewood. This deal also stalled. But when the city filed a suit against Boyar & Weingart and the Hellmans in May 1954, a settlement was reached: the city would drop the suit in return for a guarantee the homes would be built.

It's possible the Lakewood Park group was overextended. It was negotiating to build a six-thousand-home development in the west San Fernando Valley and also dealing with an investigation into the financing of its Lakewood projects, which had stretched some federal financing regulations more than intended.

While the Hellman land remained vacant, other things were changing. In 1957, the First Baptist Church of Seal Beach became the town's third church when it bought the Garden of Allah and replaced its hot jazz with hymns.

The town still offered entertainment. In 1951, two local girls, Cynthia and Kay Strother, recorded "Bermuda," a song written by sixteen-year-old Cynthia. After performing it on a local TV show, *Peter Potter's Search for a Song*, the sisters were signed by RCA Records. Calling themselves the Bell Sisters (using their mother's maiden name), they toured that year with Bob Hope,

In 1951, Seal Beach sisters Cynthia and Kay Strother performed sixteen-year-old Cynthia's song "Bermuda" on a local TV show and were soon signed by RCA Records as the Bell Sisters (their mother's maiden name). Their recording sold over one million copies, and they toured with Bob Hope, Bing Crosby and Dinah Shore and even played in Las Vegas.

Bing Crosby and Dinah Shore and even played in Las Vegas (coincidentally, at the Last Frontier Hotel), ending their show with "Bermuda," which by now had sold over one million copies. The sisters performed another two years, playing at clubs, military bases, county fairs and scout jamborees. In January 1953, the Seal Beach Chamber of Commerce sponsored a float in the Tournament of Roses parade, and Cynthia rode on it.[289]

Between movies, TV shows, Vegas and even a movie, sixteen-year-old Cynthia attended Huntington Beach High School, and twelve-year-old Kay was still at Seal Beach Elementary. Both were living in a four-bedroom bungalow on Fifth Street with their fourteen-year-old sister, Sharon, and their parents, Edith and Gene Strother. The latter two had been born in Kentucky and moved to Seal Beach in 1947 when Gene, a former Ohio State University and minor league baseball player, took a job as an electrician at the North American Aviation plant in Downey.

Gene put his baseball skills to good use in early 1956 when he and other local dads formed the Seal Beach Kids Baseball Association with three divisions. League president Ed Sukla, Jack Krebs, Charles Tozer and Strother would manage teams in the twelve- to thirteen-year-old bracket. Farris Van Zandt and Whitey Wakefield would run the thirteen- to fourteen-year-old group, and Bob Dalton, Bud Johnson, George Lynch, Harry Rhinehart and

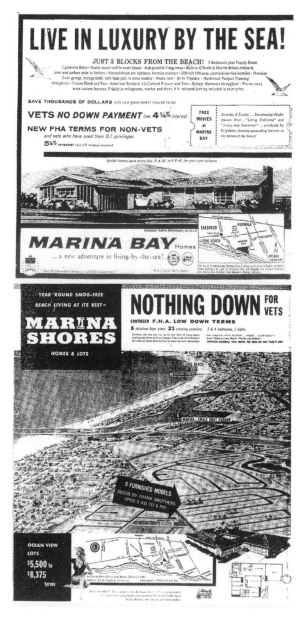

In the 1950s, the "Hill" was opened for the construction of two tracts, both built by companies with Lakewood connections. Marina Bay and Marina Shores both used proximity to the new Alamitos Bay small boat marina as a marketing point.

Blackie August would operate the midget division. The Women's Auxiliary would be led by Mary Johnson and Joyce Lynch.

The league would experience rapid growth because in the following year, 1957, the Lakewood Park group made good on its promise to build homes on the Hill. Lakewood Park was originally formed from two companies—Boyar and Weingart's Aetna Construction and Biltmore Homes, owned by Mark Taper (as in the Los Angeles Music Center's Mark Taper Forum). In 1956, a former Taper employee, Joseph Bolker, formed Brighton-Bilt Homes and optioned the triangle south of Bolsa Avenue to build the 150-home Marina Bay tract (the "Coves").

Bolker would eventually build over seven thousand residences in Southern California, become a major donor to the arts himself and become a U.S. consul general to Senegal. For his Seal Beach architect, he hired Earl Kaltenbach, who had recently designed Disneyland's Tomorrowland and the first phases of Ross Cortese's Rossmoor subdivision.

By mid-1957, Marina Bay had competition from Marina Shores just across Bolsa on the Hill. Mark Taper retained some of the lots (even naming a street after himself), but the primary builder was Butler-Harbour Construction Company, which also had Lakewood Park roots.

The builders targeted boating enthusiasts attracted to the growing Alamitos Bay small-craft marina. The Brighton-Bilt group even held boat shows in front of its Marina Bay model homes, as well as free movies made by the Frigidaire Company, depicting and emphasizing the futuristic "miracles of modern cookery and kitchen convenience."

The marketing must have worked. Within a few years, two smaller tracts, Marina View and Marina Vista, went on the market.[290]

For a while, many assumed the Navy would close the naval weapons station and return Anaheim Bay to public use. Others hoped to develop the shoreline around the Surfside Colony into a small-craft marina within the city limits. Even more ambitious boosters proposed turning the city's entire beach frontage into a small-craft harbor by extending and wrapping around the existing jetties on Anaheim and Alamitos Bay. Initially, the chamber of commerce endorsed this last plan, noting it would also solve the city's beach erosion problem. Others noted the legal argument that a marina would give the city three additional miles of jurisdiction and would force oil island operators to negotiate with the city. But these plans all went nowhere. Too many things were up in the air—the biggest being the future plans of the naval station and the location of future freeways.

Still, the area grew. New families meant more children. And children were always looking for new and different things to do. One new and different thing Seal Beach offered was surfing.

CHAPTER 11

THE SURF AND
THE SPHINX

Surfing in Seal Beach went back to at least 1916, when the Bayside Land Company touted the surfing skills of "young local" Mary Reeves. Original surfboards were made of solid redwood or similar lumber and weighed between 90 and 140 pounds. In the 1920s, hollowed-out surfboards dropped that down to about 40 pounds. These were mainly used by older adolescents or adults, usually working as lifeguards.

The introduction of balsa in the early 1950s and then foam-core boards in the late 1950s made it easier for younger kids to use surfboards. The sport was quickly adopted by teens, recently "liberated" from their parents' culture by television, the advent of rock and roll, transistor radios and their own cars.

Seal Beach bred many world-class surfers in the 1950s, including "local watermen" Lloyd Murray, Jack and Mike Haley, Denny and Sam Buehl, Harry Schurz, Billy Fury, Rich Chew, Pete Kobzev, Dave Privett, Robert Harbour, Harold Walker and Tim McElrath,[291] not to mention three surfers who would implant the sport on the national consciousness. Harry Severson and Steve Pezman would found and edit *Surfer* magazine. Bruce Brown was a self-taught filmmaker whose *Endless Summer*, even after almost fifty years, is still the definitive surf movie, a tour de force that brought the aloha spirit to Wichita, Kansas; New York City; and all places figuratively and spiritually in between.

Locals were joined on the beaches by students from Long Beach State and even by surfers from beach towns to the south. They'd test the breaks at

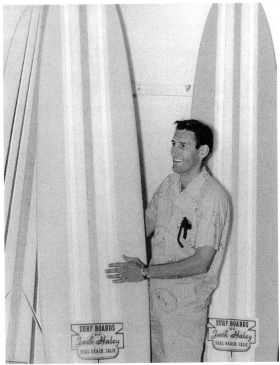

The beachfront home of Pat and Orrall "Blackie" August (shown above) was the center of the developing Seal Beach surf scene. Blackie reportedly learned surfing from Duke Kahanomoku himself, and Pat cooked for virtually whoever showed up at her house, including legendary surfer/lifeguard/restaurant owner Jack Haley (left) who credited Blackie with helping him win the first National Surfing Championship in 1959. Pat and Blackie's son, Robert August, would be one of the stars of the 1966 surf classic, *Endless Summer*.

Crabs off the west jetty, Ray Bay and, most especially, at Thirteenth Street, in front of the home of Pat and Blackie August.

Orral "Blackie" August (he got his name from his involvement with the oil business) was the guru of the local surf scene, reportedly trained by Duke Kahanamoku himself.[292] Blackie passed the traditions and surfing gestalt down to the next generation,[293] especially his son, Robert, who began surfing at the age of six. Boards were always around their home, and sometime after 1956, so was the "Surf Sphinx," a borrowed architectural statue that had been liberated one night from its Long Beach prison by a herd of about a dozen local surfers all no doubt under the influence of "Green Death" (as they labeled their preferred beverage of Carling's Black Ale).

Forty years later, Jack Haley recalled that the sphinx originally sat overlooking the ocean from its perch on the Villa Riviera Hotel. Others said it was ensconced at a tall apartment building in Venice or Santa Monica.

All versions seem to agree that wherever the sphinx was, when the surfers—about ten of them—arrived to liberate it, the guard was sleeping. On hands and knees, they snuck by him to the stairwell and made their way to the roof where, says Haley, the surfers climbed onto the ledge and lifted the heavy structure, carried it down the stairs, past the sleeping guard and into their car.[294]

Blackie and Pat August's son, Robert (a nine year old who would go on to star in the surfing classic *Endless Summer* and become one of the sport's legendary figures) remembers being "woken by a bunch of drunken surfers carrying a sphinx…who thought it would be a good idea to bring it to my parents' house. In true Blackie and Pat fashion, my dad opened up a couple bottles of wine and my mom started cooking up a storm. The party then rounded up a bunch of ladders and they hoisted the cement sphinx up on the roof of the house."[295]

The next day, Lloyd Murray, the lifeguard captain and thus deserving of great respect and powers, came down to help properly consecrate the sphinx in a mock ceremony. "I remember standing out there with a bed sheet over me, praying to the Kahuna," he says. "We poured wine on a surfboard and we were going to light it on fire and get four virgins to take it out [to sea], but we couldn't find four virgins."

The Sphinx's legend grew among the surfing community. Once when some neighbor got upset that the female portion of the sphinx was too prominent, Blackie placed a training bra on its ample charms. Over the years, to maintain it, he'd replaster the sphinx's green skin. This wasn't just any sphinx: this was the "Surf Sphinx," and aspiring wave riders came from all over to pay it proper homage. It made the Thirteenth Street waves at Seal Beach as the place to surf.

It was a different time then. Surfing wasn't yet an industry. Lifeguards weren't so militant, and surfers didn't fight over waves. They slept all night on the beach after partying and shared bonfires and wine to stay warm after surfing in winter. Tim Dorsey, another early surfer and longtime head of the city lifeguards, remembers, "We didn't have Disneyland. We didn't have cars. Our playground was the ocean, and Blackie introduced us to that playground."

Pat August was equally legendary, cooking for virtually whoever showed up at her house and sometimes feeding the lifeguards. Jack Haley remembered sitting in the cold sand before there was a tower at Thirteenth Street. "Pat would come out with a sandwich and give it to you. Or she'd invite you into her home to go to the bathroom. What people they were…Full aloha spirit, just 100 percent."

Corky Carroll, a future national champion, compared Pat to Harriett Nelson. "Being able to deal with two dudes like Blackie and Robert could not have been a walk in the park, but she always seemed happy."[296]

"Not everyone surfed," remembered Libby Appelgate, who moved to Seal Beach in 1953, after graduating from La Canada High School. "The surfers were actually just a small group from Seal and a bunch from the peninsula. But they were a crazy, fun group."

Appelgate invited a friend from La Canada down to visit, and she took her to the burger stand at Main and Coast Highway, across from Lawhead's gas station. She told her friend, "Just wait." Within five or so minutes, the girls spotted a surfer running naked down Main Street in response to the latest dare from his surfing buddies. "I didn't know what, I just knew something crazy would show up," laughed Appelgate. The au naturel sprinter was Chuck Hasley, a lifeguard who was also the son of a local preacherman and apparently hadn't been listening to his father's sermons that closely. "Of course, there weren't many people in town in those days so probably nobody but us saw him," said Appelgate.

The Haleys, the sons of deep-sea diver Francis "Jack" Haley, who had married Virginia John, would win the first national level surfing championships[297]—Jack in 1959 and Mike in 1960. Jack would also become the central figure in many legendary stories and pranks, as well as the captain of the Seal Beach lifeguards and owner of the popular Captain Jack's Seafood House in Sunset Beach.

Harry Schurz later became the first to surf Hawaii's Waimea Bay. Tim Dorsey, who succeeded Lloyd Murray and Jack as chief of lifeguards, was always laughing and loved by all.[298] Among those who idolized these guys were two kids who grew up on Thirteenth Street: Robert August and Rich Harbour.

Robert August surfed "pretty much every free moment I had," which apparently wasn't a lot, because he had good grades, was the president of his class at Huntington Beach High School and was a pole vaulter on the track and field team. In what spare time he did have, he appeared in some of Bruce Brown's surf movies—"small lecture movies that were narrated by a surfer"—which, back then, cost a quarter to see. In mid-1962, he was prepping for college to be a dentist when Brown, a frequent houseguest at Casa August, convinced him to be in a movie in which a pair of surfers chased "the perfect wave." In 1963, *Endless Summer* became the quintessential surf movie, articulating the California pop surf culture that had been partially introduced to the nation by the Beach Boys and the studio manufactured *Gidget* movies only a few years before.

Rich Harbour started shaping surfboards in his garage and became one of the most respected surfboard craftsmen in the world. "Uncle Harbie," says Carroll, "was the one constant factor between the surfboard generations from the early '60s through now."

Other local businesses became known for their surf gear and sponsoring surf teams. Nancy and Walter Katin and seamstress Sato Hughes began sewing durable swim trunks out of canvas sailcloth in their Kanvas by Katin shop in the mid-1950s.

Seal Beach surf had limitations. Because of its sand bottoms, the shape of the waves was not as perfect as the reef breaks elsewhere, but under the right conditions, there were excellent waves. "Best of all," according to Carroll, who grew up in nearby Surfside (now a part of Seal Beach), "it was pretty much left to the locals. It was the perfect surf town."

There were other things to do besides surf, like riding the pier tram along, checking out the newest movie at the Bay Theater or grabbing a hamburger. Nighttime offered another diversion for the older teens: dancing on the "Hill." Libby Appelgate recalled, "When every guy who owned a car, four to be exact, would park in a circle with their lights on and the same radio station blaring with dance music. Where the lights shone was where we danced."

"The local policeman, Benny Garza, would make sure everyone remained in Seal Beach—you'd get arrested if you were caught drinking outside the city. Then at midnight Benny told us it was time to go home."

But those days would not last long. Soon kids who had moved into all the new tract homes in Lakewood, Long Beach and Rossmoor were discovering the joys of the beach. From a quiet town with barely anybody in it, Seal Beach was starting to get quite crowded.

But it hadn't seen anything yet.

CHAPTER 12

EXPANSION AND
GROWING PAINS

The 1960 election signaled Bill Robertson's last attempt to confuse the electorate, split the vote and slip some of "his" candidates back into city hall. But a coalition of voters from the new subdivisions and the Good Government League (working with some Old Towners) drove the final nail into gambling's coffin.

Voters on the Hill now made up half of the city's votes, and many weren't happy with the old way of doing business, especially when the council released one of the Hill's tract builders from an obligation to build a sound wall along the Coast Highway.

In 1960, Hill residents voted in two of their own: Dean Gemmill and thirty-two-year-old Norma Brandel Gibbs. The Chicago-born Gibbs, an assistant professor at Long Beach State, soon became Seal Beach's second female mayor, and she, too, received nationwide attention for her stand against gambling and civic corruption. But the addition of two non–Old Town residents totally changed Seal Beach politics, and they would change even more.

A few miles to the north, Ross Cortese's 3,500-home Rossmoor development was grabbing headlines.

For Rossmoor, Cortese targeted second-time homebuyers—professionals, managers and professors at nearby Long Beach State. His marketing machine extolled the tract's wider streets and larger lots and all-electric kitchens and celebrated the women's club and the Little League in four straight years of full-page ads in the Sunday *Los Angeles Times*.

Rossmoor soon had a population twice that of Seal Beach and three times Los Alamitos and Cypress. Rossmoor also had an active homeowners association, which organized an incorporation attempt in April 1960. Rossmoor's proposed boundaries included two-thirds of present Seal Beach—College Parks West and East, the northern half of Leisure World and most of the Navy weapons station and national wildlife refuge. Fortunately for Seal Beach, in June 1960, Rossmoor residents failed to incorporate by a vote of 1,615 to 1,315.

When the Rossmoor homes sold out on May 7, 1961, Cortese took out one last full-page newspaper ad: "a Thank You to all who made Rossmoor Southern California's nicest new suburb."

He closed the ad by humbly stating that his next project "will be the most revolutionary series of housing developments since World War II." It further promised "a totally new concept in Senior Citizen housing, completely unlike anything yet attempted in the United States" and stated that "the first of these new developments will be in Orange County." He called his project Leisure World.

America's first seniors-only community (in modern terms[299]) was Youngtown, built by Ben Schliefer, an Arizona real estate developer, who in 1954 began a series of small cottages about thirty miles northwest of Phoenix as an alternative to nursing homes. He banned kids for the same reason nursing homes do—they were too noisy.[300]

Word of Youngtown soon got out: seniors didn't have to move into nursing homes or in with their kids—retirement could be fun. By late 1959, Youngtown was home to over six thousand seniors.

Its success caught the attention of Cortese and another builder, Del E. Webb, who both recognized the potential of this over fifty-five market. In 1900, those sixty-five and older comprised 4 percent of the population. By 1950, it was 8 percent and would grow to 11 percent by 1980.

Webb was already a well-known builder of casinos, hotels, motels and military bases, as well as a co-owner of the New York Yankees and the Sahara Hotel & Casino in Las Vegas. Later, his company built Madison Square Garden and the Houston Space Complex.

Webb optioned land near Youngtown and developed his first Sun City unit on a relatively small scale. He spent only $2 million dollars on it. Using a strong marketing campaign—his company coined the term "Golden Years"—he built slightly larger but still modest tract homes with golf courses, a small shopping area, a rec center with bowling alleys and shuffleboard and swimming pools. On New Year's Day 1960, over 100,000 people showed up to Sun City's grand opening. It was ten times more than expected, and the two-mile-long traffic jam earned national headlines. Perhaps motivated by this, Cortese dropped all his conventional housing projects to focus on the senior market.[301]

He had already selected a site just south of Rossmoor on 541 undeveloped acres on the Hellman Ranch that had also been prone to flooding every few years until the San Gabriel and Coyote Creek had been channeled with concrete after the 1952 floods. The property had been available for a while, but existing laws required subdividers to set aside approved school sites. At least three would be necessary on a parcel this size. But the property was in the Los Al Naval Air Base's take-off zone, and it was illegal to build a school in such places.

However, Cortese's proposal for a seniors-only tract with no school-age children—in fact, no residents under the age of fifty-two—made that point moot.

On April 10, 1961, Cortese contracted to pay the Hellman heirs $6,225,000 for the 541 acres. Two days later, Seal Beach and Cortese announced an agreement for the city to annex his parcel and the balance of the Hellman land, which included three thousand acres of the adjacent navy station. Cortese's new project would be a $150 million dollar community for seniors, which would include three golf courses, an amphitheater that could seat 2,500, a shopping center and a fully staffed medical center.[302]

As a result of the Congressional hearings into the use of FHA loans for Lakewood, Cortese had to deal with a far stricter set of government regulations that required a builder to separate the building processes. While Cortese's Rossmoor Corporation could be the provider and developer of the land, it could have no part in the building, sales or management of same.

The building part was easy. That would be done by Murry Ward's Frematic Corporation. The Missouri-born Ward, an infantryman under George Patton in World War II, had become a subdivision chief at the Lakewood development and then struck out for himself. In 1952, Cortese convinced Ward to join him for the Lakewood Ranchos, and as the head of Frematic Construction, Ward oversaw construction of almost every Cortese project over the next thirty years.

The sales part would be handled by another longtime associate, William Brangham, whose advertising firm created the marketing for Cortese's Lakewood Rancho and Anaheim subdivisions and the "walled city of Rossmoor" campaign.[303] To meet Cortese's FHA requirements for Leisure World, Brangham created his own new company, New Horizons.[304]

To manage Leisure World, Cortese formed two separate not-for-profit corporations. The Leisure World Foundation would sponsor, merchandise, administer and manage the Rossmoor Leisure Worlds. The Golden Rain Foundation (named after one of Cortese's favorite flowers) would be owner and/or trustee for assets and common facilities of the Leisure World Mutuals. It would also provide communitywide services such as recreation and security.

By May, construction crews had staked out lots, paved the streets, run sewer lines and poured the concrete pads and foundations for the new units.

By July, new salesmen were hired and then underwent a six-week training program involving three to four nights a week of classroom study and sessions with a psychologist who covered "the most advanced psychological and motivating techniques" that would help the salesman tap into the "buyer's deepest emotions" and make the sales pitch resonate with the prospect.

At industry roundtables, Brangham described the goal of such training: "We never sell the product, we sell the picture—the way of life. Whatever distinctly emotional or romantic trappings can be put into the project, that is the thing to merchandise, not the square footage."

An early sales brochure describes Leisure World as "the country club city for happy people 52 years of age and older." A cooperative apartment sold for $9,000 to $11,000 with down payments ranging from $680 to $769. The monthly payments of $92.50 to $103.50 covered all services, as well as principal, taxes, insurance and medical insurance.[305] Prospective buyers were informed that Seal Beach Leisure World would free them from landscape maintenance. Amenities included all-electric appliances, extra-wide halls, sit-down showers, individually temperature controlled rooms, electric sockets twenty-four inches above the baseboards (much easier to reach than the standard twelve inches) and private patios and gardens. The community would have three clubhouses (a fourth was added in 1974 and a fifth in 1997), an amphitheater, a nine-hole golf course, its own bus transportation system, a nearby shopping center, rolled curbs, extra-wide sidewalks and a security force.

The first parcel of land to be developed—the 844 units of Mutual Number One—was officially opened for showing in late October 1961, although 500 sales had already been "made" for at least a week before at private appointments.[306] A reported 25,000 people (again subject to real estate developers' propensity for inflation) showed up at the official opening.

The first thing anyone saw at the front gate was the four-story-high, thirty-feet-in-diameter globe of the world. Cortese called it a "unisphere—symbolizing the universal significance of the $150 million

541-acre development." The structure weighed over fourteen tons and revolved in a pool of water fifty feet in diameter. Sixty submerged floodlights bathed the globe in a spill of continuously changing colors.[307]

As with Rossmoor, buyers were given a free newspaper, the *Leisure World News*, whose articles detailed the community's virtues, including the medical care plan that was included in the monthly fees. Subsequent issues included short biographies of buyers, demonstrating the qualities of the new residents. Mutual Number One sold out in nine weeks, raising nearly $8.5 million in sales—a feat deserving of yet another full-page ad in local newspapers.

The first residents moved in on June 8, 1962, with Brangham's organization scheduling new occupation at eighteen units a day.

Leisure World's first year numbers more than doubled Sun City's equivalent sales figures—1,472 houses and 262 apartments. By November 1962, the development had over 3,000 residents, and the Leisure World Medical Clinic and the amphitheater (reportedly patterned after the Hollywood Bowl) had opened. By March 1963, over 8,500 residents were living in 4,418 units.

Rossmoor Leisure World would eventually have 6,750 cooperative apartments in fifteen mutual, plus churches, recreational facilities, shopping and transportation needs and an amphitheater modeled after the Hollywood Bowl, all topped off with an 18,000-square-foot medical center housing ten doctors. It was a complete senior citizen center. No detail was overlooked regarding customization for its elderly inhabitants—ramps, safety lights, electric outlets and even a medical care package were all provided.

Most important for Seal Beach was the quality of people and the collective experience the new development brought to Seal Beach.

"It was a great bonus," said former city manager Dennis Courtemarche. "Think of the quality of people who were becoming part of your town. People with business experience, government experience, educators. Smart, well-educated people. It was a real benefit for Seal Beach."

Even before the first potential homeowner viewed a Leisure World unit, Cortese knew he was onto something. Within a year, he was developing three more Leisure Worlds in Laguna Hills, near San Francisco and one in Santa Barbara.

While the last never happened, expansion continued. In 1964, Cortese was also developing Rossmoor Leisure Worlds in New Jersey, Maryland and near Chicago. Cortese told reporters he had over half a dozen projects underway, as well as options on land in foreign countries to take the Leisure World concept there.[308]

Leisure World wasn't the only new construction in Seal Beach in the early 1960s. There were also freeways. Construction finally began on the 605 Freeway as it headed south from the Santa Ana Freeway in Downey. A 1966 map prepared by the city of Seal Beach shows that the city expected the 605 Freeway to continue south past the San Diego Freeway (the 405), keeping west of Leisure World until a little south of Westminster. It would connect with the proposed Pacific Coast Freeway that would skirt the top of the wetlands as it paralleled the coastline through Long Beach, Seal Beach and Huntington Beach and eventually through Newport Beach and down to San Juan Capistrano. But while backed by business groups, the freeway was opposed by enough residents in the coastal cities that it never became a reality.

This master planned network accounted for everything but human nature. Once people discovered the benefits of life along the coast, they didn't want more freeways bringing more people and more traffic.

Two freeways that were constructed were the San Diego and Garden Grove freeways, each sporting an amazing three lanes in each direction.[309] Many of the cars that traveled it each day were carrying workers to the many aerospace firms in the area.

Many engineers at Douglas (later McDonnell-Douglas) in Long Beach, as well as Grumman (with plants in Pico Rivera and El Segundo), Rockwell, North American, Hughes, General Electric and TRW made their homes in Seal Beach, Los Alamitos and Rossmoor.

But soon Orange County was hosting its own defense/aerospace sites, thirteen of them by 1964, each employing at least five hundred workers. John F. Kennedy's May 1961 commitment to have a man on the moon by the end of the decade provided another boost to the industry. On September 11, 1961, North American Aviation was awarded a contract to build the second stage of the Saturn rocket that would send a man to the moon.[310] The company was already making the powerful F-2 rockets that would be used in the second stage, but North American's plant in Downey wasn't big enough to accommodate the size necessary to meet NASA's increasingly more demanding requirements.

In January 1962, North American announced it would construct a $5 million plant on thirty-nine acres of Navy land in Seal Beach. No actual firing of the Saturn's behemoth engines would be conducted there—that would happen in Canoga Park. The Seal Beach site would be used only to assemble the final eight-story-tall structure.[311]

After breaking ground in August 1962, the facility was on line by March 1963. North American workers would assemble twenty-five second stages of the

Saturn rocket that would help propel American astronauts to the moon. Some of those astronauts had been jet pilots at Los Alamitos only a few years earlier.[312]

After assembly, the eight-story, eighty-three-thousand-pound stage had to be trucked a mile and a half down a widened Bay Boulevard to the Navy's Anaheim Landing dock, where it could be loaded aboard a specially-converted barge for the seventeen-day trip to New Orleans and NASA's Mississippi Test Facility.[313]

To accommodate the missile's thirty-three-foot diameter, Bay Boulevard's southbound lanes were widened to forty feet in width, and the traffic light poles were constructed so they could be swung back to provide clearance as the Saturn moved down the road at a non–space age five miles per hour.[314]

All that work paid off on July 17, 1969, when Apollo 11 was launched. The S-II's five engines ignited forty miles up and lifted the spacecraft to earth orbital altitude one hundred miles up. Four days later, Neil Armstrong and Buzz Aldrin became the first humans to set foot on the moon.

The Seal Beach facility wasn't the only one to play a part in the moon launch. Two miles away, McDonnell-Douglas's Huntington Beach division, which employed many Seal Beach residents, participated in the development and construction of the rocket's third stage.

But as the two aerospace companies gained attention, so did the Naval Weapons Station located between them. Rather than be decommissioned and returned to public use, the base's mission had grown. It's command now included the Naval Weapons Depot at Fallbrook (on the back side of Camp Pendleton) and others would later be added (including the detachment at Norco, which hosted the Surface Warfare Testing center). More noticeably, the base provided ordnance for the increasingly unpopular war in Vietnam, loading ships at its dock or increasingly often via helicopters to ships moored off the coast. Many suspected the site also stored nuclear weapons, an assertion the Navy has neither confirmed nor denied to this day.[315]

But even as protests intensified over the next decades, locals seemed more concerned that the defense and aerospace sites provided much-needed jobs. In 1966, the weapons station employed over 900 persons with a payroll of over $7 million and a budget of $11 million, which was slated to grow to $14 million as the war escalated. Labor statistics showed that 42,700 workers in Orange County—1 in 6—were employed by companies performing work for aerospace.[316] At its peak, the North American plant in Seal Beach employed almost 1,200 workers and expanded, beginning in late 1965, to an additional 124-acre campus across Bay Boulevard.

All these workers needed homes, and more were being made available around Seal Beach. Many moved into homes on the new marina development of Huntington Harbor on Anaheim Bay, just east of the Weapons Station and Surfside. Those seeking less expensive housing looked north.

Under the leadership of Preston Hotchkis,[317] the Bixby Ranch Company looked to develop the rest of its two-mile wide strip of property that ran from the California State University–Long Beach campus (most of which it had donated to the state) east to Stanton.

Part of that strip was already under option to Ross Cortese's Rossmoor projects. But for the rest, Bixby Ranch cast its lot with Nathan Shapell and his S&S Homes.

Shapell was a Polish Holocaust survivor who came to Southern California in the early 1950s. Despite not speaking English, he soon learned the language and the homebuilding industry and eventually constructed almost eighty thousand homes from San Diego to San Francisco.

In 1955, Shapell joined his brother and brother-in law to form S&S Homes. Their first projects were typical one-thousand-square-foot homes marketed to veterans in Norwalk and Downey. In the late 1950s, S&S contracted with the Bixby Ranch Company to build College Estates northeast of Seventh and Studebaker.[318] It would be the first of many deals with the Bixbys, which included Bixby Knolls, Bixby Village and Bixby Riviera. Working with the Rancho Los Cerritos branch of the Bixbys, S&S also built El Dorado Park Estates and College Park North in Long Beach and Los Alamitos. The company also built two parcels in Seal Beach—College Park West and College Park East.

The latter's roots began in 1963, when the Bixby Ranch Company optioned most of its land east of Los Alamitos Boulevard to S&S for its Garden Park Estates project. The first homes were built in Garden Grove west of Knott and just north of Garden Grove Boulevard. Slowly, the company began working its way west.

It was the College Park parcels that first got the attention of the Seal Beach city staff, which, since 1961, was under the watchful eye of the town's first city manager, John Williams.

City managers are in the business of providing quality services to residents at the best possible price. Retail and property taxes help achieve this. Those big and available parcels of land north of town could translate into a slew of potential sales taxes and property taxes.

This land was owned by the Bixby Ranch Company. In 1960, the potential city of Rossmoor had been given first claim to this parcel, but voters turned down incorporation—twice. For historical reasons, Los Alamitos leaders viewed the property as their's to annex, once the Bixbys and their partners, presumably S&S Homes, finally started improvements to the land. But Los Alamitos city leaders were reluctant to do anything at this point. Annexation would make them financially responsible for putting in water and sewer lines, and it also might alienate Rossmoor, which they still saw as an inevitable partner.

Williams leaped at the opportunity and made it clear to the owners and developers that Seal Beach would offer favorable terms regarding zonings and utilities.

Seal Beach's display of interest came at a perfect time for the Bixbys and S&S. They were nearing the end of their available property within Garden Grove, and the annexation made continuing west on to the next parcel little more than a formality.

In August 1964, Seal Beach filed an annexation petition for a nine-hundred-acre "F-shaped parcel of land" that included College Park West (then being built) as well as the still-to-be built College Park East, the Old Ranch Golf Course and the Bixby Office Center—everything north of the present city boundary and south of Los Alamitos and "the Rossmoor subdivision." This annexation did not include the fifty-acre Rossmoor Business Center.

Los Alamitos leaders protested, citing the historical argument and more compelling ones: the area was already part of the Los Alamitos School District, as well as the Los Alamitos Water District and sewer district and that the new freeway was a natural boundary. But the annexation was approved and took place on December 31, 1964, clearing the way for 1,890 single family homes, 240 multiple units, commercial zoning and a golf course."[319]

Formal groundbreaking for the College Park East project construction took place in mid-November 1965, but interested potential buyers could already view the College Park East models at the Garden Park Estates model homes off Valley View, south of Lampson. Same builder, same models, same floor plans—at first.

The tract's first phase, the northeast quarter off Lampson, resembled the Garden Grove models, with all homes fronted by parkways. But as this phase ended (on Elder Avenue in some cases, Fir and Guava in others), S&S began building streets and homes without parkways. The housing industry was suffering the worst credit crunch since World War II. Borrowing money for construction cost more, and prices had to be cut to attract buyers. Eliminating the parkways and adjusting streets allowed

In 1962, North American Aviation was contracted by NASA to construct the second stage of the Saturn rocket that would help propel American astronauts to the moon. After assembly, the eight-story, eighty-three-thousand-pound stage had to be trucked a mile and a half down a widened Bay Boulevard to the navy's Anaheim Landing.

Opposite: High school students view North American's massive Saturn II Stage 2 booster before it is to be shipped from Anaheim Landing to a NASA testing facility in Mississippi.

Shapell's group to fit an additional twenty homes into the tract, a financial benefit that offset the higher cost of credit. To make this more acceptable, they changed to seven upgraded models and promised a community pool to be built at what is now Almond Park. (Although promised, the pool was never built.)

The first residents in College Park East were Tommy and Keiko Sugihara, who moved in June 15, 1966. The neighborhood was lonely and isolated at first—the next homeowners didn't move in until July 1, and the Lampson Avenue connection to Los Alamitos Boulevard (now Seal Beach Boulevard) wasn't open. The only way in and out of the tract was via Valley View Street.

While Old Town was no longer the center of political power, it was the center of a growing nightlife. Even though the Garden of Allah shut down, Dixieland lived for awhile at Rouge et Noir (originally on Main near Ocean and then later at 143 Main), opened by the Nikas Brothers, George and Teddy, among the sharpest club owners in Orange County.[320] By 1959 the folk scene was picking up and Ted converted Rouge et Noir to a "hip/beat" club featuring an eclectic mix of three-song acts doing folk and folk-rock, mixed in with comics and poets who hoped to bring their

175

Model 21 · Split Level

Three Bedrooms ▪ Three Baths ▪ Family Room ▪ Separate Dining Room

Split-level Plan Adds Another Dimension of Elegance to This Exciting Home

Three levels of interior beauty provide spacious surroundings for the better family life. The living room-dining room area is perfect for more formal functions, while a giant family room and nook serve the day-to-day family activities. The upper level houses two generous bedrooms and a bath, plus the master's suite and private bath, all laid out in the grand manner.

CUSTOM QUALITY FEATURES: Lath & Plaster Construction ▪ 5' Block Wall enclosed Rear Yard ▪ Concrete Driveways ▪ Red Cedar Shingle Roof (Shake Roof Optional) ▪ Entire Yard Seeded ▪ Parkway Tree ▪ Decorator Hardware ▪ Custom Light Fixtures ▪ Fireplace with Log Lighter ▪ Built-in TV Outlets ▪ Cabinets over Washer-Dryer Space ▪ Genuine Ceramic Tile ▪ Cultured Marble Pullman Tops ▪ Tempered Safety Glass in Sliding Glass Doors ▪ 100% Continuous Filament Nylon Carpeting Throughout ▪ Built-in Oven & Range ▪ Built-in Disposer ▪ Dish-Quik Dish Rinser ▪ Built-in Dishwasher ▪ All Utilities Underground

College Park East opened in 1967 as a continuation of S&S Homes' Garden Park tract in Garden Grove. When the economy went bad, the builders stopped building parkways and cut back on a promised park to squeeze more houses and more revenue out of the development.

inspiration forward. The club gave early breaks to newcomers Steve Martin and Jackson Browne, who played there with the nascent Nitty Gritty Dirt Band. Other performers who played there were Jennifer Warnes, Hoyt Axton and Jose Feliciano.[321]

By the mid-1960s Rouge had been revamped to Cosmos, still serving no liquor but now bringing in "headline" acts, usually under an exclusive contract to the Nikas Brothers.

At the other end of Main Street, manager Kenneth Cobb was establishing an equally eclectic reputation at the Bay Theatre, which, in addition to regular cinema fare, would twice a month feature three-night sets of acclaimed foreign films. It was a labor of love for Cobb, who held down a regular day job before coming to the Bay and personally welcoming patrons. His foreign films drew regular attendees from as far away as Laguna and Santa Monica, and over four thousand film lovers were on his mailing list.[322]

Meanwhile, at Dovalis 101, Greek music (inspired by the success of the film *Zorba the Greek*) was the thought of the day.

Seal Beach was also home to a soulful rock joint called the Bayou, which—when it wasn't hosting wet t-shirt contests—featured performers like the Righteous Brothers, whose later recording of "You've Lost That Lovin' Feeling" became an all-time music classic.

Even though gambling wasn't allowed, there was still life left in the old Airport Club. Owner Bill Robertson—in association with his son Bob—turned the Quonset huts into a quasi-rock and roll legend: the Marina Palace.

Beginning in 1964 (and running through 1970), the Marina Palace played host to a bunch of notable rock acts, including Jimmy Reed, the Strawberry Alarm Clock, the Seeds and Alice Cooper, plus reportedly the Byrds. (Some claim the Doors also played there, but Doors historians have done a thorough job refuting this claim.)[323]

Although the Robertsons marketed the club as a haven for the city's youth, Seal Beach's adults remembered it more for its police record. From '64 through '70, there had been ninety-seven arrests at the club, sixty-one of them juveniles, for offenses ranging from lewd conduct to illegal possession of alcohol and drugs.

Local youth, however, remember its purple Quonset huts with the rotating stage. As one band finished their last song, the stage would begin to rotate, and the next band would come around already playing their first song. The music literally never stopped, and some swear you were guaranteed to hear "Smoke on the Water" at least three times a night.

Other arts were finding a home on the revived Main Street, where the new Seal Beach Artists League, organized by Pat Jones, obtained the use of the old Bayside Land Company building at Main and Ocean for exhibits that drew big crowds and enticed big-name artists to come and teach. The league was one of the most active businesses on Main Street throughout the 1960s, and it played a huge role in making people think of something besides gambling when they did think about Seal Beach.

Another growing tradition was the "Finnegan's Wake" celebration on St. Patrick's Day.[324] This began with drinks at a Belmont Pier bar, after which poor Finnegan, a dummy dressed like a leprechaun, was placed in a mock coffin and carried to Seal Beach. The procession, growing larger with each block (or bar), proceeded down Second Street through Belmont Shore and Naples and then down PCH to Seal Beach and Main Street's many Irish bars. Originally, the Elks used the event to collect green for their handicapped children's fund, but over the years, the fun grew into rowdiness and lots of police overtime.[325]

Also getting a little out of hand were activities on the beach. With a growing popularity thanks to music and movies, surfing became an industry that put an end to much of the aloha spirit as testosterone-laden young surfers fought over spots. The writing was on the wall when Surfside asked to ban surfing in 1966. Seal Beach would soon be limiting surfing hours as well.

Dealing with the city's problems now fell on the shoulders of Lee Risner, who took over as city manager on February 1, 1966. In addition to the beach battles, Risner dealt with developing a plan to annex Surfside,[326] replenishment of sand berms at the beach, the growing St. Patrick's Day craziness, shutting down an independent movie production whose unpermitted motorcycle activity was driving away business,[327] a sewage spill into the San Gabriel River and beach waters, rowdiness at the Marina Palace and topless bars.[328]

In between this he found time to attend ceremonies for some key road openings.

On June 30, 1966, fifteen local beauty queens helped open the new 10.6-mile section of the San Gabriel Freeway between the Santa Ana (I-5) and San Diego (I-405) freeways. And soon after, on July 21, the 2-mile stretch of Lampson Avenue was opened between Valley View and Los Alamitos Boulevard. S&S Construction bore half of the $265,000 construction costs. The city and county shared the rest.

On November 15, 1966, a small article appeared in the *Press-Telegram* about another annexation. The headline read "Rossmoor Center: Annexation filed."

By now, Ross Cortese was no longer involved with Rossmoor. His Seal Beach and Laguna Hills retirement communities were successful, but the others had problems. The New Jersey unit had issues with labor unions with ties to New York City's Gambino crime family. But the biggest challenge was the national credit crunch. The same one that made Nathan Shapell cut out parkways in his College Park East project also strained Cortese's finances. Cortese needed cash.[329] He stopped the Chicago project and sold the land and other assets of his partially completed Walnut Creek site and other land under his control, including the Rossmoor Business Center.

The northernmost parcel was sold to a developer who built the Rossmoor Townhomes. The rest was sold to the Los Coyotes Land Company, which included Cortese's former partner, Judge Alfred Gittelson, but the principal partner now was Zygmaunt (Zig) Taube.

Forty-three acres of the shopping center were already developed. Fifteen acres fronting Montecito Road sat unimproved, and the new owners wanted to remedy that with condominiums and apartments. A vocal number of Rossmoor residents opposed this.

Making things more complicated, two months before, Rossmoor and Los Alamitos had gone to the polls on yet another annexation/merger. This one was very carefully orchestrated and Los Alamitos leaders felt it had made a number of "sweetheart" concessions, but Rossmoor residents still rejected the measure by a 2–1 margin. Whether there was bitterness against Rossmoor is unknown, but it was certainly an understandable possibility.

After the vote, Los Alamitos city leaders say they were approached by Rossmoor Center owners who were willing to be annexed if Los Alamitos would forward fund sewer and water lines for projects on the undeveloped lands.[330] Los Alamitos Race Track owner Frank Vessels had made a similar request in 1954. Just as they had back then, the Los Alamitos leaders declined the request, believing it was wrong to do something they weren't doing for others.

On November 14, 1966, Seal Beach filed its annexation request with Orange County's Local Agency Formation Commission (LAFCO), the state-chartered agency that dealt with local government formations and annexations. Papers reported that that Seal Beach would gain about $60,000 in sales tax and another $20,000 in property taxes annually.

Risner downplayed the request, as he had many other items to deal with. Rossmoor residents didn't care about those other items. Going back to April 1961, they had been eating at the Kress lunch counter, buying the latest fashions at the Boston Store, throwing gutter balls at the Rossmoor Bowl, borrowing books at the Los Alamitos-Rossmoor Library, having cocktails and dancing at the Rossmoor Inn, shopping at the Food King or Rossmoor Pastries and watching movies at the Fox (at least since July 1964). They were very attached to their center. It was the Rossmoor Center, for cryin' out loud! It belonged in Rossmoor.

On November 30, the homeowners association held a meeting at the Rossmoor School auditorium, and residents voiced their outrage.[331] One compared the annexation to "cutting out Rossmoor's heart." Others cheered when a woman called for a "token boycott" against the shopping center.

But just how many Rossmoor residents actually objected to the annexation is impossible to say. Only 150 residents showed up at the protest meeting—out of 3,500 Rossmoor households.

The Los Alamitos City Council filed a formal objection, and some Rossmoor residents carried the battle forward to a contentious two-hour LAFCO hearing. But ultimately, LAFCO's three-member "city" majority of mayors from Garden Grove, Anaheim and Laguna Beach approved the annexation.

At the March 6, 1967 Seal Beach City Council meeting, the Rossmoor Center officially became part of Seal Beach. Not a word of opposition came from the audience of seven persons.

In reality, the annexation made little difference for Rossmoor. Although shopping center tax revenues now went to Seal Beach, they still paid for the same roads, stoplights and police coverage in the area (in the latter case, it probably meant one additional officer closer to Rossmoor during a high-priority call.). But other big expenses of fire, library and especially schools (almost 80 percent of property tax) were unaffected.

Yes, some of the tax revenue money was now diverted to help out Old Town and other areas, but it had been diverted to help out other areas of the county before that.

Most significantly, the annexation finalized a process that ended Seal Beach's isolation. On its west, the development of the marina made the transition from Long Beach to Seal Beach almost seamless. With the Leisure World and North American developments, the Hellman Ranch was no longer the impermeable barrier it had been.

With its new borders, Seal Beach now reached up to the center of Rossmoor and into Los Alamitos. One could stand at the corner of Bradbury and Los Alamitos Boulevard and literally be in all three jurisdictions.

They were still three separate governments—with unique identities—but in many ways, Seal Beach, Los Alamitos and Rossmoor had become one community.

The story of that greater community is for a later time.

ILLUSTRATIONS

U nless otherwise acknowledged, all photographs were provided by the Orange County archives. Many are from the Tom Tully Postcard Collection. Most of the 1915–21 images of the Joy Zone, Main Street and Anaheim Landing were photographed by noted Orange County photographer Edward Cochems. Many institutions now have these photos—the copyright has expired and they are in the public domain—but the Cochems family donated his original negatives to the University of California–Irvine. If images were advertisements or publicity photos that ran in many newspapers, I did not give credit.

Pages 19, 70–71: California Historical Society
Page 21: Anaheim Public Library
Pages 25, 26: Los Angeles Public Library
Page 33: Metro Transportation Library and Archive
Page 36: Rancho Los Alamitos
Pages 40–41, 59, 62, 63, 82: Orange County Public Library, Seal Beach Branch
Pages 43, 61, 89, 102: Long Beach Public Library
Pages 44, 118, 119: Don Watts
Page 76 (top): First American Financial Corporation, Orange County Archives
Pages 80, 81: Long Beach Airport Archives
Pages 84–85: Library of Congress
Pages 89, 125, 143: U.S. Navy
Page 92: Stan Berry, www.sbfoundersday.wordpress.com

Pages 101, 102, 120, 134: Michael Dobkins

Pages 103, 148, 149: *Long Beach Press-Telegram*

Pages 109, 111: Ernest Marquez Collection

Page 115: *Popular Aviation Magazine*

Pages 131, 147: Libby Appelgate

Page 157: Bell Sisters website

Page 161 (top): Robert August blog

Page 161 (bottom): Virginia Haley, Libby Appelgate

Pages 174, 175: Boeing Company Archives, U.S. Navy

NOTES

CHAPTER 1

1. U.S. Coast and Geodetic Survey Map, 1949.
2. Gumprecht, *Los Angeles River.*
3. Some "experts" say Hokan is a hypothetical linguistic family. The controversy deserves its own book and examination, but I'll let someone else write that.
4. The floodwaters of Alamitos Bay and the San Gabriel River were cut off from the Seal Beach area when the last four thousand feet of the San Gabriel River was straightened and encased in rock in 1931.
5. Besides Los Alamitos, Stearns's properties included Ranchos La Laguna, Los Coyotes, La Habra, parts of Las Bolsas, 6,800 acres of La Bolsa Chica, fractional interests in the Rancho Temescal (near Corona) and Ranchos San Juan Cajon de Santa Ana, Santiago de Santa Ana and La Jurupa.
6. William M. Kramer, "The Stingiest Man in San Francisco," *Western States Jewish Historical Quarterly* 5, no. 4 (July 1973); *New York Times*, Michael Reis obituary, August 12, 1878. Michael Reis (Reese) (1816–1878) was legendary for being San Francisco's wealthiest—and stingiest—man. Born in Bavaria, Germany, he came to America in the late 1830s and "displayed a genius for money-making" and a reputation for frugality. His office was an eight-foot by twelve-foot room in a building he owned. He ate day-old donuts. He made his bride-to-be pay for their wedding license (and, after then deciding not to marry, was successfully sued for breach of promise). The biggest legend is that when he returned to Bavaria and visited the cemetery where his parents were buried, he died while climbing the

cemetery fence rather than pay a tollgate. Eyewitness accounts refute this, but such was Reese's legend that it was accepted as truth.

7. The skulls of dead cattle from the drought were found around what is now northern Seal Beach, Los Alamitos and beyond even into the early 1900s.

8. The Alvarado Sugar Factory near present-day Fremont, California, was the nation's first successful beet sugar factory.

9. Lewellyn's first wife, Sarah, was also a Hathaway sister.

10. The Farmers & Merchants Bank of Los Angeles, founded in 1871, was the leading bank of Los Angeles through the early 1930s. In the 1950s, it merged with the Security First National Bank, which became Security Pacific and was eventually bought by Bank of America. This is not to be confused with the Farmers & Merchants Bank of Long Beach, which was started by C.J. Walker in 1907.

11. Of the $125,000 purchase price, $80,000 was mortgage.

CHAPTER 2

12. A San Francisco newspaper, the *Daily Alta California*, of August 4, 1866, lists Anaheim Landing as a regular stop for two newer steamers.

13. Lucille E. Dickson, "The Founding and Early History of Anaheim, California," *Annual Publication of the Historical Society of Southern California* 11, no. 2 (1919): 26–37.

14. By measuring this "mile and a half" from the known Anaheim Landing, the most logical place for the first Anaheim Landing would be near present Island Village.

15. *Los Angeles Herald*, January 7, 1874; January 8, 1874.

16. Henryk Sienkewicz, *Life and Death and Other Legends and Stories* (Boston: Little, Brown and Company, 1904), 42–46.

17. *Los Angeles Times*, "Anaheim Landing: A Seaside Resort Where Joy Is Unconfined," July 29, 1883.

18. Interview with Ora Groom, "Pioneer Tales," Orange County Historical Research Project, 1936.

19. *Los Angeles Herald*, August 17, 1879.

20. *Los Angeles Times*, "Soldiering By the Sea: The Grand Army Encampment at Anaheim Landing," August 15, 1888. The layout of the camp is discussed in detail. The August 16, 1888 *Los Angeles Times* states that the campground reached the outlet of the San Gabriel River, which, at that time, entered the ocean a little farther north than it does now.

21. Ibid.

22. Leo J. Friis, *Orange County Through Four Centuries* (Orange County, CA: Pioneer Press, 1965), 54; cit. *Santa Ana Register*, "Flirted With Death on Treacherous Anaheim Bay Bar Four Years, '71–'75: the Recollections of James D. Ott, Once Agent of the Anaheim Lighter Company, Leroy Doig, Village of Garden Grove," March 20, 1920.

CHAPTER 3

23. Hellman's extensive correspondence is located in the California Historical Society in San Francisco.

24. Letter from Harrison Gray Otis to I.W. Hellman, Hellman Collection, California Historical Society; *Los Angeles Herald*, July 23, 1898. "It is rumored that Mr. Hellman, of Los Angeles, has in contemplation the erection of a sugar factory come here between Long Beach and Anaheim Landing, and the efforts on the part of his agent to remove all squatters on his property there is regarded as a good sign."

25. In August 1900, soon after San Pedro was confirmed as the primary port of Los Angeles, the Clarks acquired controlling interest in the Los Angeles Terminal Island Railroad, which connected downtown Los Angeles with Terminal Island via Long Beach. This would be the western leg of a route to Salt Lake City. The Clarks' purchase also gave them some oceanfront property, some of which became Brighton Beach, a resort that "rivaled Santa Monica and Coronado for the business of the elite." Brighton Beach was home to two yacht clubs and compared to Newport, Rhode Island.

26. Letter from Hellman to Henry Huntington, May 21, 1901, California Historical Society, Hellman Collection, MS 981, 27:270–71.

27. *Los Angeles Times*, September 3, 1901.

28. Ibid., April 18, 1903.

29. Ibid., May 5, 1903.

30. Orange County Archives, 1903, Grantor-Grantees book.

31. A 1930 newspaper ad offered the Bayside Land Company for sale, due in part "to the death of two of its largest shareholders," Lothian and Huntington.

32. *Los Angeles Times*, September 4, 1903; *Los Angeles Herald*, September 6, 1903; *Santa Ana Evening Blade*, September 11, 1903. The railroad only reached Alamitos Bay, and the new town site could only be accessed by ferry or via the Anaheim Landing road.

33. *Los Angeles Times*, July 23, 1905; *Los Angeles Herald*, "Bay City Developments," August 6, 1905.

34. This misinformation can be traced back to the second version of Samuel Armor's *History of Orange County*, originally written in 1911 and updated in 1920. In 1919, Amor wrote to the Seal Beach council requesting information, and Ord was assigned to provide it.

35. *Los Angeles Times*, June 21, 1904. This article on the court ruling approving eviction of squatters at Anaheim Landing noted there were over forty cottages of residents at the landing, many going back over twenty years.

36. The *Santa Ana Blade*, September 7, 1903, noted that J.H. McConnell and Doc McConnell were brought up on charges of illegally selling liquor before Justice of the Peace Ord. Ord was the justice of the peace when a Mosinio Nevaez broke his windows to pay off an old grudge, according to the *Los Angeles Times* of January 6, 1904.

37. *Long Beach Press*, July 1, 1904.

38. Worth considering is that by this point, Hellman had already gotten one big thing he probably wanted—the extension of the electric railroad through his lands in Orange County.

39. *Los Angeles Herald*, "Bay City Developments," August 6, 1905.

40. The Bay City pier's length of 1,500 feet was well short of the 1,950-foot-long Stearns Wharf Pier in Santa Barbara and the original Avila Beach (San Luis Obispo) pier at 1,800 feet. By the time it was lengthened in 1916, it was also shorter than Santa Monica's 1,600-foot pier (1909) and the 2,745-foot pier built in 1914 in Santa Cruz.

41. Some writers of Seal Beach history have incorrectly stated that Seal Beach's small lot sizes were determined by the tent cities. But the narrow twenty-five-foot lot sizes, typical of most "downtown" lots in those days, are clearly visible on Finley's original 1903 town survey. But with no zoning restrictions, some of these deep, narrow lots were further subdivided by individual homeowners, especially the streets closest to Anaheim Landing.

CHAPTER 4

42. Jeff Stanton, "Founding of Ocean Park," http://www.westland.net/venicehistory/articles/oceanpark.htm (accessed July 20, 2013).

43. Surfing had technically been introduced years earlier by three Hawaiian teenagers who were students in California, but Freeth popularized the sport with his regular demonstrations first at Venice in 1908, and then Redondo Beach in 1909.

44. *Los Angeles Herald*, "Expansion of Naples Project," July 16, 1905; *Los Angeles Times*, "Now For Naples: Henry E. Huntington Will Take a Hand in Making a Seaside Resort at This Point," September 15, 1905; *Los Angeles Herald*, "Wonder Pleasure

Resort for Pacific Coast," October 8, 1905. Huntington's investment was in an entity called the Naples Extension Company, which also included both Parsons and *LA Times* publisher Harry Chandler as investors and directors.

45. *Los Angeles Herald*, August 6, 1905. With the arrival of the Pacific Electric line at Newport, the Newport Beach Investment Company announced plans to develop Balboa as a resort area, beginning with a large pavilion.

46. Friedericks, *Henry Huntington*, 99. Huntington began negotiating with the Southern Pacific for the sale of his Pacific Electric and Los Angeles Interurban stock in 1907. The final deal called for him to gain exclusive control the downtown Los Angeles Railway. It did not affect the Redondo Beach Railway, which Huntington already owned outright.

47. *Electric Railway Journal* (April 18, 1916): 715; James W. Walker, *Lines of Pacific Electric, Southern and Western Districts* (Claremont, CA: Inter-Urban Press, 1975, rep. 1976), 187. In return, the Pacific Electric probably got promises to make it very difficult for jitney buses to operate in these areas. Jitneys had taken much of the businesses from the PE trains in the Long Beach area and company officials complained they weren't even making enough money to pay for the electricity to carry the cars over the tracks. As a result, the PE had already cut back much of its service and was already abandoning lines.

48. *Long Beach Daily Telegram*, "Big Changes at Bay City," October 11, 1912.

49. Ibid. Architect Burnsides Sturges had recently migrated from Toledo, Ohio, and would later make a name for himself designing homes, including the acclaimed Hancock Park home of Warner Brothers co-founder, Harry Warner.

50. Guy M. Rush came to Los Angeles in 1909 and became the region's "subdivision specialist." His company promoted new subdivisions like Lawndale (1910), Riverbank (1911), Subway Tract (1911), Burleigh (near Inglewood, 1911), Brooklyn West (1913) and Marygold Acres (1917). A 1914 acquisition of a large real estate firm did not work out, and the Rush Company scaled back its activities, including Seal Beach. When Rush returned from a World War I tour in France, he focused on real estate in the Glendale-Pasadena area. After World War II, he assisted in the formation and leadership of the Freedoms Foundation of Valley Forge, an organization that promoted the America way of life.

51. *Billboard*, July 19, 1913. The "Park, Aviation & Skating News" section included reports that the Rush Company would put the entire property on the market.

52. Seals (actually California sea lions) lived in large numbers up and down the California and Baja Coast. Numbers of the creatures often showed up on the rocks, docks and mudflats around Alamitos and Anaheim Bay. Local fishermen complained frequently about the thieving skills of the pinnipeds and often shot them.

53. *Los Angeles Times*, July 18, 1913.

54. Henri Gilbert DeKruif (1882–1944) was Michigan born and trained in art at the Art Institute of Chicago and New York Arts Students league. After working at the Grand Rapids Advertising Company, he migrated to Los Angeles in 1911 and started work for the Merril Advertising Company, which apparently got Guy M. Rush's contract for advertising Seal Beach. He later became a noted impressionist watercolor painter and prominent in the Laguna art colony. Long Beach historian Claudine Burnett has done an excellent study and review of the entire ad campaign "The Seal-ing of Seal Beach" at her blog, www.historicalsealbeach.blogspot.com.

55. Robert Burns Armstrong was an Iowa-born newspaper advertising salesman who worked in Chicago, Des Moines, New York and later Washington, D.C. (where he worked as an assistant secretary of the treasury to fellow Iowan L.M. Shaw). Armstrong came to Los Angeles in 1909 and began working for Guy M. Rush in 1912, soon becoming the company's general manager. The ever-optimistic Armstrong wrote columns, gave speeches and even wrote an advice book for salesmen under the Rush banner and seems to have overseen the Seal Beach account almost from the beginning. After the big Rush Company newspaper advertising campaign ended in 1914 (with less-than-hoped-for results), Armstrong, who resided in Pasadena, continued to oversee Seal Beach's marketing under his own name.

56. *Long Beach Press-Telegram*, "New Car Line Ready Sept 9; Long Beach-Seal Beach Connection Almost Done," September 2, 1913; "Seal Beach, Eastern Suburb, Officially on Map Today; Connection with Long Beach by Means of Street Railway Made Gala Occasion," September 9, 1913.

57. *California Railroad Decisions Records*, May 5, 1915. When Santa Monica and Venice merchants complained in 1914 that the flat round-trip rate of fifty cents to any beach town was discriminatory to their towns (which were closer to downtown), the commission pointed out that "there is nothing at Anaheim Landing to attract excursionists, and there is little or no travel to that point" and that the real competition for the northern resorts (Santa Monica, Ocean Park and Venice) was Long Beach, which was equal distance to their towns.

58. *Los Angeles Times*, December 7, 1913; January 25, 1914.

59. Ibid., March 29, 1914.

60. Ibid., January 31, 1914. The legal transaction, like all of Hellman's Anaheim Landing sales, was handled by attorney Jackson Graves, who later wrote that the money Hellman received for just the thirty-three acres brought in "about ten thousand dollars more than twice as much as he paid for his original interest in the entire rancho." Graves, *Seventy Years in California*, 158.

61. Frank Todd, *Story of the Exposition* (San Francisco: Panama-Pacific International Exposition Company, 1921), 343. Courtesy of Walter D'Arcy Ryan, the

exposition's innovative "Illuminating Engineer"—and employee of the General Electric company, which wanted to showcase its new line of lighting products.

62. *Los Angeles Times*, "Wet-Dry Issue Looming Large," September 8, 1915.

63. Elected as trustees (city council members) were Judge John C. Ord (ninety-eight votes), James H. Blagge (seventy-eight), Harry G. Magee (seventy-six), Herman Eichorn (seventy-one) and C.A. Little (seventy-nine). Not elected but getting votes were Russell (twenty), R.D. Richards (eighteen), Reader (eighteen) and Herbert (nineteen). One other candidate, Ira Patterson, who correctly said the community didn't have five hundred residents, didn't get many votes of the residents it did have, netting only eighteen votes himself.

64. *Long Beach Daily Telegram*, October 20, 1915. The Balboa Company's presence at the Seal Beach celebration led to incorrect reports that the entire Seal Beach celebration was filmed. The original article left unsaid whether Bracken's crews shot any of the official proceedings. Also unknown is the veracity of the claim that this was the first scene of its kind ever taken at night. Figuring it would take an additional couple months before the film could be distributed, it seems most likely that the film in question using the footage could be *The Shrine of Happiness*, which was released in February 1916. We've never seen a synopsis for this film, so we have no idea if this is a correct assumption.

65. *Los Angeles Times*, "Plan Pleasure Mecca By the Sea," November 10, 1925.

66. The exact length of the Seal Beach coaster's paper-clipped shaped track is unknown, but it definitely was NOT two miles in length. Amusement manager Bert St. John said it "was almost a mile in length," a figure consistent with the footprint on the Sanborn Fire Insurance Maps and similar to the length of the coasters at other resorts. (A two-mile track would have taken about four minutes to complete, empty and re-load, a time not cost-efficient for ride operators.) Another press release described The Derby as "the largest, longest and most unique type of roller coasters ever built," a trick statement meaning it was the longest 'safety' coaster yet built, it being one of the first to have wheels both above and below the rail. "A speed of a mile a minute is attained, but so scientifical [*sic*] is it constructed, that danger from the excessive speed is entirely eliminated." The *Long Beach Press*, July 1, 1916, unintentionally phrased it to read "lacking the element of danger." The *Ontario Daily Report* of July 1 described the Derby as "one of the longest and safest ever built."

67. *Salt Lake Tribune*, "Colorado Cullings," November 3, 1896; *Salt Lake Tribune*, "Attempts at Suicide: Mrs. Annie Abbott Takes a Dose of Chloroform," July 16, 1897; *Los Angeles Times*, "He Grew Up on Thrills," April 4, 1920; *Seal Beach Post & Wave*, "Things, This and That," February 23, 1945. "Things, This and That" was a column by longtime *Post & Wave* editor-publisher A.W. Armstrong, who met Abbott when both were living in Denver. Colorado. The above article was

excerpted in the Seal Beach Historical & Cultural Society newsletter, July–August 2005. Multiple family histories confirm the Hogbin surname.

68. *Salt Lake Tribune,* "Colorado Cullings"; *Colorado Springs Weekly Gazette,* September 19, 1901; *Lincoln Evening Journal,* "Fireworks Explode," February 4, 1914; *Los Angeles Times,* "He Grew Up on Thrills," April 4, 1920.

69. *Los Angeles Times,* November 28, 1915.

70. *Santa Ana Register,* June 8, 1915.

71. *Electric World* 67, no. 21:1186

72. *Los Angeles Times,* March 19, 1916.

73. Stanton, Bayside and Burt had apparently assumed operation of the Jewel Amusement Company by this time. Except for a 1918 city council resolution to revoke Edwards and Tarpey's license to operate the roller coaster unless some improvements were made to the arched passages under the coaster at Tenth and Eleventh Streets, little more is heard of Edwards and Tarpey at Seal Beach, as Edwards had gotten into building racing cars and flying airplanes.

74. *Los Angeles Times,* April 23, 1916. Labb had also been arrested for passing a bad check a year earlier in Ocean Park, and in 1920 would be sued for making fraudulent stock claims while raising money for a new manufacturing company. *Los Angeles Times,* October 17, 1915; July 1, 1920.

75. *Los Angeles Times,* "Rousing Talks Wakes Up Seal Beach Folk," May 22, 1916.

76. The assumption of tent hangars is due to aerial photos that show little evidence of permanent structures along the beach west of the pier.

77. The race was between Daugherty and Harry Christofferson. Overall, aviation was a young activity. The Wright brothers' first practical flight had occured just over ten years earlier.

78. *Long Beach Daily Telegram,* "Daugherty Gets Contract for Two Weeks Exhibition at Seal Beach," May 4, 1916; "Loop Flyer Signs Up for Exhibitions Here and at Seal Beach," May 5, 1916; *Long Beach Press,* "Local Birdmen Wing Their Way to Seal Beach," May 15, 1916.

79. *Long Beach Daily Telegram,* "Big Crowds Attend Seal Beach Opening," May 29, 1916.

80. The *Santa Ana Register* June 8, 1916 special section on Seal Beach actually wasn't *that* special. The previous week the paper did a special on Laguna Beach and Dana Point. Then on June 16 and 23, it did eight-page special editions on Huntington Beach and Newport Beach/Balboa. These are great for comparing the Orange County beach areas.

81. The Loughheep (Lockheed) Brothers decided against Seal Beach and chose Burbank.

82. The plunge joined the long list of promised attractions that were never built.

83. Santa Ana *Register,* June 8, 1916. A "cafe chantant" was a French term, for a cafe with musical entertainment.

84. Frank Morton Todd, *Story of the Exposition*. San Francisco, Panama-Pacific International Exposition Company, 1921, 148-49. The Seal Beach coaster did have some good heritage. It's San Francisco predecessor was designed and built by LaMarcus Thompson, who at Coney Island in 1884 built the world's first amusement railway. After that, he built coasters or scenic railways all over the world, at parks in London, Petrograd, Paris, Berlin, Vienna, Madrid, Venice and Copenhagen and even one on the beachfront at Santa Monica's Arcadia Hotel, the first roller coaster in Southern California. Much of Thompson's reputation was built on the fact that no one had died on one of his coasters. Thompson did not participate in the Seal Beach venture. City records show that Tarpey & Edwards possessed the roller coaster operator's license, and newspaper articles and mechanics' liens state the Seal Beach coaster was constructed by the Ingersoll Company, owned by Frederick Ingersoll, which constructed 277 coasters, mainly between 1890 and 1920.

85. Ibid., 93. While the Seal Beach owners hint they came down from Panama-Pacific Exposition, the 1915 directory for San Francisco Chamber of Commerce Activities list the exhibit's original owner as E.A. Wasserman.

86. Ibid.

87. *The Story of the Exposition*, 353. "The prize and male instinct to hurl a missile was strong enough that some men would invest ten or fifteen dollars [in a Kelly game] at a time in its gratification."

88. Ibid., 352.

89. Samuel Armor, *History of Orange County* (Los Angeles: Historic Record Company, 1921), 872–73.

90. *Long Beach Daily Telegram*, May 31, 1916.

91. Ibid., "Aviator Was Willing to Take Pretty Girl Aloft, But Authorities Objected," August 25, 1916; *Los Angeles Evening Express*, "Town Marshal Bans Loop-Loop Flights as Feminine Pursuit," August 25, 1916.

92. *Los Angeles Times, Herald, Examiner*, et al, July 16, 1916.

93. The electriquette was the venture of Clyde Osborne, a San Diego attorney who operated a fleet of 200 cars at San Diego. He apparently sold 150 electricquettes to J. Paulding Edwards, a consulting engineer on electric railways, who earned gross receipts over $112,000 at the San Francisco event. They came in two models: a three-wheeler that carried two people and a four-wheeler designed for four but sometimes seen wandering about with seven passengers. The electriquettes were charged with a lead storage battery and could travel at four or five miles per hour. Although first publicly used on the beach boardwalks of Venice and Santa Monica, a few may have been at Seal Beach by mid-1914. DeKruif drew an electriquette in an August 1914 Seal Beach ad and even alluded to the upcoming San Diego and San Francisco Expositions. After the success at the 1915 San Francisco Panama-

Pacific International Exposition, Paulding Edwards and an in-law, A.B. Tarpey, became the original major investors and officers in the Jewel City Amusement Company, which obtained a "long-term lease" to operate "numerous high class concessions" at Seal Beach. They had the city license to operate the roller coaster.

94. Handwritten reporter's notes saved in the Seal Beach scrapbook in the Seal Beach Library. The author found no evidence that this story ever made it into print.

95. *Seal Beach Post*, July 14, 1916; *Long Beach Press*, July 14, 1916.

96. *Orange County Post*, July 21, 1916. The actual mechanics lien was for $4,770.51 of a $9,185.02 bill and was filed against the Bayside Land Company, the Jewel City Amusement Company and the Ingersoll Engineering Company, the world's leading builder of roller coasters.

97. *Los Angeles Express*, August 18, 1916.

98. *San Bernardino Index*, August 4, 1916.

99. Fredrick L. Bird and Frances M. Ryan, *The Recall of Public Officers: A Study of the Operation of the Recall in California* (New York: Macmillan Company, 1930), 107–108.

100. *Corona Independent*, "Seal Beach to Have Real Snow Battles," March 20, 1917.

101. *Moving Picture World*, November 4, 1916. Also known as *The Circus Girl*, the Walter Wright–directed film was released in March 1917.

102. Ibid., June 16, 1917; July 17, 1917.

103. *Los Angeles Times*, "He Grew Up on Thrills," April 4, 1920.

104. Balboa likes to claim it held the county's first bathing beauty pageant, but its first event was in 1920.

105. Jim Sleeper, *Great Movies of Orange County* (Trabuco Canyon, CA: California Classics, 1980), 42, 118. Sleeper's book shows an August 2, 1918 *Santa Ana Register* ad for the film, with a second run airing the week of September 25, 1918. As the film is not listed in any major distribution exchanges, it is probable it had few, if any, showings outside Southern California.

106. *New York Herald*, August 11, 1918; Tom Dardis, *Keaton: The Man Who Wouldn't Lie Down* (London: Deutsch, 1979), 53.

107. The rental rate was that of the Tent City down the road at Huntington Beach, as shown in a display ad in the *Santa Ana Register*'s Huntington Beach supplement on June 16, 1916.

108. *Los Angeles Times*, "Thrills Promised for Aerial Circus," December 19, 1921.

109. Daniel S. Levy, *Two-Gun Cohen* (New York: St. Martin's Press, 1997), 124–25; *North China Herald*, "American Aviator in Hong Kong: His Daring, Ill Luck and Final Triumph," July 29, 1924.

110. Daniel S. Levy, *Two-Gun Cohen* (New York: St. Martin's Press, 1997), 124–25; *North China Herald*, "American Aviator in Hong Kong: His Daring, Ill Luck and Final Triumph," July 29, 1924.

111. *Santa Cruz Sentinel,* "Museum Boasts Collection of Indian Chief's Regalia," March 5, 1939; Raylene Abbott e-mail to author, February 6, 2014; A.W. Armstrong, "Things, This and That" column, *Seal Beach Post & Wave,* February 23, 1945. Armstrong also said that as part of the Liberty War Bond Drive, Abbott parachuted off the Washington Monument, but there is no record of anybody ever parachuting from that structure.

112. *Wid's Film Daily,* "Another Film Colony," July 8, 1919, 3.

CHAPTER 5

113. The Pacific Studios were in business from 1921 to 1924, when Burt left and then died later that year.

114. This information came from a notebook of press clippings provided to the author by Kathleen O'Sullivan Matthews, great-niece of Grace O'Sullivan Stanton. P.A. and Grace had no children, but some Seal Beach historians mistook Grace's younger brother, John (Jack) O'Sullivan, for Stanton's son.

115. *Los Angeles Times,* 1921.

116. Frances Catherine Smiley, *Educational Survey of Orange County* (Berkeley: University of California, May 1921).

117. Jim Sleeper, *Great Movies Shot in Orange County* (Trabuco Canyon, CA: California Classics, 1980), 88–89.

118. Ibid., 92; Virginia Jones Hadley, oral history interview, Seal Beach Red Car Museum.

119. By this time, Patterson had apparently given up construction and returned to being a storekeeper at a shop three doors from Central. The store also held amateur nights when movies weren't available.

120. Virginia Haley, oral interview, December 1993.

121. *Los Angeles Times,* "Lots Not for Sale," December 1, 1919.

122. *Los Angeles Times,* May 23, 1920, display ad.

123. This was mainly the Hellman land located in the Alamitos Bay wetlands.

124. Virginia Haley, interview, *History of Seal Beach* TV series, Seal Beach TV, 2012, cited in Joe Segura, "Stories of Seal Beach of Old," *Long Beach Press-Telegram,* November 22, 2011.

125. *Los Angeles Times,* "New Seal Beach Church Opened," August 23, 1937.

126. A 1925 *Time* magazine report tallied the costs as "a case at Rum Row, $25[;] on the beach, $40; to the retail bootlegger, $50; to the consumer, $70, or $6 a bottle."

127. Jack Dragna (1891–1956), called by Governor Earl Warren the "Capone of California," was connected to the New York Sicilian "Black Hand" Society. He

settled in Los Angeles in 1914 and soon became number two to Los Angeles mob boss Frank Ardizonne. During Prohibition, they built up their illegal liquor business and then expanded into the local bookmaking and gambling operations. After Ardizonne's mysterious death in 1931, Dragna became the crime boss of Los Angeles, frequently maintaining power by working with rivals and challengers like Bugsy Siegel and Mickey Cohen, who challenged him in the late 1930s.

128. Although the man most associated with gambling ships, Cornero did not run a gambling ship until 1935. After being indicted for rum-running in 1926, he fled the United States and did not return until 1929, when he turned himself in. After release from prison in 1931, he went to Las Vegas and built the Meadows, one of the first luxurious casinos. After returning from Las Vegas in 1935, he became one of many partners in the *Tango*, controlled by Clarence Blazier, who had been involved with most of the earlier gambling ships. In early 1938, Cornero, upset when Blazier ignored his suggestions, challenged him to roll the dice for each other's share. Blazier accepted, and Cornero lost. Within a couple months, Cornero's new gambling ship, the *Rex*, opened for business in Santa Monica Bay. Because Cornero, who was independent of organized crime, sought publicity and was so open about his gambling ship operations, he soon became the "face" of the gambling ships.

129. *Los Angeles Times*, "Beauty Captured in Liquor Raid," March 25, 1923.

130. The international limit was originally a three-mile limit until 1924, when the United States got all nations to agree on a twelve-mile limit, approximately a one-hour boat ride.

131. *Los Angeles Times*, "Tower Café Is Raided," June 12, 1922.

132. Ibid. "Deal Beach Soon Will Be Dried Up," December 22, 1922.

133. Ibid., "Six Indicted in Huge Rum Plot," June 17, 1927; "More Accused in Liquor Plot," June 18, 1927.

134. Claudine Burnett, *Prohibition Madness* (Bloomington, IN: Authorhouse, 2013), 60.

135. *Los Angeles Times*, "Suspect in Rum War Arrested," August 5, 1925.

136. Ibid., "Retired Admiral Routed Hoodlums," December 11, 1960.

137. *Seal Beach Journal*, 1985 (sixtieth anniversary series issue). In Gise's early days, he was reportedly also an assistant manager at the Seal Inn, one of the establishments operated by local gambling "kingpin" Ballard Barron.

138. *Los Angeles Times*, "Retired Admiral Routed Hoodlums," December 11, 1960; Willard Hanzlik, interview by Libby Appelgate, November 5, 2003, courtesy SBHCS.

139. *Los Angeles Times*, "Thirty Nabbed in Beach Raids," April 23, 1923; *Long Beach Press*, "Apply Sponge to Seal Beach," April 23, 1923.

140. *Los Angeles Times*, "Seal Beach Resorts in Liquor Raid," April 30, 1923. Arrested were Seal Inn co-owner (and brothel madam) Mrs. H.M. Blankenship and her

assistant manager, Lew Weston. Nabbed at the Jewel Café were proprietor Jack Smith, headwaiter Charles Zander and two patrons from Long Beach.

141. Ibid., "Rum Ship Seized in Chase," July 23, 1923.

142. Ibid., "Dry Squad to Search Boat," November 24, 1923.

143. Ibid., "Liquor Cargo Seized on Pier," January 13, 1932.

144. Ibid., "Scores Held in Week-End Raids," July 27, 1925. The Captain's Inn was located at 111½ Thirteenth Street, per Flagg's 1926 South OC Directory, Fullerton Public Library.

145. *Reports of Cases Determined in the Courts of Appeal of the State of California* 48:257–62, *People v. Bayside Land Company*. It was charged that the Tower Café proprietor, Louie White, had used the building, furniture, fixtures and musicians for the purpose of lewdness and for encouraging and allowing lewdness and prostitution and that although no acts of prostitution took place on the premises, on November 30, 1918, Beatrice Swanner, Viola Johnson and Irena Fucha used the building for solicitation of prostitution. The court also charged that the Seal Inn was where rooms were rented to complete the act of prostitution, and even if the proprietor Louie White and the property owner (the Bayside Land Company) did not know about the lewd conduct of its guests, they did nothing about once learning of it. Nine witnesses testified that the Tower Café's general reputation was "bad" and "unsavory." Also convicted were Doc Smith and F.C. Blankenship, proprietors of the Seal Café and its upstairs sixteen-room Seal Inn.

146. Seal Beach Council Minutes, book 1; *Long Beach Press-Telegram*, January 6, 1927.

147. *Radio Digest* (January 9, 1926): 30; *Radio Doings* (February 5, 1927): 70.

148. *Long Beach Press*, "Flames Sweep Seal Beach Play Zone: Historic Panama Pacific Relics Saved by Firemen from This City," August 31, 1923; *Los Angeles Times*, "Origin of Seal Beach Fire is Investigated," September 1, 1923. Interestingly, this fire received no little play in the Long Beach, Los Angeles or Orange County newspapers. The coaster continued to run on special occasions.

149. *Long Beach Press-Telegram*, May 29, 1927. R.D. Richards survived for a long time in Seal Beach as a "dry" in a "wet town." But in May 1927, he traded his home on Fourteenth Street for a hardware store in Norwalk, where he lived the rest of his life. During his twenty-two years in Seal Beach, Richards represented it on the Associated Chambers of Orange County "almost from the beginning in 1912" and also served on the Republican Central Committee from 1908 to 1926. He opened the rebuilt bathhouse and bowling alley in 1905 but sold that interest in 1916 and got into the hardware business.

150. *Los Angeles Times*, November 8, 1923; Long Beach Press, "Seal Beach Is to Close on Sundays; Lid Clamped Down on All Amusements by Bayside Land Company," December 24, 1923.

151. Fredrick L. Bird and Frances M. Ryan, *The Recall of Public Officers: A Study of the Operation of the Recall in California* (New York: Macmillan, 1930), 108, 127–28, 147.

152. Richard Nixon, *In the Arena: A Memoir of Victory, Defeat, and Renewal* (New York, Simon & Schuster, 1990) 83.

153. Seal Beach City Council Minutes, 2:273. June 19, 1930.

154. *Los Angeles Times*, "Seaside Cities Prepare to Celebrate as New State Coastline Highway Nears Completion," March 25, 1925.

155. *Long Beach Press-Telegram*, March 24, 1925; April 16, 1925.

156. *Los Angeles Times*, January 12, 1929; *Long Beach Press-Telegram*, January 7, 1929; February 19, 1929; March 1, 1929; March 29, 1929; June 1, 1929; July 1, 1929.

157. Rancho Los Alamitos records; Florence Tyler, interview, Seal Beach Historical Society.

158. Ruth Ellyn Taylor, ed., *Legacy*, Orange County Register seventy-fifth anniversary publication (Santa Ana, CA: Orange County Register, 1980), 112.

159. Interviews with many Japanese farmers of Orange County, California State University–Fullerton, Japanese Oral History Project Collection, http://coph. fullerton.edu/JAOHPAbout.asp.

160. Joan Stegman, oral interview with Libby Appelgate, November 8, 2000, Seal Beach Historical and Cultural Society (SCHCS). Stegman, whose grandparents ran the Willard Hotel, described the Seal Beach artesian well tap water as "nasty…yellow…tasted and smelled like sulphur." Even though "bad and horrible to drink and bathe in," she noted that "you still got a great shampoo."

161. *Los Angeles Times*, "Weed Case May Go to Higher Court," September 15, 1927. The midway area, especially the big coaster, was run down, and weeds grew unmolested on the company's numerous unsold lots. Finally, the council ordered city workers to remove the weeds and charge the company. Stanton took the matter to court but lost.

162. Advertisement appearing in the *Los Angeles Times* and other area newspapers, May 18, 1930.

163. *Los Angeles Times*, "Seal Beach to Vote on City Hall Bonds," January 5, 1929.

164. Seal Beach Council Minutes, book 1 (September 20, 1923): 641.

165. Robert Righter, *Wind Energy in America: A History* (Norman: University of Oklahoma Press, 1996), 87–90; Peter Asmus, *Reaping the Wind: How Mechanical Wizards, Visionaries, and Profiteers Helped Shape Our Energy Future* (Washington, D.C.: Island Press, 2001), 112–14. George Worthen Sperry Knighton was a painter by trade and tinkerer by avocation. He was the chief electrical engineer on a late-1920s project by one-time Seal Beach real estate salesman Dew Oliver to harness wind power. Oliver, who came to Seal Beach in 1925, "could talk a person out of the gold in his teeth." After his real estate business failed, he got an idea to harness the wind to produce energy. Using engines first obtained from the old

Seal Beach roller coaster and then the Pacific Electric Railroad Company, Oliver and Knighton built just east of Banning what was called at the time "a giant blunderbuss"—a bell-shaped wind machine that stretched seventy feet. The wind would turn the blades and funnel through the machine, compressing it by a factor of twelve, and generators beneath that produced two hundred horsepower of electricity. The effort was one of the earliest efforts to produce energy from wind. Unfortunately, Oliver played a little fast and loose with security laws and ended up getting sent to prison for three years. The judge commuted the sentence to three months, in part because the machine worked (it worked so well that it blew out the old roller coaster engine), and on the condition that Oliver abstain from liquor and stay out of places where it was sold. This pretty much prevented him from returning to Seal Beach.

166. *Long Beach Press-Telegram*, "Antique Engine Cranked Up for Fifth Annual Fire Event," August 22, 1935. Although mainly promoting the Fifth Annual Firemen's Ball, the article also gives a short history of the department. The ball, to be held at the Jewel City Inn, was under the direction of Knighton, "with help from Fred Thomas, Orville Glenn, and Ray Wilkinson." Other members of the department were Milden Eckberg, Earl Wade, Elwood Brenner, Cyrus Shepherd, Byron Haas, Russell Weber, Henry Smith and some names too difficult to make out.

167. *Los Angeles Times*, August 13, 1917. Through the spin of a wheel, players could win "candy, cigars, chewing gum, sofa pillows, silk stockings or other items of like value."

168. William F. Robertson, 1940 testimony before the Los Angeles Police Commission. Investigations revealed that in the second half of the 1930s, he had worked as a guard at both the Inter-City and Bees.

169. The Kefauver report and FBI files note that Binion was involved with a number of suspicious deaths in the Dallas, Texas area, including the wife of a rival who died in an explosion when she drove a car that her husband usually drove.

170. Lester "Benny" Binion, 1973 interview in *Some Recollections of a Texas and Las Vegas Hotel Operator* by Mary Ellen Glass (Reno: University of Nevada Oral History Program, 1976).

171. Morton Saiger (longtime Las Vegas figure and former employee of Barron's at the Last Frontier Hotel), interview, University of Nevada Oral History Program, http://www.knowledgecenter.unr.edu/materials/specoll/oralhistory/PDFs/S/saiger.pdf (accessed on July 29, 2013). Freedman (also spelled Friedman) was a "big time Houston gambler-horse breeder-oilman" who fronted the group that opened the Sands Hotel in 1952. The rumored real owner was New York mob boss Frank Costello.

172. *Los Angeles Times*, "Orange Gaming Ban Announced; Action Follows 23 Seal Beach Arrests," July 26, 1934.

173. *Long Beach Independent Press-Telegram*, "Seal Beach...Calm Except for Stars, Gambling and Bootlegging," March 20, 1976; This article is mainly about the recollections of longtime Seal Beach resident Ray Gise.

174. Seal Beach Historical Society newsletter (May–June 2000): 1, 3.

175. *Los Angeles Times,* August 4, 1934; August 5, 1934; September 7, 1934; September 8, 1934.

176. *San Bernardino Sun*, "Nine Arrested on Game Ship Acquitted," June 24, 1934; *Los Angeles Times*, "Fight Launched by OC DA to Make Gambling Charge Felony," September 8, 1934; *Los Angeles Times*, "Seal Beach Leaders Aid Chip Games," September 8, 1934.

177. *Los Angeles Times*, "Orange County Grand Jury Report Bristling With Criticism," February 18, 1936.

178. Virginia Haley, oral interview, SBCHS.

179. *Long Beach Independent Press-Telegram*, March 20, 1976.

180. *Articles from the Attic* (May–June 2000): 1, 3.

181. *Los Angeles Times*, "Girl Rescued in Hotel Raid," February 19, 1933.

182. Ibid., "New Facts Promised in Shooting," March 13, 1936.

183. The "City Hall gang" was run by Charlie Crawford, who had backed the right candidates for city offices and basically ran the town in the 1920s. A key confederate was LAPD Vice Squad head Guy McAfee, who oversaw most of the gambling, prostitution and illegal bars in town, often working with rumrunning and gambling kingpin "Farmer" Page. Page and Cornero had some rumrunning shoot-outs in the mid-1920s, and McAfee used his connections to get Cornero indicted and put in prison for a few years. When Fletcher Bowron became mayor in 1938, McAfee, Page and the rest of the City Hall group were basically run out of town to Las Vegas where, for the most part, they (not Bugsy Siegel) started big-time Las Vegas gambling. When Cornero got out of prison, he went to Nevada and opened the Meadows in 1931, Las Vegas' first "carpet joint" (a plush casino with carpet instead of sawdust on the floor). The Meadows burned down after a year.

184. *Los Angeles Times*, "Gambling Ship Resumes Career Off Seal Beach," November 27, 1929.

185. Another account says the *Johanna Smith* removed its propeller, making it a barge and not subject to shipping laws. Choose your sources carefully.

186. Ernest Marquez, *Noir Afloat* (Santa Monica, CA: Angel City Press, 2011), 171; Marquez references a *Long Beach Morning Sun* twelve-part series that reported a government estimation that the ships earned a day's expenses in an hour and could pay for a week's expenses in a little over five hours.

187. *Los Angeles Times*, "Gamblers Scoff at Law in Their Floating Haven," April 13, 1930.

188. Ibid., "Sea Gamblers Battle with Guns for Control of Floating Palace," May 22, 1930; Marquez, "Noir Afloat."

189. *Dallas Morning News*, "Gamblers on Floating Hall of Chance Escape as Craft Blazes, but $50,000 Sinks," September 1, 1930.

190. Marquez, *Noir Afloat*, 169. The *Monte Carlo* was the biggest of the ships, three hundred feet in length, and its owners eagerly anticipated the influx of crowds for the 1932 Olympics. Marine Stadium in Long Beach would play host to the rowing events.

191. *Los Angeles Times*, "Gaming Ship to Be Dismantled," May 5, 1934. The district attorney chartered a barge, boarded the *Monte Carlo*, "anchored off Long Beach" and removed gambling paraphernalia valued at $50,000; Ibid, "Gambling Ship Out of Danger," April 26, 1930. Many in LA wanted DA Z.B. West to draw a line from the Palos Verdes Peninsula to Malibu, which would make all the waters inside that area a bay and thus within the three mile limit. West declined, saying he couldn't win the case. Later that decade, Los Angeles officials tried to do the same with Tony Cornero's new *Rex* ship. He went to court, argued that Santa Monica Bay was actually a bight, not fitting the legal definition of a bay as a protected inlet. An appeals court agreed and threw out the state's case, but the California Supreme Court later ruled in favor of the county, and Cornero threw in the towel.

192. Ibid., "Gambling Ship Inquiry Looms," July 24, 1932.

193. Marquez, *Noir Afloat*, 172–75; *Los Angeles Times*, "Gaming Ship Dismantled," May 5, 1934; *San Bernardino Sun*, "Nine Arrested on Game Ship Acquitted," June 24, 1934.

194. *Los Angeles Times*, July 30 and August 1, 1938; 1950, U.S. Senate, Kefauver Investigation into Organized Crime, testimony of William Moore, owner of the Last Frontier Hotel; Marquez, *Noir Afloat*, 182–86. The raid is most remembered for Tony Cornero holding off authorities with a fire hose for a day or two before giving in. Rarely reported is that the owners of the *Sho-Boat*, off Seal Beach, did the same thing a few days later when authorities tried to take its gambling equipment. The *Sho-Boat* was the only ship that succeeded in keeping its gambling equipment.

CHAPTER 6

195. *Los Angeles Times*, August 10, 1917. The mock fort held its own though, when one of its gunners inadvertently fired a shot that struck Prest's engine, ripping holes in the back seat and the wing and shattering the propeller. "By cool maneuvering," Prest glided the plane through a three-hundred-foot drop back to Earth.

196. *San Bernardino Sun*, "Prest Reaches Altitude of Over 18,000 Feet," August 14, 1917. The spotters from the California Aero Club had grown tired of waiting and left. Witnessing part of Prest's attempt was balloonist/parachutist Wayne Abbott, who rode with Prest to eight thousand feet, then leaped overboard and floated to the audience below with a documented record (properly witnessed by Prest).

197. *Los Angeles Times*, "He Grew Up On Thrills," April 4, 1920. Other details are confirmed in an Internet comment by Harry's son, noted aviation man Dan San Abbott, who was born in China when Harry was hired to help organize the Nationalist Chinese air force.

198. Bragunier's logbook, page 6, clearly lists the August 25, 1919 date, duration sixty-five minutes. http://www.dmairfield.org/people/bragunier_ac/19180204-19280930_Bragunier_Log1Cropt.pdf.

199. Claudine Burnett, *Soaring Skyward* (Bloomington, IN: Authorhouse, 2011), 124. Wesley May became one of the most well-known barnstormers until he was killed during a parachute stunt in mid-1922.

200. *Los Angeles Times*, August 27, 1927.

201. Ibid., October 9, 1927; November 19, 1927; *Financial Handbook of the American Aviation Industry* (New York: Commercial National Bank and Trust Company of New York, 1929), 60.

202. *Los Angeles Times*, "In the Air at Local Airports," December 9, 1928. The Hamilton syndicate of Nogales, New Mexico, ordered three planes from Crawford to be equipped for refrigeration, with an option for fifteen more, if the experiment was successful.

203. "Douglas Company Recapitalizes for Expansion Purposes," *Air Travel News* 3 (February 1929): 44.

204. Gerald R. Burtnett, "Training in a Powered Glider," *Popular Aviation* (August 1930): 31–32.

205. Ibid.

206. *Long Beach Independent Press-Telegram*, "He's Been Up in the Air Most of His Life," January 19, 1958.

207. The airfield was by now interchangeably called Crawford Field and Seal Beach Airport. Commerce Bulletin No. 4 of 1932 says "*Crawford Airport*, one-fourth of a mile northeast of *Seal Beach*, is no longer available for the use of commercial aircraft." Although the Federal Aviation books call it Crawford Airport until at least 1934, the 1932 Orange County directory refers to it as Seal Beach Airport.

208. Ryan Aeronautical School of San Diego 1938 directory.

209. Joseph Watts was one of the earliest to buy a lot in Los Alamitos and was followed to town by his two brothers, who ran the town's main store for years, and in 1910 by his father, Reverend Benjamin Watts, who became Los Alamitos' first

full-time minister, serving at the Congregational Church on Katella from about 1910 to 1923.

210. Gus Strodthof came from an early Anaheim family that had spent many warm days at Anaheim Landing. He was one of the very first employees of the Los Alamitos Sugar Company and eventually became the factory and company's general manager in 1925 and ran it until the heirs decided to sell it off in 1949. Strodthof was the last president, and the man who finalized the sale of the property to Louie Boyar, Ben Weinberg and Mark Taper who would build the city of Lakewood. Strodthof and his wife, Una, lived on Ocean Avenue in Seal Beach for quite some time in the 1930s. She lived there when she rode her horse in the Tournament of Roses Parade. They later moved to Ocean Avenue in Long Beach.

211. Conversation with Don Watts, nephew and sole heir of both Nina and Una Watts.

212. *Los Angeles Times*, "Navy Base Site Offered," July 11, 1934; *Long Beach Press-Telegram*, "Big Naval Base East of City Furthered; 16,000 Acre Tract between Long Beach and Bolsa Chica Is Proposed," July 10, 1934; *Long Beach Press-Telegram*, "Coast Body to Back Anaheim Landing as Site for Naval Base," July 19, 1934. The proposal seems to have been the brainchild of Phillip Stanton, who was desperate to unload his Seal Beach properties. Significantly, it apparently did not include the Fred H. Bixby property but did include the property inherited by his sister, Susannah Bixby Bryant, which is located where the Alamitos Power Plant is now just east of Studebaker.

213. Norma Reed Pranter, interview, "Norma Pranter Recalls Old Days in Seal Beach," *Seal Beach Journal*, April 10, 1985.

214. Benny Olsen, interview, 1985, *Seal Beach Journal*.

215. Marge Ordway, SBHCS oral history, interview in *Seal Beach Journal*, 1985.

216. Community gardens, sometimes called Relief Gardens and Welfare Gardens, were a common sight during the Great Depression. They were originally pushed by the Hoover administration and then even more by the Franklin Roosevelt administration. Although they were fairly successful, government financial aid to these gardens stopped in 1935.

217. *Seal Beach Journal*, "Pioneers Russ and Harriett Carley Look to Future," April 17, 1985.

218. Ibid., interview with Marge Schmidt Ordway by William G. Quinn, April 24, 1985,.

219. Marge Ordway, interview, *Seal Beach Journal*, April 24, 1985.

220. *Los Angeles Times*, April 23, 1933; June 4, 1933.

221. Ibid., "Voters Reject School Bonds," June 20, 1933.

222. Ibid., "New Horse Racing Plant Planned," May 24, 1933.

Chapter 7

223. *Los Angeles Herald*, "Slowly Take Testimony: Several Witnesses Give Evidence in Bolsa Bay Land Spit Case," November 7, 1905.

224. By the early 1930s, any concerns were long forgotten. Stanton was listed as president of the Ord Land Company in newspaper ads for Surfside, plus he had all the company documents in his possession (which were passed on to family members after his death).

225. *Los Angeles Times*, June 26, 1927; October 27, 1929; http://malibucomplete. com/mc_history_dev_colony.php (accessed September 9, 2013). Although some local historians have billed Surfside as the first gated beach community, the Malibu Colony predates it by a few years, having been formally opened in 1927. To access the area, visitors had to use the Rindge family's guarded gate at Las Flores Canyon.

226. *Los Angeles Times*, May 19, 1929; June 23, 1929; August 25, 1929. The initial articles call the Phillips-Hambaugh deal for the Oxnard property "the largest transaction in the history of Ventura County." The principal partner in the project was M. Penn Phillips, a very active Southern California realtor. Phillips and Hambaugh organized in 1922, and one of their biggest projects appears to be Rancho Vista (now Vista) in northern San Diego County.

227. *Los Angeles Times*, "Area's Growth Described," August 23, 1931.

228. Ibid., "Beach Land to Be Used for Colony;" May 26, 1929; Virginia Adell Blake, Darla Austin Funk and Donna Metzger Kettler, *Surfside Colony: History, Legend, Lore* (Seal Beach, CA: privately published for Surfside residents: 2006), 23–24.

229. *Los Angeles Times*, "Beach Property Interest Grows," June 21, 1936.

230. Blake, Funk and Kettler, *Surfside Colony*, 20, 42.

231. Ibid., 20, 42.

Chapter 8

232. The last reference I could find regarding the coaster being operative was a *Los Angeles Times* article on August 18, 1929, when the Elks Club's Big Brother committee hosted a day at the beach for Los Angeles area orphans. The article stated, "The roller coaster was turned over to the orphans."

233. Marge Ordway, interview. Others talk about putting a stick under the wheel. After most had jumped in a car, one would kick the stick out to send them hurtling down the slope.

234. Jean Dorr, *Seal Beach* (Seal Beach, CA: Whale & Eagle for the City of Seal Beach, 1976), 12.

235. George Brown, oral history, Seal Beach Historical Society.

236. Marge Ordway, interview, oral history project, Seal Beach Historical Society.

237. Joan Stegman and George Brown, oral histories, Seal Beach Historical Society.

238. Dorr, *Seal Beach*, 9.

239. E-mail comment by Pat Gray, posted on www.losalhistory.com, article "Anaheim Landing Was Area's First Settlement."

240. The usual starting line in 1927 was Beanblossom (right field), Lebarron (shortstop), Lewis (left field) Thompson (second base), Mitchell (third), H. Ecker and C. Ecker (splitting time at first), McGinnis (pitcher), Flanders (catcher) and Ingalls (center fielder), who batted ninth. The team played their games on Sunday afternoon and the *Long Beach Press-Telegram* ran box scores the following day throughout the spring and summer.

241. In an 8–7 loss to the Corona Cubs in 1938, the lineup included Davis (left field), Trenton (second base), James (short stop), Scott (first base), Webis (right field), Starty (thrd base), Davis (catcher), Graves (center field) and Luckett was the pitcher. In the loss to Corona, James hit a homer to no avail.

242. Terry Lee Rioux, *DeForest Kelley: From Sawdust to Stardust* (New York: Pocket Books, 2005), 18.

243. Jeanne Gaye Pool, *Peggy Gilbert & Her All-Girl Band* (Lanham, MD: Scarecrow Press, 2008), 126. Peggy Gilbert, a top-notch musician, led all-girl bands under various names, including Peggy Gilbert and Her Symphonics or Her Coeds, but when quality female musicians weren't available, Gilbert hired men and called her band "the Jacks and Jills." The Long Beach Pleasure Guide for November 14–21, 1945, said, "The Garden of Allah brings after-dark pleasure seekers to within its walls for gay dinner-dancing and to pay homage to Peggy Gilbert and her 'Jacks and Jills' who reign supreme in the art of supplying dance tempos to the enthusiastic customer."

244. *Long Beach Independent*, December 8, 1939; April 3, 1940.

245. *Los Angeles Times*, "Ten Arrested in Gambling Raid at Seal Beach," September 18, 1941. This article does not name the Garden of Allah specifically, but the restaurant was named ten days later on September 28, 1941, by the *Long Beach Independent*, "10, Seized in Seal Beach Gambling Raid, Plead Guilty Fined $100," and in a follow-up in the October 3, 1941 issue of the Corona *Independent*, which reported that the sheriff would destroy $15,000 of gambling equipment confiscated in the raid.

246. By this time, Stanton was the Bayside Land Company, and the company seemed to have no purpose other than not spend any more money than it had to. In addition, Stanton's health was not good at this time. In December 1934, he was reported "near death due to toxic poisoning" and remained an invalid at least through May 1935, according to the *Los Angeles Times* of May 17, 1935. In mid-1934, Huntington heirs began a thirteen-month appeal before a Federal Tax

Board, and the value of the Bayside Land Company was reported as one of the "principle items in dispute." *Los Angeles Times*, May 13, 1935; November 15, 1937.

247. *Ogden Standard-Examiner*, "Twenty Saved From Waves," July 3, 1935; *Los Angeles Times*, "Seal Beach Pier Rescue May Speed Replacement," July 4, 1935.

248. One source describes this as the largest foreclosure in Orange County, but in truth it was only half the dollar figure of the Bastanchury Ranch foreclosure of February 1933.

249. *Long Beach Press-Telegram*, "Bank Acquires 900 lots in Seal Beach," August 31, 1935. The sale was conducted by the Los Angeles Trust and Deposit Corporation and endorsed by P.A. Stanton and Bayside secretary J.P. Transue. Typical of the Bayside Land Company's luck, the article noted that at one time, $1 million had been offered for the oceanfront property alone.

250. *Los Angeles Times*, "Hobby Brings Cheer to Civil War Veteran," December 2, 1935.

251. Ibid., "Seal Beach Activity Slated: Purchase of Land Valued at $500,000," October 16, 1938.

252. Ibid., July 29, 1938.

253. Ibid., July 17, 1938.

254. *Corona Daily Independent*, "View Storm Damage," September 30, 1939. An eyewitness report of a Corona resident, Officer William Patterson, who took an automobile trip through the damaged area. *Newspaper Archive*.

255. *Seal Beach Journal*, interview with Wes Carroll, December 21, 1977.

256. Ibid.

CHAPTER 9

257. *Long Beach Independent*, June 7, 1940; *Los Angeles Times*, June 23, 1940.

258. Homer DeSadeleer obituary, *Seal Beach Sun*, November 24, 1988.

259. *Fresno Bee*, "7 Americans, 15 Others Killed in British Air Crash," August 12, 1941.

260. *Los Angeles Times*, "Submarine Shells Southland Oil Field," February 24, 1942; *Los Angeles Times*, "Secrets of '42 LA 'Air Raid' Related," October 29, 1945.

261. *Long Beach Independent*, December 16, 1941.

262. *Seal Beach Post & Wave*, "Silk Stockings Vitally Needed By Government," December 3, 1942.

263. Alan Harbour, memoir in *Seal Beach Sun*, September 24, 2010.

264. *Long Beach Independent*, "Mrs. Jessie Reed, New Seal Beach Mayor, Promises 'Clean City,'" May 5, 1942.

265. United States Senate Investigation of Organized Crime In Interstate Commerce (Kefauver Hearings), 1950, Testimony of W.L. Burt, tax consultant, Long Beach, California, 306. Burt testified that he helped "Long Beach bookmakers" like Dick Rains. "Well, over at Seal Beach Mr. Rains there, for the Garden of Allah, tells me he wants some phones and I assisted him as much as I could in getting the phones, and also Travis, the contractor's. Of course, those fellows that gambles, they have other ways too, and I helped him secure some phones."

266. *Los Angeles Times,* "Navy Starts Negotiations for Ordnance Depot Land," January 23, 1944; City Council Minutes, January 24, 1944.

267. *Seal Beach Sun,* Lynne Pranter Phipps interview.

268. *Long Beach Independent*, November 19, 1944; *Los Angeles Times*, November 19, 1944.

269. Carolyn Dame, letter, August 28, 2013. As a young child, Carolyn would vacuum Stanton's two-story house on Saturdays and receive five dollars each time. Carolyn's mother owned Ruby Belle's Beauty Salon on Main Street, and her grandparents once owned the Jewel City Café.

Chapter 10

270. *Hawarden (IA) Independent,* August 16, 1945. Oscar Johnson was a native of Hudson, Iowa, where he was apparently also involved with theaters. When building the Beach, he brought out a friend, Seal Van Sickle, to decorate and paint the new theater's interiors. Van Sickle had done the same for theaters in Iowa.

271. *Seal Beach Post & Wave,* November 23, 1945.

272. *Long Beach Independent,* June 23, 1946.

273. Ibid., July 14, 1946. The ad text also says, "It's all yours and worth waiting for! Three weeks of strenuous activity now brings you the ultra-modern new Bay Theater." Below that, it gushes, "This modernized and revitalized theater with its rich new hangings, luxurious appointments—all befitting its new dignity as 'the pace [*sic*] to go.'" The theater was outfitted with new RCA sound equipment, a new screen, new acoustic treatments and new floor coverings.

274. *Sentimental Journey* was a 1946 Twentieth Century Fox film starring John Payne and Maureen O'Hara, whom audiences found so appealing that they were reunited the following year in the Christmas classic *A Miracle on 34ᵗʰ Street. Miss Susie Slagles* (Paramount, 1946) was a turn-of-the-century medical drama starring Veronica Lake, Sonny Tufts and a young Lloyd Bridges.

275. Minutes of Seal Beach Lions' Club, October 16, 1946, accessed at http://sealbeachlions.com/ClubInfo/About/history/1939-93.html.

276. *Los Angeles Times*, August 7, 1946.

277. Jimmy Utley, one of Jack Dragna's top lieutenants and a part owner of a tango parlor on Seal Beach's Main Street and other towns, was pistol whipped by Cohen in front of Lucy's El Adobe, a restaurant across the street from the Paramount Studios, in 1946.

278. *Long Beach Press-Telegram*, November 15, 1954. Barron came to Las Vegas when investors like Griffith viewed the casino as a sideline to the hotel business, so his suggestions like moving casinos closer to the front were minimized—even more so after Griffith died and his theater company partners back in Texas assumed control. Ten years later, better-designed hotel-casinos like the Desert Inn captured much of the betting action, and the Last Frontier's days were numbered. In 1952, the theater owners sold out, and Barron retired to Beverly Hills. In 1954, he suffered a heart attack and died in Long Beach. Interestingly, his obituary in the *Press-Telegram* called him only a Long Beach oil man and never mentioned his Seal Beach gambling past.

279. United States Senate Investigation of Organized Crime in Interstate Commerce (Kefauver hearings), 1950, Testimony of W.L. Burt, tax consultant, Long Beach, California, 306. In the Kefauver hearings, a tax accountant, W.L. Burt, testified that he helped "Long Beach bookmakers" like Dick Rains. "Well, over at Seal Beach Mr. Rains there, for the Garden of Allah, tells me he wants some phones and I assisted him as much as I could in getting the phones, and also Travis, the contractor's. Of course, those fellows that gambles, they have other ways too, and I helped him secure some phones."

280. Testimony at a 1940 Police Commission hearing revealed that in 1936 he received $38,000 from the Inter-City Athletic and Social Club of Seal Beach. In 1939, he received $6,500 from the Bees, a club owned by Ballard Baron. Robertson also earned money at clubs owned by Paul Tapper, one of LA's top bookies, and probably at one partially owned by Jimmy Utley, one of Jack Dragna's top lieutenants.

281. *Los Angeles Times*, "Police Detective Under Fire Over Large Income Resigns," December 27, 1940.

282. Ibid. Robertson refused to answer some questions about his unusually large income and resigned. These facts were brought out the 1950 U.S. Senate Investigation into Organized Crime (Kefauver Hearings), and Robertson was again questioned about how he had acquired so much money for a police detective.

283. Utley was also involved with card parlors in Venice and Gardena as well as bookmaking, prostitution and abortion mills and was well known as a guy with connections in the police and sheriff's offices.

284. The story, related by former Seal Beach mayor Charles Antos, makes sense. The late 1930s was the beginning of Bugsy Siegel's and Mickey Cohen's takeover of the

Los Angeles bookmaking operations, and the race wire—which provided timely results of the nation's horse races—was a key element for the area's 1,800 bookies.

285. *Los Angeles Times*, "Fathers, Sons to Dine," November 24, 1947.

286. Draw poker was legal for two reasons: it was not specifically mentioned in the anti-gambling statute, and its selective, thought-out (and thus "skilled") discards omitted it from the law's "other games of chance" provision.

287. *Long Beach Independent*, "Seal Beach Will Ballot Tuesday to Decide Robertson Club's Fate," April 12, 1953.

288. Henry Kaiser had honed mass-production techniques while building Boulder Dam (now Hoover Dam) and then thousands of Liberty ships in World War II.

289. Pat Jones Crow, letter, www.bellsisters.com. Her parents owned the Seal Inn (newer version), and she managed it for them. Her dad was also president of the Seal Beach Chamber of Commerce. Crow recalls the rose parade theme as American Indian, and Cynthia was dressed as a squaw and wore a wig. Early in the parade, she momentarily removed the wig and people laughed at the blond Indian.

290. *Los Angeles Times*, "Fireplace in Bedroom Held Interest Factor," September 10, 1961; *Surf and Sun*, letter from Norma Gibbs, mayor of Seal Beach, November 23, 1961.

CHAPTER 11

291. Corky Carroll, e-mail to author, August 18, 2013; *Sun*, interview with Libby Appelgate, August 15, 2013.

292. Blackie August was a champion swimmer at Poly High School in Long Beach and met Kahanamoku, an Olympic champion swimmer, when the latter trained in Poly's Olympic-size pool. Blackie's son Robert would go on to star in director Bruce Brown's the 1966 surf classic *Endless Summer* and become a surfing legend throughout the world.

293. Tim Dorsey, quoted in *Press-Telegram*, "Surf's Still Up in Seal Beach," March 23, 1976; Corky Caroll, e-mail, August 17, 2013.

294. *Long Beach Press-Telegram*, "Mystery of the Surf Sphinx," September 9, 1999. In another article, Tim McElrath says it was just him and Dick Thomas who did the lifting.

295. Robert August Surf Blog, http://robertaugustsurf.wordpress.com/2013/03/02/the-sphinx.

296. Corky Caroll, e-mail to author, August 17, 2013.

297. It was originally called the West Coast Surfing Championship and changed its name to the U.S. Surfing Championships in 1961.

298. Corky Carroll, e-mail to author, August 18, 2013; *Sun,* interview with Libby Appelgate, August 15, 2013.

CHAPTER 12

299. Leisure World was marketed as the first seniors-only community *"of its type"* (which would be a large, complete community). Some "senior communities" like in Kearsley, Pennsylvania, trace their lineage back over one hundred years, but these were not complete communities with golf courses, stores, churches for multiple faiths and other amenities allowing an "active lifestyle."

300. Andrew Blechman, *Leisureville: America's New Retirement Utopias* (New York: Atlantic Monthly Press, 2008). Some reports say that Schliefer was "an idealistic Russian Jewish immigrant who wanted to construct a kibbutz-like community where older citizens could age affordably and gracefully."

301. In May 1960, newspapers reported that Cortese was planning a $50 million 2,400-home walled development between Springdale and Bolsa Chica and Bolsa and Smeltzer (now Edinger), where Marina High School is now located. Within a year, most of the land had been sold to William Lyon, who built another of his many Dutch Haven communities there.

302. *Long Beach Press-Telegram,* April 13, 1961; *Los Angeles Times,* August 6, 1961. The initial report used a dollar amount of $70 million, but subsequent press releases always used the $150 million figure.

303. Brangham originally worked for Fallon & Co. and after his success became the managing partner of Fallon, Brangham & Moon.

304. Over the next twenty years, Brangham became one of the nation's most influential housing marketers. Besides Cortese's Leisure Worlds, Brangham worked on the planned city of Reston, Virginia, and then in 1968 returned to California to become head of sales for the Larwin Co., developers of the Tanglewood and Greenbrook subdivisions off Bloomfield and Ball in Los Alamitos.

305. *Long Beach Independent Press-Telegram,* "A Leisure World's Medical Plan," Southland Magazine supplement, February 18, 1962. The original medical plan included "1. diagnosis and treatment by a licensed physician; 2. upon order of a physician, laboratory and x-ray examinations, drugs, physical therapy treatments, visiting nurse service to apartments, and ambulance service."

306. *Los Angeles Times,* "Unique City Opening Today," October 29, 1961. The article noted, "'Prior to today's official opening, some 500 apartments were sold in the first week by private appointment,' William G. Brangham, general sales manager, said."

307. Ibid., "Huge Globe Will Mark Entranceway to Project," August 6, 1961. Some claim the the Leisure World unisphere is a copy of the 1964 New York World's Fair unisphere. The Leisure World globe predated the New York Unisphere by over two years, although word of the New York structure and its name, which had been publicly announced just a few weeks before this article, was known in the building and architectural community.

308. Robert Peterson, syndicated column, "LIFE Begins at Forty," *Traverse City (MI) Record-Eagle*, September 11, 1964. The Rossmoor Leisure World ad on the back page of the Seal Beach fiftieth anniversary book listed only the Seal Beach, Laguna Hills and Walnut Creek communities and the following future Leisure World communities and projected populations: near Princeton New Jersey (fifty thousand residents); Olney, Maryland (seventeen thousand resident); Chicago (fifty-one thousand residents); and Lugano, Switzerland (five hundred acres).

309. *Los Angeles Times*, May 28, 1955.

310. Saturn Illustrated Chronology, Part 2, January 1961 through December 1961, http://history.nasa.gov/MHR-5/part-2.htm.

311. *Los Angeles Times*, "Rocket Plant Site Will be Annexed," February 4, 1962; "Big Saturn Facility Set For Seal Beach," May 24, 1962; "Space Agency Approves Moon Rocket Center," May 27, 1962.

312. Neil Armstrong had flown weekends with a reserve unit at Los Alamitos while working during the week as a test pilot at Edwards Air Force Base. John Glenn had taken off from Los Alamitos on his record-breaking transcontinental flight in 1957.

313. After leaving Seal Beach, the Saturn rockets were transported to what is now the John C. Stennis Test Center in Hancock County, Mississippi. Located on the Pearl River, rockets could be floated on barges right to testing platforms.

314. *Los Angeles Times*, "Seal Beach Send Off: Moving Saturn Rocket Tougher Than Getting It to the Moon," January 3, 1966.

315. Ibid., "Seal Beach Stores Deadly Shells," July 30, 1967.

316. Ibid., "One Worker Out of Six in County Employed in Aerospace Industry," September 23, 1965.

317. Hotchkis's wife, Katharine, was the oldest daughter of Fred H. Bixby. Katharine had grown up on the Rancho Los Alamitos, but she and Preston lived in San Marino. He built up a strong insurance company and led many chamber of commerce and war bond campaigns during the 1940s and 1950s. He would later become a key member of Ronald Reagan's cabinet of California advisors.

318. *Long Beach Independent Press-Telegram*, February 15, 1959.

319. *Los Angeles Times*, "Annex Bid by Seal Beach Gains Support," October 11, 1964.

320. The Nikas Brothers also owned the Prisoner of Socrates in Newport, the Mecca in Buena Park and the Golden Bear in Huntington Beach. Jackson Browne mentions Rouge et Noir in his song "The Barricade of Heaven."

321. Steve Martin, *Born Standing Up* (New York: Scribner, 2007), 66, 70.

322. *Long Beach Independent Press-Telegram*, May 10, 1959.

323. http://www.thedoorsguide.com/research/marinapalace.html.

324. *Finnegan's Wake* was author James Joyce's last work. Experimental, ambitious and largely unread, it is remembered more for its name than content.

325. *Long Beach Independent Press-Telegram*, March 17, 1967.

326. Ibid., "Planners Vote OK of Surfside Annex," March 3, 1967.

327. This was probably *The Born Losers*, an American International biker film notable as the first appearance of Tom Laughlin's Billy Jack character. It had a three-week shooting schedule and was first released in summer 1967.

328. *Long Beach Press-Telegram*, "Seal Beach Squabble: Go-Go Bar Hit for Rowdy Crowd," March 10, 1966. Goldfinger's Go-Go at 800 Pacific Coast Highway was not winning friends and influencing people in its immediate neighborhood.

329. *Oakland Tribune*, "Rossmoor Land Sale Expected," May 5, 1968. The credit crunch also forced Cortese to forego payments (donations) to the Rossmoor-Cortese Gerontology Center at USC, which wasted little time dropping his name (1969) and finding a new donor, Ethel Percy Andrus (1970).

330. Former mayors and city councilmen Jim Bell and Chuck Long, interviewed 1988 for Los Al TV *History of Los Alamitos*.

331. *Long Beach Press-Telegram*, December 1, 1966.

SUGGESTED READING

A challenge in doing Seal Beach research is that there is not one great repository of Seal Beach information, and that many of its key characters (e.g., Bixbys, Hellman, Huntington, Stanton, Cortese) usually resided elsewhere and their records and correspondence are spread all around. But the following sources are great starting points.

GEOLOGY, THE RIVERS AND THE WETLANDS

Gumprecht, Blake. *The Los Angeles River: Its Life, Death and Possible Rebirth (Creating the North American Landscape)*. Baltimore, MD: Johns Hopkins University Press, 1999.

Stein, Eric D. *Historical Excology of the Southern California Wetlands*. N.p.: Southern California Coast Waters Research Project, Technical Report, 2007.

RANCHO DAYS

Cleland, Robert. *Cattle on a Thousand Hills*. San Marino, CA: Huntington Library, 1951.

Newmark, Harris. *Sixty Years in Southern California*. New York: Houghton-Mifflin, 1930.

The Bixbys and the Long Beach/West Orange County Area in the Late 1800s

Flint, Dr. Thomas. *Diary of Dr. Thomas Flint: California to Maine and Return, 1851–1855.* Claremont, CA: Historical Society of Southern California, 1924.

Jurmain, Claudia, David Lavender, and Larry L. Meyer. *Rancho Los Alamitos: Ever Changing Always the Same.* Berkeley, CA: Heyday Books, 2011.

Lavender, David. *Rancho Los Alamitos: A Historical Perspective.* Berkeley, CA: Heyday Books, 2011.

Smith, Sarah Bixby Smith. *Adobe Days.* Cedar Rapids, IA: Torch Press, 1925. The library resources of the wonderful Rancho Los Alamitos (thanks again to Pamela Seager and curator Pamela Lee) and the Rancho Los Cerritos will also provide further information.

Bay City, the Pacific Electric and I.W. Hellman

Dinkelspiel, Frances. *Towers of Gold: How One Jewish Immigrant Named Isais W. Hellman Invented California.* New York: St. Martins Press, 2008.

Friedericks, William. *Henry Huntington and the Creation of Southern California.* Columbus: Ohio State University Press, 1992.

The California Historical Society's large collection of the letters and papers of Isais W. Hellman, especially Hellman's correspondence with Philip A. Stanton, Fred H. Bixby, and Henry E. Huntington, is very revealing of life around Anaheim Landing, the development of the Pacific Electric Railroad, and Bay City/Seal Beach 1890–1905.

Seal Beach and the Joy Zone

Most of my information was culled from the archives of the *Los Angeles Times*, and the numerous Long Beach newspapers (the *Press*, the *Daily Telegram*, the combined *Press-Telegram* and its sister publication, the *Independent*). Fortunately, The *Times* is available online through most local libraries. Post-1945 issues of the Long Beach papers are online through www.newspaperarchive.com and www.newspapers.com. The *Press-Telegram* can be viewed either on microfilm at the Long Beach Public Downtown Library or (post-1925 issues) at the Historical Society of Long Beach. Pre-1945 issues of the Long Beach papers are on microfilm at the downtown Long Beach Main Library.

Also of value are online archives for entertainment industry trade papers like *Billboard*, *Motion Picture World* and *Wid's Film Daily.*

The Seal Beach Mary Wilson Library has a valuable book of newspaper clippings, but these are basically rehashes of Bayside Land Company press releases that cover only a short period of time and provide a skewed company view of the amusement park days.

SEAL BEACH, RUM-RUNNING AND GAMBLING

Criminals did not recognize political boundaries except when it was to their advantage, so to understand rum-running and gambling in Seal Beach, one has to understand how it operated throughout the entire Southern California area. This involves the City Hall Gang, Tony Cornero, the growth of the Los Angeles Mafia and the growing power of Bugsy Siegel and Mickey Cohen, and there are many books on these figures, although most are sensationalist rehashes and get many events out of order. The news clippings of the *Times* and the *Press-Telegram* are a must to place a proper chronological frame of reference on these events.

The best-researched study on the gambling ships is Ernest Marquez, *Noir Afloat*, Santa Monica: Angel City Press, 2011.

POSTWAR SUBURBIA

Through the development of Ross Cortese's Rossmoor and Leisure World, the S&S Homes at the College Parks and the Lakewood Company influence on The Hill, this area was a microcosm for the growth and spread of postwar suburbia. But studies of our little corner of Orange County seem to have been overlooked for the later, larger and more southerly Orange County developments such as Irvine, Laguna Hills and the second Leisure World. While it is touched upon in many books, there, unfortunately, is no one great source that thoroughly covers this area.

INDEX

ABOUT THE AUTHOR

Larry Strawther has been writing professionally for over forty years for newspapers, movies and television. His television writing and producing credits include the television classics *Happy Days*, *Laverne & Shirley* and *Night Court*; the cult comedy hit *MXC (Most Extreme Elimination Challenge)*; and even being the head writer on *Jeopardy!* in the late 1970s.

He has also written for movies (*Without a Clue*, *Mighty Ducks*) and been a sportswriter in the San Francisco Bay Area.

In recent years, he has indulged his lifelong interest in local history with two haphazard but fact-filled websites: www.losalhistory.com and www.historysb.com. In 2012, he wrote his first book, *A Brief History of Los Alamitos and Rossmoor*, about Seal Beach's neighboring communities to the north.

He lives in Rossmoor, California, with his wife, Nancy. They have three children: Megan, Michael and Mallory.